Trial of Dea

(Editor: William Roughead)

Alpha Editions

This edition published in 2024

ISBN : 9789362092663

Design and Setting By
Alpha Editions
www.alphaedis.com
Email - info@alphaedis.com

PREFATORY NOTE.

THE following report of this interesting trial is prepared from the original record, with additional particulars from contemporary sources. No connected account of the life of William Brodie having hitherto been attempted, the Editor has endeavoured to give in the introduction as complete a view as is now possible of his remarkable career.

To Sheriff Moffatt, Lanark, and Mr. William Brown and Mr. John A. Fairley, Edinburgh, the Editor is under obligation for the use of MSS., books, and prints in connection with the subject. His thanks are also due to Dr. Joseph Anderson, Keeper of the Scottish National Museum of Antiquities, who has allowed him to photograph Deacon Brodie's lantern and keys and to make excerpts from the records of the Cape Club. For permission to publish for the first time facsimiles of Brodie's letter to the Duchess of Buccleuch and the MS. register in his Family Bible, the Editor is respectively indebted to the courtesy of Mr. Alexander Anderson, Librarian of the Edinburgh University Library, and the Plans and Works Committee of Edinburgh Town Council.

Mr. Bruce J. Home has not only kindly permitted the reproduction of two drawings from his well-known work, "Old Houses in Edinburgh," but has made a drawing of the old Excise Office, Chessel's Court, expressly for the present volume.

W. R.

EDINBURGH, *November, 1906.*

INTRODUCTION.

FEW cities have preserved more faithfully than Edinburgh the traditions of former days, and none is richer in the material of romance. Throughout the length of the Royal mile extending from Holyrood to the Castle Hill, each tortuous wynd and narrow close owns its peculiar association, each obscure court and towering "land" has contributed, if but by a footnote, to the volume of the city's history. And where these visible memorials have perished beneath the slow assault of time, or succumbed to the more lethal methods of modern improvement, the legends which they embodied survive their dissolution and serve in turn to perpetuate their fame.

Of the many memories that haunt the lover of old Edinburgh, wandering to-day among the vestiges of her romantic and insanitary past, perhaps the most curious is that of William Brodie, Deacon of the Wrights and doyen of the double life; by day "a considerable house carpenter" and member of the Town Council; by night a housebreaker and the companion of thieves.

It is nearly a hundred and twenty years since Deacon Brodie played out his twofold part at the west end of the Luckenbooths one grey October afternoon in 1788; but the close in the Lawnmarket which bears his name remains to this day. Here he was born and lived, man and boy, robber and decent burgess, for many reputable years; here his old father passed away, happy in the possession of so excellent a son; and from hence did the son essay that "last fatal" adventure, the issue of which was, for him, discovery and the scaffold.

The house itself has long since vanished—a victim to the indiscriminate destruction which has swept away so much else worthy of preservation. You can no longer see the heavy oaken door with the cunning lock of the Deacon's own contriving, and the turnpike stair down which, with mask and lantern, he so often stole at midnight upon his secret and criminous affairs. But if you follow him in fancy down the High Street and past the Nether Bow, to where a gloomy "pend" leads into Chessel's Court, you will find the tall front of the old Excise Office still rising within its "palisadoes," behind which lurked the trembling Ainslie; and if it be about the dusk of the evening, and your imagination is informed with the spirit of the place, you may even see the man rush wildly forth from the doorway up the court, and hear, in the succeeding silence, the three blasts of an ivory whistle.

The trial of Deacon Brodie has many claims upon the attention of a later age. It is of value to the antiquarian for the vivid picture it presents of the manners and customs of our forbears at a time when the life of Edinburgh yet flowed in the ancient arteries of the old city on the ridge, although beginning to circulate more freely in the spacious thoroughfares of the New Town already invading the fields across the valley. To the lawyer it is notable as affording a singularly graphic view of the old-time practice of our criminal Courts, as well as for the galaxy of legal talent engaged upon its conduct—with such men as Braxfield on the bench and Henry Erskine and John Clerk at the bar the proceedings could lack neither picturesqueness nor importance. The psychologic interest of the chief actor's character and the dramatic elements in which his career abounds make a more general appeal; and so long as human nature remains the same will the story of the Deacon's downfall be accorded an indulgent hearing.

That story had for Robert Louis Stevenson a strong attraction. As early as 1864 he prepared the draft of a play founded upon it, which—after being at various times re-cast—finally took shape in the melodrama, "Deacon Brodie, or the Double Life," written in collaboration with the late W. E. Henley, and published in 1892. It may even be that the conception of "Dr. Jekyll and Mr. Hyde" was suggested to Stevenson by his study of the dual nature so strikingly exemplified in his earlier hero; while in other of his writings he has touched the Deacon with a felicitous and kindly hand.

The birth of Deacon Brodie is thus recorded in the Register of Births for the city of Edinburgh—

"Monday, 28th September, 1741. To Francis Brodie, wright, burgess, and Cecil Grant, his spouse, a son named William. Witnesses—William Grant, writer in Edinburgh, and Ludovick Brodie, Writer to the Signet. Born the same day."

It is an inexplicable circumstance, although by no means uncommon, that so goodly a family tree as that of the Brodies should, in due course of nature, bear such degenerate fruit as the subject of this entry was destined to prove. His great-grandfather, Francis Brodie of Milnton, Elginshire, was a member of a family well known in the North of Scotland, and his grandfather, Ludovick Brodie of Whytfield, was a much respected Writer to the Signet in Edinburgh, who, on his death in 1758, was the oldest member of the Society. His father, Francis Brodie, was born in 1708, and in 1740 married Cecil, daughter of William Grant, writer in Edinburgh, with whose family he was already connected. Both the Deacon's grandfathers, therefore, were members of the legal profession.

There will be found in the Appendix a copy of a MS. Register of Births and Deaths kept by Francis Brodie in his family Bible, together with some account of that interesting volume, from which it appears that William was the eldest of eleven children, most of whom died in infancy. The entry relating to his birth has been cut out of the Register, presumably on his public disgrace some forty-seven years later.

Francis Brodie was a substantial wright and cabinetmaker in the Lawnmarket of Edinburgh, where he carried on an extensive and prosperous business. In 1735 he was made a Burgess, and in 1763, a Guild Brother of his native burgh. That he stood high in the estimation of his fellow-craftsmen is evidenced by his being, in 1775 and 1776, elected a member of the Town Council as Deacon of the Incorporation of Wrights, and again in 1779 and 1780, in the same capacity; while in 1776 he also represented the Incorporated Trades of the city as their Deacon Convener. A further proof of the position and circumstances of the family is to be found in the fact that the close in which their house was situated became known by their name.

This mansion, the most important in the close, was originally the town residence of the Littles of Craigmillar, having been built by William Little, a magistrate of Edinburgh, in 1570, whose brother, Clement Little, was the founder of the University Library. In the earlier titles of the property the close bears the name of its old residenters; but in Edgar's map of 1742 it appears as Lord Cullen's Close, from the eminent judge, Sir Francis Grant of Cullen, who in turn resided there. Brodie's Close was formerly a "throwgang" or thoroughfare passing from the Lawnmarket to the Cowgate, the upper portion of which alone has escaped the "improvements" that have so effectively changed the features of this part of the Old Town. The area occupied by the Deacon's dwelling is now covered by Victoria Terrace, the building having been demolished about 1835, when the principal carved stones of the mansion were transported by Clement Little's descendants, in whose possession the property remained, to the garden of the family seat, Inch House, near Liberton, as relics of the habitation of their ancestors. The lower extremity of the close, in which were situated the Deacon's workshops and woodyard, survived until a later date, the last traces of it disappearing to make way for the foundations of the Free Library.

In the fine old tenement at the head of the close—often erroneously described as Brodie's residence—is still to be seen the decorated hall of the Roman Eagle Lodge, a famous Masonic society of the eighteenth century, immediately beyond which, on the east side of an open court, stood the Deacon's house. It is thus described by Chambers in his "Traditions of Edinburgh" as it existed in 1825—'Brodie's house is to be found in its original state, first door up a turnpike stair in the south-east corner of a small court near the foot of the close. The outer door is remarkable for its curious, elaborate workmanship. The house is well built, and the rooms exhibit some decorations of taste. The principal apartment, of which the ceiling is remarkably high, contains a large panel painting of the 'Adoration of the Wise Men,' and has an uncommonly large arched window to the west." What became of this painting, which was attributed to Alexander Runciman, is now unknown.

Of the early years of William Brodie we have, unfortunately, no record, but it may be assumed that he received an education suitable for the son of a well-to-do burgess. He was apprenticed

Foot of Brodie's Close, Cowgate.
(From a Drawing by Bruce J. Home.)

to his father's trade, and in due time became associated with him in his thriving business. In those days no self-denying ordinance obtained in the Town Council, and Francis Brodie's municipal connection secured for him and his son the most of the city work. The young man had the ball at his foot, as the saying goes, and only good behaviour and application to business were required for the attainment of an assured position. Unhappily for himself, however, he soon exhibited that taste for dissipation which ultimately led to such dire results; and while his days were occupied in following his respectable employment, in which he speedily obtained proficiency, his nights were largely devoted to gambling and kindred pursuits.

The social customs of the time were not conducive to steadiness and sobriety among the youthful citizens. It was the Edinburgh of Humphrey Clinker and of Topham's Letters; the "Auld Reikie" of Fergusson's convivial muse—

Auld Reikie! wale o' ilka town
That Scotland kens beneath the moon;
Whare couthy chiels at e'ening meet
Their bizzing craigs and mou's to weet:
And blythly gar auld Care gae bye
Wi' blinkit and wi' bleering eye.

The early hours of the evening were at that period universally spent by Edinburgh tradesmen in one or other of the innumerable taverns of the old town. So soon as the business of the day was over, as Fergusson tells us—

When auld Saunt Giles, at aught o'clock,
Gars merchant louns their shopies lock,
There we adjourn wi' hearty fock
To birle our bodies,
And get wharewi' to crack our joke,
And clear our noddles.

"All the shops in the town," says Chambers, "were then shut at eight o'clock, and from that hour until ten—when the drum of the Town Guard announced at once a sort of licence for the deluging of the streets with nuisances, and a warning of the inhabitants home to their beds— unrestrained scope was given to the delights of the table." At the latter hour the more reputable roysterers sought their homes; but it was then that the clubs, which formed so prominent a feature of the old city life, began the business of the evening. Fergusson, who has given us in his incomparable "Auld Reikie" a glowing picture of the Edinburgh of his day, thus alludes to the subject—

Now Night, that's cunzied chief for fun,
Is wi' her usual rites begun;
Thro' ilka gate the torches blaze,
And globes send out their blinking rays.

Now some to porter, some to punch,
Some to their wife, and some their wench,
Retire, while noisy ten-hours drum
Gars a' your trades gae dandring home.
Now mony a club, jocose and free,

Gi'e a' to merriment and glee;
Wi' sang and glass, they fley the pow'r
O' care that wad harass the hour.

But chief, O Cape! we crave thy aid,
To get our cares and poortith laid:
Sincerity, and genius true,
Of Knights have ever been the due:
Mirth, music, porter deepest dy'd,
Are never here to worth deny'd;
And health, o' happiness the queen,
Blinks bonny, wi' her smile serene.

Of this, the most famous of the Edinburgh social clubs, Brodie was admitted a member on 25th February, 1775. The Cape Club usually held its festivals in James Mann's tavern, facetiously known as "The Isle of Man Arms," situated in Craig's Close. The roll of the Knights Companions of the Cape contains many celebrated names, including those of David Herd, the antiquarian; Robert Fergusson, the poet; Alexander Runciman, the painter; and Sir Henry Raeburn—William Brodie's election occurring four months after Fergusson's death. Each member was required to assume some fanciful title, Brodie taking that of "Sir Lluyd." On the margin of the roll prefixed to the minute-book an ingenious member has drawn a representation of his last public appearance on the new drop, some thirteen years later. The insignia of the Sovereign of the Cape are in the possession of the Society of Antiquaries, together with the club records, excerpts from which relating to Deacon Brodie will be found in the Appendix.

Had young Brodie been satisfied with the legitimate and very ample convivialities afforded by the Cape Club it would have been better for himself. But he became a frequenter of a disreputable tavern kept by James Clark, vintner, at the head of the Fleshmarket Close, where gambling by means of

Thus we poor Cocks, exert our Skill & Bravery
For idle Gulls, and Kites, *that trade in Knavery*

Cock-fighting Match between the Counties of Lanark and Haddington in 1785, at which Deacon Brodie was present. (After Kay.)

dice was nightly practised in a select company of sharpers and their dupes. It is probable that this house still survives in the truncated portion of the close remaining between the High Street and Cockburn Street. He also developed, among other "gentlemanly vices," a passion for cock-fighting, at that time a fashionable recreation among the young bloods of the capital, and was a regular attender at the *mains* held in the cock-pit belonging to Michael Henderson, stabler in the Grass-market, of whom we shall hear further in the sequel. Brodie, who is said to have lost large sums in betting on his favourite sport, was present, among other "eminent cockers," at the historic match between the counties of Lanark and Haddington, of which an account is given in "Kay's Portraits." In allusion to this contest, Kay observes—"It cannot but appear surprising that noblemen and gentlemen, who upon any other occasion will hardly show the smallest degree of condescension to their inferiors, will, in the prosecution of this barbarous amusement, demean themselves so far as to associate with the very lowest characters in society." Brodie himself kept game-cocks in a pen in his woodyard, and retained to the last his attachment to the "art of cocking." Between his bets at the cock-pits and his gambling at Clark's, the young man must have got rid of a good deal of money; and it is believed that he had already begun to supplement his income by the nefarious means which later he certainly employed.

One night in August, 1768, the counting-house of Johnston & Smith, bankers in the Exchange, was entered by means of a false key, and upwards of £800 in bank notes carried off. Two nights afterwards £225 of the money was found, wrapped in paper, at the door of the Council Chamber; but the balance was never recovered, and no clue to the delinquent could be obtained. The discovery, many years afterwards, of Deacon Brodie's exploits induced a strong suspicion that he was concerned in the affair. It was then recollected that, prior to the robbery, the Deacon had been employed in making various repairs on the premises, and had frequent occasion to be in the bank. The key of the outer door, from which it was ascertained he had taken an impression in putty, usually hung in the passage, a custom of which the Deacon, as we shall find, often afterwards took unscrupulous advantage.

At this time, however, no one dreamt of suspecting Brodie, whose secret dissipations were known only to his disreputable associates. Outwardly he was following worthily in his father's footsteps, and, on 9th February, 1763, was, like him, made a Burgess and Guild Brother of Edinburgh. In September, 1781, he also became a member of the Town Council as Deacon of the Incorporation of Wrights, and his connection with the Council continued from that date till the year before his apprehension, as follows:— Deacon of the Wrights in 1782 and 1783; Trades Councillor in 1784, and, again, Deacon of the Wrights in 1786 and 1787. In 1785 he was not a member of the Town Council. Robert Fergusson, in his poem, "The Election," has, with his usual felicity, portrayed the humours of an Edinburgh municipal election according to the old mode, when—

... Deacons at the counsel stent
To get themsel's presentit:
For towmonths twa their saul is lent,
For the town's gude indentit.

The minute of Deacon Brodie's last election, on 20th September, 1786, will be found in the Appendix, together with other excerpts from the Council records, bearing upon his official life.

In the new Deacon's first year of office occurred the political contest between Sir Laurence Dundas, who had represented the city in Parliament from 1760 to 1780, and William Miller, afterwards Lord Glenlee. The Town Council was divided into two hostile camps, and extraordinary efforts were made by each party to secure the return of its own candidate. Both claimed to have been duly elected member for Edinburgh; but, as the result of a parliamentary inquiry, Sir Laurence retained the seat. Deacon Brodie made a conspicuous figure in this election by keeping back his promise to vote for either party, in consequence of which he became a man of great moment to both the candidates, because upon his vote the election turned.

On 1st June, 1782, Convener Francis Brodie "died of the Palsy att his own house in Edinburgh, att 5 o'clock afternoon, in the 74th year of his age"; and William, his son, reigned in his stead. We read in the *Annual Register* for 1788—"However extraordinary it may appear, it is a certain fact that Mr. Brodie at the death of his father, which happened about six years ago, inherited a considerable estate in houses in the city of Edinburgh, together with £10,000 in specie; but by an unhappy connection and a too great propensity to that destructive, though too predominant passion, gaming, he is reduced to his present deplorable situation." That the Deacon owned some heritable property other than the family mansion in Brodie's Close, appears from a statement by the author of "Kay's Portraits" (1877, vol. I., pp. 141-2). It is there said that a house in Gourlay's Land, Old Bank Close, was purchased from the trustee for the Deacon's creditors in 1789 by William Martin, bookseller and auctioneer in Edinburgh, who subsequently sold the property to the Bank of Scotland in 1793. From the state of affairs, which he prepared at a later date as aftermentioned, it is evident that Brodie owned, in addition to this property, three other tenements, respectively situated in Horse Wynd, at the Nether Bow, and in World's End Close. We also find from the Council records that, in 1785, he was speculating in the building lots of the New Town.

The "unhappy connection" above mentioned refers to the Deacon's two mistresses, Anne Grant and Jean Watt. Anne Grant resided in Cant's Close, and her relations with William Brodie must have been long continued, for she had borne three children to him, the eldest, Cecil, being a girl of twelve at the time of his trial. To Anne Grant he addressed one of the letters written after his escape from Scotland, by which, as will be seen, he was traced and brought to justice. Jean Watt, by whom he had two boys, lived in Libberton's Wynd, close to his own house, and was the principal witness to the *alibi* attempted to be set up for him at his trial. Each of these women was presumably ignorant of the other's existence, and the Deacon's connection with both appears to have been unknown to his family and friends. After his father's death his sister, Jean Brodie, presided over his household; his other sister, Jacobina, to whom he refers in his letters as "Jamie," having married Matthew Sheriff, an upholsterer in Edinburgh.

It seems incredible, regard being had to the confined and crowded stage on which the old city life was played, that Deacon Brodie's protracted peccadilloes escaped the notice of those "stairhead critics," who, Fergusson tells us—

Wi' glowring eye,
Their neighbours' sma'est faults descry.

But, if the facts were generally known, the estimable reputation which he nevertheless enjoyed is characteristic of the social conventions of his day.

Had it not been for the Deacon's unhappy propensity for gambling and dissipation, his circumstances at this time should have been highly satisfactory. During his term of office he was regularly employed by his fellow-Councillors to execute wrightwork in connection with the town—his accounts for the year 1782-3, for instance, amounting to upwards of £600. In addition to the city work, his social and official position had secured for him the best cabinetmaking business in Edinburgh; but, notwithstanding these advantages, he was frequently at a loss for money.

Deacon Brodie was already, in Stevenson's striking phrase, "a man harassed below a mountain of duplicity," and to one so circumstanced it is not surprising that the idea occurred of putting his professional opportunities to an unlawful use. He knew the locks and bolts of all the houses of his customers; was familiar with their internal arrangements and the habits of the owners; and could, without incurring remark, exhibit in such matters a professional interest in the houses of his friends and acquaintances. No doubt he was sometimes consulted, at a later stage, as to the best means of defence against his own infraction. He was shortly, as we shall see, to become the leader of a gang of robbers, whose mysterious depredations, under his skilful conduct, were, during eighteen months, to baffle the authorities and strike terror to the hearts of wealthy burgesses; but at the outset of his career of crime the Deacon worked alone.

"Many a citizen," says Stevenson, "was proud to welcome the Deacon to supper, and dismissed him with regret at a timeous hour, who would have been vastly disconcerted had he known how soon, and in what guise, his visitor returned. Many stories are told of this redoubtable Edinburgh burglar, but the one I have in my mind most vividly gives the key of all the rest. A friend of Brodie's, nesting some way towards heaven in one of these great 'lands,' had told him of a projected visit to the country, and afterwards, detained by some affairs, put it off and stayed the night in town. The good man had lain some time awake; it was far on in the small hours by the Tron bell; when suddenly there came a creak, a jar, a faint light. Softly he clambered out of bed and up to a false window which looked upon another room, and there, by the glimmer of a thieves' lantern, was his good friend the Deacon in a mask."

Another story, illustrative of the methods of this pioneer of amateur cracksmen, is as follows:—One Sunday an old lady, precluded by indisposition from attending the kirk, was quietly reading her Bible at home. She was alone in the house—her servant having gone to church—when she was startled by the apparition of a man, with a crape over his face, in the room where she was sitting. The stranger quietly lifted the keys which were lying on the table beside her, opened her bureau, from which he took out a large sum of money, and then, having locked it and replaced the keys upon the table, retired with a respectful bow. The old lady, meanwhile, had looked on in speechless amazement, but no sooner was she left alone than she exclaimed, "Surely that was Deacon Brodie!"—which subsequent events proved to be the fact.

On both of these occasions it is to be noted that, although the Deacon was recognised, no action was taken by his victims. In the first instance the man hesitated to denounce his friend; in the second the old lady preferred to doubt the evidence of her senses—a striking proof of the advantages conferred by a respectable reputation.

Apart altogether from the question of gain, it is probable that Deacon Brodie, in adopting these criminal courses, was influenced by the dramatic possibilities of his new part. The minor duplicities which hitherto he had so successfully practised would thus be capable of development upon a larger stage; and, to one of his peculiar temperament, the prospect doubtless afforded fascinating opportunities for deception. To rob a friend's house of an evening, and in the morning condole with him upon his loss; to carry through some daring burglary overnight, and gravely deliberate next day in the Council Chamber as to offering a reward for discovery of the perpetrator—these were situations after the Deacon's heart.

Throughout the whole course of the robberies which we are about to consider, it is to be kept in view that Deacon Brodie retained the respect and esteem of his fellow-citizens—for his reputation among the associates of his secret life is immaterial; daily pursued his lawful avocations; and regularly attended the meetings of the Council, taking his share in the conduct of the town's affairs. And so masterly was his performance of this dual *rôle* that no suspicion of the Deacon's integrity was aroused, until the failure of the "last fatal" business of the Excise Office and the treachery of an accomplice shattered, at once and for ever, the elaborate fabric of his deceit.

We can form a vivid impression of the appearance of Deacon Brodie about this time from the description of him which was circulated some two years later. From this it appears that he was a small man—"about 5 feet 4 inches"—of a slender build, and looking younger than his age. He had "dark brown, full eyes, with large black eyebrows, and a cast with his eye that gave him somewhat the look of a Jew," a sallow complexion, and a peculiar manner of speaking, "which he did full and slow." From the minute details of his dress and toilet it is evident that the Deacon was something of a dandy, or, in the language of the day, "a macaroni." He had also "a particular air in his walk, and moved in a proud, swaggering sort of style," while the advertisement includes such particulars as the size of his ankles and the turn of his calves. We shall afterwards find that this very candid portrait was not appreciated by its original.

About the month of July, 1786, there arrived in Edinburgh a man who was to exercise a powerful influence for evil upon the Deacon's fortunes. This was George Smith, a native of Boxford, near Newburgh, in Berkshire, who was travelling the country as a hawker with a horse and cart. He was a stranger to Edinburgh, and put up at Michael Henderson's house in the Grassmarket, having heard it mentioned on the road as a traveller's inn. Soon after his arrival he fell sick, and, his illness lasting for some four months, he was reduced to selling his goods, and finally his horse, in order to support himself and his wife, for whom he had meanwhile sent into England to join him. Among the frequenters of Michael Henderson's tavern were two men, Andrew Ainslie and John Brown *alias* Humphry Moore, of whom, prior to their doings in connection with the robbing of the Excise Office, but little is known. Ainslie is designed in the Crown list of witnesses as "sometime shoemaker in Edinburgh," but his attention to his professional practice was less marked than his addiction to dicing and the company of cheats. Brown— like Smith, an Englishman—was a noted sharper, and had been convicted of theft at the Old Bailey in April, 1784, and sentenced to transportation beyond the seas for a term of seven years. He had, however, contrived to escape from justice, and was then lurking in Edinburgh, ready for any villainy that might prove remunerative.

With these two agreeable acquaintances Smith beguiled the tedium of convalescence in various games of hazard, in which, owing to the skill of the players, but little was left to the blindness of Fortune; and at this time he first made the acquaintance of Deacon Brodie, who, in connection with his cock-fighting proclivities, had long been a patron of the house. It is probable that, at this juncture, the Deacon's resources were at a low ebb. Notwithstanding the income he derived from his varied interests and pursuits, his passion for gambling was a constant drain upon his purse, and the expense of maintaining no less than three establishments at once must also have been considerable, while the success of his earlier robberies doubtless induced him to extend his future operations by the assumption of a partner.

Be that as it may, we have it from Smith's second declaration that Brodie, early in the intimacy which, in spite of the disparity in their social positions, speedily sprang up between them, suggested to him in the course of conversation "that several things could be done in this place, if prudently managed, to great advantage, and proposed that they should lay their heads together for that purpose." Smith is said to have been at one period of his career a locksmith in Birmingham, and his abilities in this direction may have first led the Deacon to select him as an accomplice. From the readiness with which Smith embraced this proposition we may assume that his past record was not so blameless as he would have us believe.

In the following account of the burglaries (other than that of the Excise Office) committed by Deacon Brodie and his associates, the details are given from the various statements made by Smith, and, so far as possible, in his own words; but there is good reason for believing that these by no means disclose the full extent of the depredations for which the gang was responsible.

When the invalid was sufficiently recovered, the new friends, "in consequence of this concert, were in use to go about together in order to find out proper places where business could be done with success." In the course of these interesting excursions, Smith relates that one evening in November, 1786, they visited a hardware shop in Bridge Street belonging to Davidson M'Kain, armed with false keys, an iron crow, and a dark lantern. Having opened the outer door, Smith entered the shop, his companion remaining outside to watch. Smith was inside for about half-an-hour, and Brodie, becoming impatient, called out what made him stay so long—was he taking an inventory of the shop? The result appears to have been disappointing; but among the goods removed was a red pocket-book, which Smith presented, as a token of gratitude, to "Michael Henderson, stabler in Grassmarket, his daughter."

About a fortnight later the two worthies again repaired to M'Kain's shop with the view of making a more thorough clearance. The same methods were adopted; but before Smith could get to work he was disturbed by movements in a neighbouring room, and fled, shutting the shop door after him. Brodie had already beaten a retreat. A little later, however, the pair walked arm-in-arm down Bridge Street to reconnoitre the premises, but, seeing a man on the watch, "and a guard soldier standing opposite at the head of the stair which goes down to the Fleshmarket, they passed along the bridge, and afterwards went to their several homes, as nothing could be done further that night." This, according to Smith, was their first joint depredation; but there is reason to believe that a much more important robbery, which was committed on 9th October, the previous month—when a goldsmith's shop near the Council Chambers was broken into and many valuable articles carried off—was also the Deacon's handiwork.

An ostensible occupation had been found for Smith, and he was established in a house in the Cowgate, where his wife and he kept a small grocery shop. Brodie had now introduced his new friend to his own favourite "howff"—

Clark, the vintner's at the head of the Fleshmarket Close—where it was their habit to foregather nightly for the purpose of gambling and discussing future opportunities for the exercise of their felonious talents. Hither, also, came Ainslie and Brown, from the lodging which they occupied together at the foot of Burnet's Close, but who were not yet admitted to share the others' councils. On 8th December, we read that "the shop of John Law, tobacconist in the Enchange, was broken into, and a cannister containing between ten and twelve pounds of money carried off." This robbery, though not confessed to by Smith, was probably committed by him and Brodie.

Stimulated to further efforts by the inadequate results of these operations, the Deacon now proposed to Smith a more important undertaking. He had recently been employed by the magistrates, in consequence of the lowering of the streets, to alter the door of the shop in Bridge Street belonging to Messrs. John & Andrew Bruce, jewellers, there. This, he said, "would be a very proper shop for breaking into," as it contained valuable goods, and his familiarity with the lock would make it an easy matter to effect an entrance. It was accordingly agreed that they should meet at Clark's on the evening of Saturday, 24th December, for the purpose of carrying out the robbery. Arriving there, they fell to playing hazard with other members of "the club," as it was called by the questionable characters who frequented the house, and Smith, the luck being against him, soon lost all his money. Brodie, on the other hand, was winning steadily, and refused to leave, turning a deaf ear to his friend's repeated reminders that business should come before pleasure and their work awaited them. It was nearly four in the morning when Smith decided to wait no longer, "as the time for doing their business was going," and started by himself upon the exploit. The lock presented no difficulties, and, by the light of his dark lantern, he was able to reap an excellent harvest. "Ten watches, five of them gold, three silver, with the whole rings, lockets, and other jewellery and gold trinkets in the show-boxes," were all stuffed into two old black stockings and carried by Smith to the hospitable Mr. Henderson's stable, where he hid them in a manger, and was at last free to seek the shelter of his grocery establishment in the Cowgate.

Smith was up betimes on the Sunday, and by eight o'clock was "tirling" at the door in Brodie's Close, to inform the Deacon of what he had missed. The maid told him, however, that her master was still in bed, so Smith left a message that he wanted to see him, and returned home. Later in the day the Deacon called upon him, and Smith, having meantime fetched the black stockings from the Grassmarket, poured out upon the bed their glittering contents, remarking, "You see what luck I have been in; you might have been there, but, as you did not go, you cannot expect a full share. But there are the goods; pick out what you choose for yourself"—which certainly seems handsome behaviour on Smith's part, although Brodie afterwards complained that he had been treated badly in the matter. The Deacon accordingly selected for his own use a gold seal, a gold watch-key set with garnet stones, and two gold rings. They valued the whole articles at £350 sterling, and must have been good judges, for that was the figure which the owners themselves subsequently put upon the goods.

That same day they walked past Bruce's shop several times to see if the robbery had been discovered, but found everything as they had left it. Delighted at the success of his coup, Smith boldly proposed returning that night "in order," as he said, "to sweep the shop clean," but Brodie dissuaded him from so hazardous an attempt. They then consulted as to the safest means of disposing of the goods, with the result that, on the following Wednesday, Smith set off with them on foot to Dunbar, and from thence took the mail-coach to Chesterfield, where he parted with them to one John Tasker *alias* Murray—who had previously been banished from Scotland—for £105. The Deacon had advanced five and a half guineas for the expenses of the journey, and, on his return, Smith repaid this sum, and entrusted Brodie with the balance to keep for him, and give him as he required it; but Brodie "gained a great part of it at play." The Deacon, therefore, did not do so badly after all.

Head of Brodie's Close, Lawnmarket.
(From a Drawing by Bruce J. Home.)

It is interesting to note in passing that during this period—the winter of 1786-7—Deacon Brodie had for an opposite neighbour no less a person than Robert Burns. While the poet was sharing his friend Richmond's lodgings in Baxter's Close, Lawnmarket, there also dwelt in the adjacent Wardrop's Court Alexander Nasmyth, the artist, whose portrait of Burns was painted at this time. It is probable that the poet, the painter, and the Deacon foregathered with other kindred spirits at Johnnie Dowie's tavern in Libberton's Wynd, the recognised resort of the Edinburgh wits of that day.

The partners seem to have rested satisfied with the substantial profits of their last transaction for a considerable time, for the next robbery of which we have any details was not carried out till 16th August, 1787. In this, for the first time, they had the advantage of Ainslie's assistance, he being taken into their confidence for that end. The three repaired to Leith, to the shop of John Carnegie, a grocer at the foot of St. Andrew Street, which Ainslie and Smith entered by means of pick-locks—Brodie remaining without to watch—and carried off "350 pounds of fine black tea," at that period a very valuable haul. Two wallets were filled from the chests in the shop, but "Ainslie being ill at this time and Brodie being weakly," they were forced to abandon one of the wallets, which they hid in a shed in a field by the Bonnington Road, where it was afterwards recovered. The Deacon objected to the other wallet being taken to his house, and what became of it is not known.

In their next undertaking the company was raised to its full strength by the accession of John Brown *alias* Humphry Moore, whose previous experiences in England eminently qualified him to take an important part in such criminal enterprises. Brown appears to have been spending the autumn in Stirlingshire, but his visit was suddenly brought to a close in September on his banishment from that county by the Justices of the Peace for a theft committed by him within their jurisdiction. This was a more boldly conceived robbery than the gang had yet attempted—no less than the theft of the silver mace belonging to the University of Edinburgh. The Deacon, in the course of those walks with Smith, in which healthful exercise was combined with an eye to business, "carried" the latter "to the College Library, where, having observed the mace standing, Brodie said that they must have it." Ainslie was accordingly sent to see where the mace was usually kept, and reported that it was in the Library, where the others had seen it. Accordingly, on the night of 29th October, 1787, the quartet proceeded to the University. "Having got access at the under gate, they opened the under door leading to the Library with a false key, which broke in the lock; and thereafter they broke open the door of the Library with an iron crow, and carried away the College mace." The magistrates offered a reward of ten guineas for a discovery of the thieves, but without success. The mace was forthwith despatched to the accommodating Tasker, of Chesterfield, at the appropriate address of the "Bird in Hand," and the macer thereof knew it no more.

Brown appears entitled to the credit of planning the next robbery, and took a leading part in its execution. In those days the merchants of Edinburgh usually resided above their business premises, and the key of the shop was hung on the inside of the door—a habit highly appreciated by the Deacon's little band. Brown brought to Smith the key of a shop belonging to one John Tapp, which, he said, also opened the door of that gentleman's house; and Smith, having cast a professional eye over same, assured him "there was nothing in it." Thereafter, one evening about Christmas time, between nine and ten o'clock, Brown dropped in upon John Tapp, whom he detained in his shop over a friendly and seasonable bottle. His associates, meanwhile, opened the house door with a false key and rifled the good man's repositories, making off with "eighteen guinea notes, and a twenty shilling one, a silver watch, some rings, and a miniature picture of a gentleman belonging to Tapp's wife, which picture they broke for the sake of the gold with which it was backed." One wonders if Mrs. Tapp mentioned the loss to her husband. These valuables accompanied the mace to Chesterfield, where John Tasker *alias* Murray seems to have driven a brisk, though illegitimate, trade, along with a letter to him, written by Brown in Smith's name, arranging for their disposal.

Soon after this the Deacon, ever on the alert for a good stroke of business, suggested to his partners the "doing" of the shop of Messrs. Inglis & Horner, silk mercers at the Cross of Edinburgh, "as the goods there were very rich and valuable, and a small bulk of them carried off would amount to a large sum." He and Smith frequently went to examine the padlock, "which they did most commonly on the Sunday forenoon when the people were in church." They found this necessary, as the lock proved to be of a difficult construction. Brodie made a key for it himself, and went one night alone to test its efficacy, probably with the view of stealing a march upon the rest, and doing a little private practice outwith the knowledge of his colleagues. When he tried the key, however, although it unlocked the padlock it would not lock it again, and he had to disclose the state of matters to the others. On learning of his attempt "they were all very angry with him, and said that he had more than likely spoilt the place after all the trouble they had been about; but Brodie told them he hoped not, as he had fixed the padlock with a bit stick in a way that it would not be discovered, and upon looking at the place afterwards, which they all did, they found the lock to be just as it was." Eventually Smith made a key that was more reliable, and on the night of 8th January, 1788, an entry was effected, and silks and cambrics to the value of between £300 and £400 successfully removed.

Next day a reward of £100 was offered by the Procurator-Fiscal for the discovery of the criminals, but, as usual, without success. The owners, however, did not let the matter rest there, and on their representations the Government, on 25th January, offered an increased reward of £150 to any one who, within six months, would give such information as should lead to the discovery and conviction of the perpetrators, and twenty guineas for the names of the offenders whether they should be convicted or not. In addition, "His Majesty's gracious pardon" was promised to any accomplice who should within the like period procure the apprehension of the guilty parties. Though this offer elicited no information at the time, it was, ultimately, as we shall see, the means of breaking up that dangerous association from whose depredations the inhabitants of the good town of Edinburgh had so long and severely suffered.

From the spoils of Inglis & Horner's shop Smith tells us that Brown selected "a piece of plain white sattin, a piece of variegated ditto, and a lead-coloured silk, in quantity about ten yards, which he gave to a girl, an acquaintance of his of the name of Johnston." One is pleased to notice in passing this indication of a gentler element in Mr. Brown's rugged nature. The remainder of the goods were concealed in a cellar which Ainslie had hired for the purpose in Stevenlaw's Close, and were subsequently despatched in two trunks—one by the Berwick carrier and the other by the Newcastle waggoner—to our old friend at the "Bird in Hand," Chesterfield. We shall hear more of them later.

The reader must have been struck, in following the account of the robberies committed by Deacon Brodie, with the singular incapacity displayed by the official guardians of the public safety. These were the Old Town Guard, a body of armed police which existed in Edinburgh from an early date until 1817, when it was finally disbanded. The corps was composed of some hundred and twenty veterans, chiefly drawn from the Highland regiments, who were in continual conflict with the youth of the capital. Fergusson, in his poems, has many a hit at the peculiarities of this "canker'd pack"—

And thou, great god of *aqua vitæ*!
Wha sways the empire of this city—
When fou we're sometimes capernoity—
Be thou prepar'd
To hedge us frae that black banditti,
The City Guard.

Indeed, so frequently does he refer to them that Scott, in "The Heart of Midlothian," calls him their poet laureate. Evidently these antiquated warriors were no match for the Deacon and his merry men.

Notwithstanding the many calls upon his time, owing to the varied character of his engagements and pursuits, Deacon Brodie managed to drop in at the club in the Fleshmarket Close of an evening as frequently as ever, and, in spite of the magnitude of his recent operations, was not above winning a few guineas from any one foolish enough to lose them. On the night of the 17th of January, therefore, Brodie, Smith, and Ainslie were at Clark's, according to their own account, "innocently amusing themselves with a game of dice over a glass of punch," when their privacy was intruded upon by John Hamilton, a master chimney-sweep in Portsburgh, who insisted on joining them at play. This person was, within a surprisingly short time, relieved by the trio of "five guinea notes, two half guineas in gold, and six shillings in silver," and being apparently a bad loser, he promptly seized the dice, which, on examination, were found to be "loaded, or false dice, filled at one end or corner with lead." Here was a pretty scandal for the respectable Deacon to be mixed up in! Outraged innocence was of no avail—the dice spoke for themselves.

But the master sweep's blood was up, and the matter was not allowed to end there. Hamilton forthwith presented to the magistrates of Edinburgh a petition and complaint against Brodie, Smith, and Ainslie, setting forth his meeting with them at Clark's, and his being invited to join them in a friendly game, with the result above narrated. The petitioner concluded with praying for a warrant to apprehend and incarcerate the said persons until they should repeat the sum of which he had been so defrauded, and pay a sum over and above in name of damages and expenses. Answers were lodged for Brodie, and separate answers for Smith and Ainslie, in which it was stated that if false dice were used it was unknown to the defenders, as the dice they played with belonged to the house; that Brodie had only gained seven and sixpence; and that "the petitioner himself was a noted adept in the science of gambling, and it was not very credible that he would have allowed himself to be imposed upon in the manner he had alleged."

Hamilton's replies to these answers are conceived in a fine vein of irony— "Mr. Brodie knows nothing of such vile tricks—not he! He never made them his study—not he! Mr. Brodie never haunted night houses, where nothing but the blackest and vilest arts were practised to catch a pigeon, nor ever was accessory, either by himself or others in his combination, to behold the poor young creature plucked alive, and not one feather left upon its wings—not he, indeed! He never was accessory to see or be concerned in fleecing the ignorant, the thoughtless, the young, and the unwary, nor ever made it his study, his anxious study, with unwearied concern, at midnight hours, to haunt the rooms where he thought of meeting with the company from which there was a possibility of fetching from a scurvy sixpence to a hundred guineas—

not he, indeed! He is unacquainted altogether either with packing or shuffling a set of cards—he is, indeed!" This, one would think, must have been painful reading for the Deacon's fellow-Councillors; but nothing further appears to have been done in the matter, and the affair blew over without damaging the worthy man's repute: a singular comment on the moral standard of the time.

In spite of the consummate skill with which Deacon Brodie had hitherto sustained his double character, one is hardly prepared, in view of his manner of life, to find him figuring in a criminal trial in any other capacity than that of the central figure. Strange as it may seem, however, his next public appearance was in the jury-box of the High Court of Justiciary, when, on 4th February, 1788, Allan M'Farlane, officer of Excise, and Richard Firmin, soldier in the 39th Regiment of Foot, were placed at the bar charged with the murder of Dougald Fergusson, ferryman at Dunoon, Argyllshire.

The facts brought out at the trial were, briefly, as follows:—A party of Excise officers, accompanied by some soldiers, had, in the previous July, gone to Dunoon and seized certain illicit stills, which they put on board their boat. Fergusson, a zealous freetrader, had rung the kirk bell, assembled a mob, who pelted the officers with stones, and, boarding the boat, had knocked down the two boatmen and attempted to carry off the stills. In these circumstances, M'Farlane ordered Firmin to fire, which he did, killing Fergusson on the spot. The charge against Firmin was abandoned by the Lord Advocate in his address, as it was proved that he had only acted under orders; and the point for the jury to consider was whether M'Farlane was justified in giving the order to fire in self-defence, in view of the danger to which the Excise party were exposed from the hostile mob behind them, had Fergusson succeeded in carrying off the boat. The jury unanimously found both panels not guilty.

Thus did the Deacon, at the very time when all Edinburgh trembled at his depredations and the authorities were straining

**The Old Excise Office, Chessel's Court, Canongate.
(From a Drawing by Bruce J. Home.)**

every nerve to discover the guilty author, calmly officiate upon a jury to judge of the crimes of others. But, although he may have laughed in his sleeve at this ironical situation—for he had a pretty wit, and doubtless relished the humour of it keenly—fate had prepared for him one yet more dramatic. A few months later he himself would sit in that dock on trial for his life, the same counsel would conduct the prosecution, the same judges occupy the bench; but the verdict would be a different one, and the sentence to follow upon it, death.

Undisturbed by any shadow of coming disaster, and emboldened by his previous successes, Deacon Brodie now decided to carry out a robbery upon a grander scale than any he had previously attempted, the daring and danger of which were commensurate with the advantages to be gained. The General Excise Office for Scotland was at that period kept in a large mansion, enclosed by a parapet wall and iron railing, situated in Chessel's Court, Canongate. The building had formerly been occupied as a dwelling-house, and was by no means a secure repository for the great sums of money which in those days were collected there from all parts of the country. The Deacon, in his professional capacity, was familiar with the arrangements of the office, his men having at various times executed repairs on the premises. A connection of his, Mr. Corbett, of Stirling, too, was in the habit of coming to Edinburgh frequently on Excise business, and Brodie took the opportunity of accompanying him upon these occasions with a view to studying how the land lay.

Having learned all that was necessary for his purpose, the Deacon went one day to the office with Smith, on pretence of inquiring for Mr. Corbett, and while he thus engaged the attention of the cashier, Smith took an impression in putty of the key of the outer door, which, according to the prevailing ingenuous custom, was hung upon a nail inside it. From this Brodie prepared a drawing of the wards, and Smith filed a key of similar pattern. The next step was to ascertain the habits of the watchman who guarded the premises, and for this purpose Ainslie—whose department seems to have been scouting—was deputed to observe the office on several successive nights. He found that it was usually closed for the day at eight o'clock; that when all the clerks had left the outer door was locked, and the key taken to Mr. Dundas, "the housekeeper," who lived in the court, and that the night watchman did not come on duty until ten o'clock. The Excise Office was thus left wholly unguarded between the hours of eight and ten at night.

Smith and Brown had already tried the efficiency of the new key, which readily opened the outer door, but the lock of the inner door to the cashier's room refused to yield to their persuasive methods. Smith was of opinion that its resistance could only be overcome by violence, observing that the coulter of a plough would be a suitable instrument for that purpose. Accordingly, on the afternoon of Friday, 28th February, Ainslie and Brown repaired to Duddingston as a likely spot for picking up such an implement. Having refreshed themselves after their walk with a bottle of porter at a house in the village, they entered a field in the neighbourhood, where they had seen a man ploughing, and, when his back was turned, removed the coulter of the plough and two iron wedges, which on their way home by the King's Park they hid in Salisbury Crags. Unfortunately for themselves and Smith, they were accompanied upon this country ramble by a black dog, belonging to the latter, named "Rodney," which, curiously enough, was at a later stage to bear testimony against its master before the Sheriff.

On Tuesday, 4th March, a final consultation was held by the four desperadoes at Smith's house in the Cowgate to arrange the details of the attack upon the Excise Office, which was fixed for the following night, when, as they had ascertained, it was the turn of an old man, who watched night about with the other porter, to be on guard. According to Smith's second declaration, "it was concerted by Brodie, in case of interruption by the man coming into the office before the business was accomplished, to conceal themselves quietly until he was gone to rest, and then to secure him; and they were, if this happened, to personate smugglers who came in search of their property that had been seized; and the declarant had a wig of Brodie's father in his pocket in order to disguise himself." Little did that decent old gentleman dream to what base uses his respectable wig would one day be assigned by his cynical and degenerate offspring. The Deacon also furnished Smith with a coil of rope to be knotted into a ladder, so that if taken by surprise they could lock the outer door of the office and make good their escape by the back windows into the garden behind. Having decided upon their plan of campaign, the meeting adjourned till the following afternoon.

Wednesday, the 5th of March, 1788, was a busy day for the Deacon. Between two and three o'clock he was back at Smith's, attired in "the white-coloured clothes he usually wore," with various requisites for the night's adventure— pick-locks, false keys, an ivory whistle, "a strong chisel with a brass virral," and a spur, which was to be left on the scene of the robbery, "to make it believed it had been done by some person on horseback, in order that it might appear, when found, to have dropped from the foot by its being torn by accident at the buckle."

By three o'clock he was presiding in his own dining-room, with the panel painting and the great arched window, at a dinner-party consisting of his aunt, his two sisters, Matthew Sheriff, his brother-in-law, and "a stranger gentleman" whose identity was not disclosed. "We drank together," says Mr. Sheriff, "from dinner to tea, which I think was brought in about six o'clock, and then the stranger gentleman went away." Probably he thought discretion the better part of valour. The brothers-in-law, however, continued the sederunt till shortly before eight o'clock, when Sheriff retired to his residence in Bunker's Hill—the name by which St. James' Square was then known. The moment his guest had gone the Deacon, hastily attiring himself in an old-fashioned black suit, a cocked hat, and a light-coloured great-coat, put his pistols and dark lantern in his pocket, and hurried off to the business of the evening.

It had been arranged that the gang should assemble at Smith's house at seven o'clock, since which hour the others had been impatiently awaiting their leader's arrival. The Deacon was in a merry mood; his spirits were high as his hopes, and the potations of the afternoon had doubtless contributed to their elation. He burst in upon his anxious friends with a pistol in his hand, singing a stave from his favourite "Beggar's Opera"—

Let us take the road;
Hark! I hear the sound of coaches!
The hour of attack approaches;
To your arms, brave boys, and load.

See the ball I hold;
Let the chemists toil like asses

Our fire their fire surpasses,
And turns our lead to gold.

It was a raw and wintry evening of a type familiar to the Edinburgh spring—
that "meteorological purgatory" of Stevenson; there had been a considerable
fall of snow, followed by an intense frost, and few people were out of doors.
Smith, Brown, and Ainslie were sitting in an upper room beguiling the time
with a light refection of herrings and chicken, washed down by draughts of
gin and "black cork," *i.e.*, Bell's beer. Ainslie and Brown had, whenever it was
sufficiently dark, brought the coulter of the plough and the iron wedges from
their hiding-place in Salisbury Crags. No time was to be lost, and so soon as
the Deacon arrived the final arrangements were quickly made. Three brace
of pistols—one of which had been obligingly lent by Michael Henderson—
were loaded by Smith with powder and ball, each member of the party,
excepting Ainslie, being armed with a pair, "as they were determined not to
be taken, whatever should be the consequence." Three crape masks were also
prepared for the use of Smith, Ainslie, and Brown. To Smith and Brown was
appointed the task of forcing the doors and rifling the premises; the Deacon
was to be stationed in the hall behind the outer door to prevent a surprise;
while it was Ainslie's duty to keep watch within the "palisadoes" outside the
office, where, concealed by the parapet wall, he could command a view of
the court and entry. Ainslie was provided with a whistle of ivory, purchased
by Brodie the night before, with which, if the watchman appeared, he was to
give one whistle, so that they might be prepared to secure him; and, if more
than one man or any appearance of danger was perceived, he was to give
three whistles, and then make the best of his way to the gardens behind, in
order to assist the others in escaping by the back windows. Brodie, on hearing
the signal, was, in turn, to give the alarm to Brown and Smith within the
building.

In pursuance of this arrangement, Ainslie left first for the scene of action in
Chessel's Court, carrying with him the coulter, and, having taken up his
position within the "palisadoes," saw the porter come out with a light and
lock the outer door behind him. Shortly thereafter Smith arrived. On hearing
that the coast was clear, he lost no time in opening the front door with his
false key and went into the office. He was followed five minutes later by
Deacon Brodie, who, learning that Smith was within, but that Brown had not
yet put in an appearance, went back up the court to look for him. They met
in the entry and returned together, Brown explaining that, on his arrival, he
had seen the old man who usually locked up the office leaving the court, and
had dogged him home as a precautionary measure. Brown then inquired of
Ainslie "whether or not he had 'Great Samuel'?"—by which playful
appellation he referred to the coulter—and Ainslie handed it to him through

the railings. The Deacon and Brown then entered the office, leaving the outer door on the latch, behind which the former ensconced himself.

Smith had meanwhile opened the spring catch of the inner door with a pair of curling irons or "toupee tongs" which he had prepared for that purpose, and was awaiting Brown in the hall. By means of the coulter and an iron crow—"Little Samuel," in Brown's humorous phraseology—the two burglars at length succeeded in forcing the door of the cashier's room, and by the light of the Deacon's lantern they proceeded to prize open every desk and press which it contained. In the cashier's desk they found and appropriated two five-pound notes, six guinea notes, and some odd silver; but after half-an-hour's diligent searching their utmost efforts failed to discover the accumulated riches which they had confidently expected to secure.

In the hurry of the search, by a curious chance, a secret drawer, concealed beneath the cashier's desk, containing no less than £600 sterling, escaped their notice.

Unwilling to accept their defeat, the two men were ransacking the desks afresh when they heard the front door open, but, supposing Brodie to be at his post, paid no attention. They were about to leave the room to prosecute their investigation of the premises when they heard some one come hastily down the stairs, "which made them stop or they must have met him." Upon this Brown whispered, "Here must be treachery; get out your pistols and cock them!" They then heard the front door close with a crash. Perceiving that something was wrong, they now hastened into the hall, when, to their amazement, they found that the Deacon had vanished, and, on opening the door, that Ainslie also had disappeared. Cursing their ill luck and the defection of their companions, the puzzled burglars hurried through the court into the Canongate; and, quite at sea as to what had happened, made the best of their way to Smith's house, leaving behind them in the office the heavy coulter and the spur which was designed to mislead the discoverers of the robbery.

We must now return to Ainslie, whom we left on the watch behind the railings. A servant girl, returning from a message to her master's house in the court, saw him looking over the wall, and, "judging him to be a light or suspicious person"—in which diagnosis she was not far wrong—sought safety within doors. He had not been long at his post when the silence of the court was broken by the sound of a man running into it from the street, and Ainslie, peering through the railings, was alarmed to see him go in at the open door of the Excise Office. At the very moment of his entrance another man rushed from the doorway and fled at full speed up the court; and before Ainslie could recover from his surprise at this unlooked-for situation, a third man, as he supposed, came immediately out of the office and also disappeared towards the Canongate after the other.

The scanty oil lamps with which in those days the city was "illuminated" after nightfall served but as feeble foils to the surrounding darkness, and to Ainslie, in the dimly-lighted court, friend and foe were equally indistinguishable. These mysterious and unlooked-for doings proved too much for the watcher's nerve; so, having hastily given the agreed-on signal of retreat by three blasts upon his whistle, he, too, made for the entry, and, turning down St. John's Street, came through the gardens of the Canongate to the back of the Excise Office. Finding no trace of his associates there, Ainslie in his turn repaired to Smith's.

The explanation of these occurrences, which had dispersed the gang in bewilderment and consternation, was singularly simple, but the issue might have been very different. Mr. James Bonar, Deputy Solicitor of Excise, had returned to the office about half-past eight o'clock to get certain papers which he had left in his room. Finding the outer door on the latch, he assumed that some of the clerks were still in the building, and was entering the office when the Deacon, who appears to have lost his usual presence of mind, bounced out from behind the door, and, brushing past him, fled hastily from the court. Mr. Bonar attached no importance to this incident, thinking the person belonged to the office, and, being pressed for time, ran upstairs to his own room, got what he wanted, and hastened from the building, slamming the outer door after him.

If Ainslie had not lost his head at the sudden entrance and exit of the Solicitor and the Deacon, but had blown his whistle, as he should have done, whenever the former appeared, Smith and Brown, rushing out with their pistols cocked, would have encountered Mr. Bonar in the lobby, and murder would doubtless have been done. As it was, that gentleman probably owed his life to the pusillanimity of Ainslie and Brodie, the latter of whom could, from his ambush, easily have closed with him as he entered the hall.

After his undignified flight from the Excise Office, Deacon Brodie reached his own house about nine o'clock, where he once more changed his attire, putting on the fine white suit he usually wore. He then hurried to the house of his mistress, Jean Watt, in Libberton's Wynd, where he remained till the following morning. Meanwhile, at Smith's house the other three were discussing the disappointing result of the night's expedition and indulging in mutual recriminations. The non-appearance of Brodie added to their uncertainty, and they parted for the night in no amiable mood, Ainslie and Brown going over to the New Town, where, in a tavern kept by one Fraser, they sought consolation in a bowl of punch. The next day—Thursday—the Deacon came to Brown and Ainslie's lodging in Burnet's Close and laughingly told them that Smith had accused him of deserting his post the previous night. He was received but sourly by Brown, who made no secret of sharing Smith's opinion. These, however, were minor matters, the vital question being whether or not suspicion would be directed to themselves. It was arranged that they should all meet at Smith's the following night, when the sixteen pounds—miserable recompense of so much risk and labour!—was to be equally divided among them.

Accordingly, upon the Friday evening, in the upper room of Smith's house, each man received his share, amounting to a little over four pounds. Ainslie, to whom Brodie owed a "debt of honour," took occasion to require payment, and got one of the five-pound notes and some gold from him. The Deacon, who had staked infinitely more, thus made less than any of them by the adventure. Brown, so soon as he had received his share, went out, like Judas, and for a similar purpose.

The reader may remember the two trunks in which the silks stolen from Inglis & Horner's shop were packed with a view to transmission to John Tasker at Chesterfield. One of these had been despatched some time before by the Berwick carrier, the other had been forwarded that week by the Newcastle waggoner, and Smith's wife was to leave for England on the Saturday in order to treat personally with the proprietor of the "Bird in Hand," who was probably a difficult customer to deal with. Smith and Ainslie therefore proceeded to the New Town, where, at the inn kept by William Drysdale, they purchased a ticket for Mrs. Smith by the mail-coach to Newcastle on the following day. The five-pound note was tendered in payment, and they received the change, less the price of the ticket.

Let us now see how prudent Mr. Brown had been improving his time. Daily since the 25th of January there had appeared in each of the three Edinburgh newspapers advertisements offering £150 reward and a free pardon to whoever should disclose the robbers of Inglis & Horner's shop. The excitement occasioned by that crime had been revived and increased tenfold by the discovery of the attack upon the Excise Office, which was made by ten o'clock on the night of its occurrence, and the vigilance of the authorities was proportionally augmented.

Brown stood in a more ticklish situation towards the outraged majesty of the law than any of his companions, for over him hung the sentence of transportation, which he had hitherto successfully evaded; and it would go hard with him if he fell into the hands of justice in connection with any of his later villainies, which might happen at any moment. He was, moreover, profoundly disgusted with the manner in which the Excise business had miscarried through no fault of his own, and would not be sorry to steal a march on his cowardly associates. He was also cunning enough to foresee that, if he turned informer, he would not only earn a handsome reward, but enjoy immunity for his past performances, as it would be necessary for the public prosecutor to obtain a pardon for his old offence also, before his evidence could be made available against his fellow-criminals.

Having carefully considered his position, therefore, and immediately after securing his dividend at Smith's, Brown proceeded to William Middleton, of the Sheriff-Clerk's Office, and informed him that he had certain discoveries to make concerning the robberies recently committed in the city. Late as it then was—eleven o'clock—Middleton at once took Brown to the Procurator-Fiscal, to whom he told the whole story, suppressing, however, in the meantime, all mention of Deacon Brodie's name in connection with the crimes. His object in taking this course was doubtless to secure a hold upon the Deacon which would enable him, at his leisure, to blackmail that respectable gentleman with impunity. At his own request the Procurator-Fiscal and Middleton went with him that same night to Salisbury Crags, where Brown pointed out a number of false keys underneath a stone, hidden there by Smith after the affair at the Excise Office, of which the Fiscal took possession.

The next morning, Saturday, 8th March, Brown, accompanied by Middleton, left for Chesterfield in pursuit of Inglis & Horner's goods by the very coach in which Mrs. Smith was to have performed the same journey. How they fared upon their errand is not recorded, but it would have been interesting to know what happened when John Tasker's unexpected guests dropped in at the "Bird in Hand."

The same day Ainslie, Smith, and his wife, and servant-maid were apprehended; and, having been examined before the Sheriff, were committed to the Tolbooth, the two women being subsequently set at liberty.

That Saturday evening the rumour of the prisoners' arrest spread like wildfire through the city, and on Deacon Brodie, confident in his fool's paradise, the intelligence must have fallen like a thunderbolt. Apart from his temporary loss of nerve at the Excise Office, he was undoubtedly a man of courage and resource, and the step he now determined to take might well have daunted a less intrepid character. This was to visit the Tolbooth in person and obtain speech with Smith and Ainslie, so as to induce them, if it were not too late, to hold their tongues. To do this, knowing nothing of where he stood or how much had come out, was to put his head into the lion's mouth; but he saw that, at all costs, he must ascertain what had happened. Accordingly, having taken his cane and cocked hat, the Deacon, with that "particular air" which characterised his walk, sallied forth upon his desperate errand. The Tolbooth was but a few paces from his own door, and he was familiar with the jail, both as a Town Councillor and in the ordinary course of his employment. Arrived there, he congratulated the officials on their capture, and expressed his curiosity to see the redoubtable burglars with whose deeds all Edinburgh was then ringing, but was informed that no one was allowed access to them. He was therefore compelled to return home no wiser than he went, where, it is probable, the owner of the house in Brodie's Close passed a sleepless and remorseful night.

Next morning, realising that the game was up, and that he must prepare for the worst—for he might now be arrested at any moment—Deacon Brodie sent for his foreman, Robert Smith, at eight o'clock, told him that he was about to leave town for a day or two on business, and gave him a message about a waistcoat and a pair of breeches he required for the journey. He then casually asked "if there were any news about the people who had broke into the Excise." The foreman answered that Smith was in custody, and that Brown had been sent to England; and, knowing his master's intimacy with these men, added that he hoped he (Brodie) was not concerned with them, to which the other made no reply.

If he was to fly the country it was essential that the Deacon should be in touch with his relations in Edinburgh, upon whose assistance he would principally have to rely. He therefore promptly called upon his cousin— whose name was considerately withheld in the subsequent proceedings—and explained the situation. This gentleman's feelings, as he listened to the disclosures of his respectable relative, may readily be imagined. But the honour of the family was at stake, and he seems to have done everything he could to further the Deacon's plans. The necessary arrangements made, early in the forenoon of Sunday, 9th March, while the good folks of Edinburgh were still in church, Deacon Brodie burnt his boats and stole secretly out of the city.

Had the Deacon's confidence in the loyalty of his late companions been stronger, it is possible he might even yet have weathered the storm, for neither Smith nor Ainslie in the declarations emitted by them on the Saturday had admitted their guilt or made any reference to his connection with them. So far, therefore, the statements of Brown were uncorroborated; and if, in modern parlance, Brodie had decided "to face the music" and remain in Edinburgh, his fortunes might have taken a different turn.

In the course of Smith's first examination before the Sheriff a curious incident occurred. He was confronted with the ploughman, John Kinnear, whose coulter had been stolen by Ainslie and Brown as before narrated, in order to try if that person could identify him. Kinnear, never having seen him before, failed to do so. At this moment, however, Smith's dog "Rodney," having followed his master to the Sheriff-Clerk's Office, came into the room, and the ploughman at once recognised it as the black dog which he had seen with the men in the field at Duddingston. The animal ran up to Smith and fawned upon him, thus, in spite of his denial, establishing the fact of his ownership. "Rodney" figures in Kay's sketch of the first meeting of Brodie and Smith.

On Monday, 10th March, Smith, learning that the Deacon had decamped, and no doubt hoping to secure more favourable terms for himself, sent for the Sheriff and informed him "that he wished to have an opportunity of making a clean breast and telling the truth." He thereupon emitted his second declaration, laying bare the whole operations of the gang, and implicating Brodie to the fullest extent, his admissions being afterwards confirmed by Ainslie.

The following paragraph appeared next day in the *Edinburgh Evening Courant*:—"The depredations that have been committed by housebreakers in and about this city for this some time past have been no less alarming than the art with which they have been executed, and the concealment that has attended them has been surprising. From a discovery, however, just made, there is reason to hope that a stop will soon be put to such acts of atrocious villainy. With what amazement must it strike every friend to virtue and honesty to find that a person is charged with a crime of the above nature who very lately held a distinguished rank among his fellow-citizens? With what pity and compunction must we view the unfortunate victim who falls a sacrifice to justice for having violated the laws of his country, to which violation he was perhaps impelled by necessity, when rank, ease, and opulence are forfeited in endeavouring to gratify the most sordid avarice? For to what other cause than avarice can we impute the late robbery committed upon the Excise Office, when the situation of the supposed perpetrator is considered? No excuse from necessity can be pled for a man in the enjoyment of thousands, who will run the risk of life, honour, and reputation in order to attain the unlawful possession of what could in a very trifling degree add to his supposed happiness.—See the advertisement from the Sheriff-Clerk's Office."

The advertisement to which this article refers—a copy of which will be found in the Appendix—was the offer by the Procurator-Fiscal of a reward of two hundred pounds for the apprehension of "William Brodie, a considerable house carpenter, and burgess of the city of Edinburgh," together with the minute and somewhat unflattering description of that gentleman's personal appearance, to which we have already alluded. So the murder was out at last, and the ex-Town Councillor became a fugitive from justice with a price upon his head.

In consequence of the revelations of Smith, the officers of justice proceeded on Monday, 10th March, to search the house in Brodie's Close. There Smith, who accompanied them, unearthed the Deacon's pistols, buried in his woodyard. His dark lantern, several pick-locks, and a parcel of false keys were also found—the first "in a pen where game-cocks had been

Deacon Brodie's Dark Lanthorn and False Keys. (From the originals in the Museum of The Society of Antiquaries of Scotland.)

kept"—together with "a black case, with a lid to it, the case full of potty," with which it had been the Deacon's amiable habit to take impressions of his friends' door keys, and of which Smith remarked that he "approved of Brodie keeping the potty in a case, as the lid prevented an impression of a key, when taken, from being defaced." On a subsequent occasion, Smith conducted the sheriff-officers to the foot of Warriston's Close, where the iron crow— "Little Samuel"—the "toupee tongs," and the false key for the Excise Office door were discovered hidden "in an old dyke." The Deacon's dark lantern and twenty-five false keys were, on 13th December, 1841, presented by the then Clerk of Justiciary to the Society of Antiquaries of Scotland, in whose museum they still remain.

On Tuesday, 11th March, George Williamson, King's Messenger for Scotland, was deputed to search for the missing Deacon. He tried several of Brodie's haunts in Edinburgh and Leith—even examining the enclosed tombs in Greyfriars Churchyard, which had more than once sheltered living offenders against the law—but without success. Prosecuting his inquiries along the London Road, Williamson first got scent of his quarry at Dunbar, which the fugitive had left at four o'clock on the Sunday afternoon in a post-chaise, and afterwards traced him to Newcastle, where he had taken the "Flying Mercury" light coach for York and London. From the coachman of that vehicle Williamson learned that Deacon Brodie had left the coach at the foot of Old Street, Moorfields, instead of proceeding to the "Bull and Mouth," where the coach stopped, and there all trace of him was lost. His pursuer repaired to the billiard tables, hazard tables, cock-pits, tennis courts, and other likely places, without hearing anything of him, and pushed his inquiries as far as Margate, Deal, and Dover, with the like result. Finally, after eighteen days' fruitless search, the King's Messenger was compelled to return to Edinburgh and confess himself at fault.

We must now, in our turn, set forth in search of Mr. Brodie; and as to his doings after leaving Edinburgh we have the evidence of his own letter to Michael Henderson. He writes—"Were I to write you all that has happened to me, and the hair-breadth escapes I made from a well-scented pack of bloodhounds, it would make a small volume. I arrived in London on Wednesday, 12th March, where I remained snug and safe in the house of an old female friend until Sunday, 23rd March (whose care for me I shall never forget, and only wish I may ever have it in my power to reward her sufficiently), within five hundred yards of Bow Street. I did not keep the house all this time, but so altered, excepting the scar under my eye, I think you could not have rapt [swore] to me. I saw Mr. Williamson twice; but although countrymen commonly shake hands when they meet from home, yet I did not choose to make so free with him notwithstanding he brought a letter to me. He is a clever man, and I give him credit for his conduct. My female gave me great uneasiness by introducing a flash man to me, but she assured me he was a true man, and he proved himself so, notwithstanding the great reward, and was useful to me. I saw my picture [his description in the newspapers] six hours before, exhibited to public view, and my intelligence of what was doing at Bow Street Office was as good as ever I had in Edinburgh. I make no doubt but that designing villain Brown is now in high favour with Mr. Cockburn [the Sheriff], for I can see some strokes of his pencil in my portrait. May God forgive him for all his crimes and falsehoods." It is evident that the impartial terms of this description were unpalatable to its subject.

The scar to which the Deacon here alludes was a souvenir of his membership of the club in the Fleshmarket Close, and the occasion of his receiving it is thus referred to in the answers of Hamilton, the master sweep, in the process before mentioned—"Mr. Brodie, in all his innocent amusements, never met with any person who, after having been fleeced of money to the amount of a hundred pounds, and detected of the vile and dishonest methods by which it had been abstracted from him, received, as a return for his moral rectitude, a very handsome incision on the eye—never he, indeed! He never was in such company, nor ever met with such an accident—not he!" This scar may be observed in the portraits of the Deacon by Kay.

Deacon Brodie had brought with him to London an introduction from his cousin to Mr. William Walker, attorney in the Adelphi, who busied himself in the fugitive's affairs, lent him twelve guineas, and arranged to have him shipped safely off to the Continent so soon as the coast was sufficiently clear.

On Sunday, 23rd March, that "constant trader," the sloop "Endeavour," of Carron, John Dent, master, bound for the port of Leith, lay at her anchor at Blackwall. About twelve o'clock that night the captain, who had gone ashore, came aboard with the owners, Messrs. Hamilton and Pinkerton, and an elderly gentleman, apparently in feeble health. After a short conversation the owners left the ship; the passenger, who had been "allotted a bed in the state-room near the fire, as he was sick," withdrew to the privacy of his cabin; and the "Endeavour" began her voyage. Off Tilbury Point, however, she went aground, and did not clear the Thames for a fortnight. No one seems to have thought this misadventure at all remarkable, and such incidents were doubtless common enough in those spacious days, when time, generally speaking, was no object.

The only other passengers on board were John Geddes, a tobacconist in Mid-Calder, and his wife, who were returning to Leith after a visit to the metropolis. The leisurely methods of the "Endeavour" afforded ample opportunity for cultivating the acquaintance of their fellow-passenger, whose name they found was Mr. John Dixon. They passed the time agreeably together, and Mr. Dixon on one occasion entertained his fellow-voyagers to dinner at a neighbouring village, though for the most part, while the vessel was aground, he remained on board.

At length, having been successfully refloated, the "Endeavour" resumed her interrupted voyage. No sooner, however, were they well out at sea than Mr. John Dixon produced and handed to Captain Dent sealed orders from the owners, wherein he was instructed to make sail for Ostend, where Mr. Dixon was to be landed, before proceeding to Leith, and the vessel was accordingly headed for the coast of Flanders. Owing to thick weather and cross winds, she failed to make that port, and finally put in to Flushing. Even this fresh delay appears in no way to have disturbed the equanimity of the easy-going Geddeses; and, having arrived on the 8th of April at their unlooked-for destination, they improved the occasion by making some purchases of contraband goods as a memento of their visit. Mr. John Dixon, meanwhile, before leaving the ship, wrote three letters—which he entrusted to the care of Geddes for delivery on his arrival in Edinburgh—directed respectively to Michael Henderson, stabler in the Grassmarket; Mrs. Anne Grant, Cant's Close; and Mr. Matthew Sheriff, upholsterer in Edinburgh. Having taken a cordial farewell of each other, Mr. Dixon and Geddes parted company, the former—in whom the astute reader has ere now discerned the perfidious

Deacon—setting out for Ostend in a skiff, and the latter resuming his protracted voyage.

When the "Endeavour" eventually arrived at Leith, where her non-appearance had caused considerable anxiety, Geddes, on perusing the newspapers, saw the Deacon's description; but, though satisfied that the letters he carried were written by the notorious William Brodie, for three weeks after making the discovery he did nothing further in the matter. Perhaps a dilatory habit had been induced by his late experiences, or his conscience may have required some persuasion. Having at last decided to open the letters, he showed them to various persons, and subsequently delivered them over to the Sheriff. In taking this course, Geddes was probably actuated less by a sense of duty to his country than by a desire to secure the reward. If so, it is satisfactory to find that he did not receive it. The authorities had now, through the Deacon's singular imprudence, obtained the necessary clue to his whereabouts, and no time was lost in following it up.

What were the contents of the letter to Anne Grant we have now no means of knowing, for that document was not produced at the trial, but the other two letters will be found at length in the following report. In all the contemporary accounts of the trial the names of persons referred to by Deacon Brodie in his letters were, for obvious reasons, omitted. These are now printed in full for the first time from the originals in the Justiciary Office, Edinburgh. In that addressed to his brother-in-law, Matthew Sheriff, dated 8th April, the Deacon writes—"My stock is seven guineas; but by I reach Ostend will be reduced to less than six. My wardrobe is all on my back, excepting two check shirts and two white ones; one of them an old rag I had from my cousin Milton, with an old hat (which I left behind). My coat, an old blue one, out at arms and elbows, I also had from him, with an old striped waistcoat and a pair of good boots. Perhaps my cousin judged right that old things were best for my purpose. However, no reflections; he is my cousin and a good prudent lad, and showed great anxiety for my safety; rather too anxious, for he would not let me take my black coat with me. I could not extract one guinea from him, although he owes me twenty-four pounds for three years past. He cannot help his natural temper." Evidently the spruce and dapper gentleman keenly felt the sartorial straits to which his cousin's parsimony had reduced him. He requests that wearing apparel, tools, and certain articles connected with his trade be forwarded to him at an address in New York; desires that his remittances may be as liberal as possible—"for without money I can make but a poor shift"; and adds in a postscript, "Let my name and destination be a profound secret, for fear of bad consequences."

To Michael Henderson he writes, on 10th April, after the passages already quoted, asking what is likely to become of "poor Ainslie, Smith, and his wife; I hope that neither you nor any of your connections has been innocently involved by these unfortunate men. Write me how the Main went; how you came on in it; if my black cock fought and gained, &c., &c."—from which we are pleased to note that the Deacon, amid the ruin of his fortunes, retained his kindly disposition and sporting instincts. One hopes that the black cock came off victorious. It is interesting to find in the *Edinburgh Evening Courant* of 5th April, 1788, the following advertisement of the "Main" to which the Deacon refers:—

COCK FIGHTING.

The LONG MAIN betwixt William Hamilton, Esq., of Wishaw, and Captain Cheap of Rossie, begins at twelve o'clock on Monday, the 7th curt., and will continue at the same hour every day during the week, at HENDERSON'S PIT, Grassmarket.

SUNLEY and SMALL, Feeders and Handlers.

Brodie concludes his letter thus—"I am very uneasy on account of Mrs. Grant and my three children by her; they will miss me more than any other in Scotland. May God in His infinite goodness stir up some friendly aid for their support, for it is not in my power at present to give them the smallest assistance. Yet I think they will not absolutely starve in a Christian land, where their father once had friends, and who was always liberal to the distressed. My eldest daughter, Cecil, should be put apprentice to the milliner or mantuamaking business; but I wish she could learn a little writing and arithmetic first. I wish to God some of my friends would take some charge of Cecil; she is a fine, sensible girl, considering the little opportunity she has had for improvement." Here we have a glimpse of another and better element in the complex character of this extraordinary man.

Information of the circumstances disclosed in these letters was instantly despatched to the authorities in London, and the Secretary of State, Lord Carmarthen, at once communicated with Sir John Potter, the British Consul at Ostend, in consequence of which Deacon Brodie was traced to Flushing and Middleburgh, and from thence to Amsterdam. Application was immediately made to Sir James Harris, British Consul there, with the result that the Deacon was apprehended in an alehouse, through the instrumentality of John Daly, an Irishman, on the eve of embarking for America.

The circumstances of his capture were as follows:—Daly, armed with an exact description of the fugitive, ascertained his whereabouts in Amsterdam from two Jews "who attend the passengers that arrive in the treck schoots." On reaching the alehouse where Brodie was lodged, the landlord told him that the gentleman he inquired for was above. Daly proceeded to the first floor, knocked once or twice at the door, and, receiving no answer, entered the room. It was seemingly empty, but a search of the apartment disclosed the unlucky tenant hiding in a cupboard. "How do you do, Captain John Dixon *alias* William Brodie?" said Daly; "come along with me"; and the Deacon, realising that resistance was useless, surrendered at discretion, and was duly lodged in the Stadthouse. It is disappointing to find our hero yielding thus tamely to his Irish captor, but it must be remembered that, physically, the Deacon was a small man, and, moreover, at this time was not in good health. Having seen his captive safely disposed of, John Daly left for London to claim and receive the reward.

On 1st July, Mr. Groves, Messenger-at-arms, was despatched from London to bring the prisoner back to England. The journal kept by Groves on this expedition—a copy of which is contained in the Appendix—gives an interesting account of the proceedings before the magistrates at Amsterdam in connection with the extradition of the Deacon. There was some difficulty in establishing the prisoner's identity, the evidence of two witnesses on oath to that effect being required by the law of Holland. One witness, who had seen Brodie in Edinburgh, stated that he had no doubt he was the same man, "but would not swear he had no doubt"—a nice distinction. The Deacon would admit nothing. Ultimately the magistrates declared themselves satisfied, and the prisoner was delivered up to Mr. Groves, who conducted his charge in triumph to Helvoetsluys.

The journey was accomplished, with all the pomp and circumstance befitting so important an occasion, in "two carriages, and four guides, with four horses in each carriage," and the poor Deacon "properly secured" inside. Next day they sailed for Harwich, the prisoner being "watched two hours alternately on board by the ship's crew, his hands and arms confined, and his meat cut up for him, &c." Mr. John Dixon must have recalled with regret the comforts of his earlier voyage.

On 11th July the pair arrived in London, where Deacon Brodie was examined at Bow Street before Sir Sampson Wright, chief magistrate, and Mr. Longlands, solicitor to the Treasury, in whose presence he admitted his identity. He was accordingly committed to Tothilfields Bridewell, pending his removal to Scotland.

At Bow Street two trunks belonging to Brodie were opened, and in one of them was found a bundle of papers. Among these were two draft letters or unsigned scrolls, afterwards produced at the trial, and printed in the following report, which throw much interesting light upon the writer's position and prospects. They were evidently intended for friends in Edinburgh, and written subsequent to the letters which he had intrusted to the treacherous

Geddes. He writes—"I hope to embark in the first ship for America, to whatever port she is bound, which will probably be Charlestown, South Carolina, as there is a ship lying-to for that port. I will settle there, if I think I can do better than at Philadelphia or New York." He asks his correspondent to inform him "what has been done with the two unfortunate men Smith and Ainslie, and the greater villain, John Brown *alias* Humphry Moore? Was John Murray *alias* Jack Tasker brought from England? I shall ever repent keeping such company; and whatever they may allege, I had no direct concern in any of their depredations, excepting *the last fatal one*, by which I lost ten pounds in cash. But I doubt not all will be laid to my charge, and some that I never heard of." The last quoted passage told strongly against him at the trial, and it is difficult to see why he had preserved such compromising documents.

In the same trunk was found an account or state of Brodie's affairs prepared by himself on 24th March, the day after he embarked in the "Endeavour." This document was founded on in the indictment and produced at the trial; but Creech tells us, in the introduction to his report, that, "although laid on the table for the inspection of the jury, yet, being of a private nature and not necessarily connected with the crime charged, the jury had too much delicacy to look into; and it is hoped the same motive will be a sufficient apology for not laying it before the public." It was, accordingly, not published in any of the contemporary accounts of the trial, and is now for the first time printed in the following report from the original MS. in the Justiciary Office. From this most interesting document we are able to learn the financial position of Deacon Brodie at the time of his flight, and it is surprising to find that he brings out a balance in his favour of upwards of £1800.

Our old friend, George Williamson, the King's Messenger, was sent from Edinburgh to conduct the reluctant Deacon back to his native city. On the journey north, Williamson tells us, "Mr. Brodie was in good spirits, and told many things that had happened to him in Holland." Among other items of interest, he mentioned that, while in Amsterdam, he had formed the acquaintance of a gentleman living in that city on the proceeds of a successful forgery committed upon the Bank of Scotland. Forgery was a branch of the learned professions which the Deacon had hitherto neglected, and he was receiving instruction from this obliging practitioner, when his studies were abruptly terminated by Mr. Daly's call. "Brodie said he was a very ingenious fellow, and that, had

George Williamson, King's Messenger for Scotland.
(After Kay.)

it not been for his own apprehension, he would have been master of the process in a week." Before arriving in Edinburgh the Deacon, ever careful of his personal appearance, was anxious to obtain a shave—a luxury to which, in the turmoil of his affairs, the dapper gentleman had been for some days a stranger. Williamson, afraid to trust a razor to one so circumstanced, himself essayed the task. His intention must have been superior to his execution, for, when the operation was over, the patient remarked, "George, if you're no better at your own business than at shaving, a person may employ you once, but I'll be d——d if ever he does so again!"

On 17th July the *Caledonian Mercury* was able to announce to its readers— "This morning early Mr. Brodie arrived from London. He was immediately carried to the house of Mr. Sheriff Cockburn, at the back of the Meadows, or Hope Park, for examination. Mr. George Williamson, Messenger, and Mr. Groves, one of Sir Sampson Wright's clerks, accompanied Mr. Brodie in a post-chaise from Tothilfields Bridewell. He was this forenoon committed to the Tolbooth. They were only fifty-four hours on the road."

While their leader was enlarging his experience of life on the Continent, Smith and Ainslie had varied the monotony of existence in the Tolbooth by a vigorous attempt to regain their liberty. We read in the *Scots Magazine* for May, 1788, that "in the night between the 4th and 5th of May, George Smith, prisoner in the Tolbooth of Edinburgh, accused of shop-breaking and theft, had the ingenuity to make his way from his own apartment to that of Andrew Ainslie, a supposed accomplice in the same crimes, though Ainslie's room was situated two storeys above that occupied by Smith. This, it would appear, was achieved by his converting the iron handle of the jack or bucket of the necessary into a pick-lock, and one of the iron hoops round the bucket into a saw. By a dextrous use of these instruments Smith took off one door from the hinges, and opened the other which led to Ainslie's apartment. They then both set to work, and cut a hole through the ceiling of Ainslie's room, as well as through the roof of the prison itself. Luckily, however, the falling of the slates and lime into the street, between three and four o'clock in the morning, attracted the attention of the sentinel upon duty, who immediately gave the alarm, and the inner keeper had them soon after properly secured. In order to let themselves down from the top of the prison they had prepared 16 fathoms of rope, which they had artfully manufactured out of the sheets of their beds."

This daring and ingenious bid for freedom deserved a better fate, and it is a testimony to Smith's skill that he was able to achieve so much by means so grotesquely inadequate. Little wonder that, with liberty and his tools, he was a competent and successful practitioner.

Mr. Brown, that unamiable informer, was, strangely enough, also at this time an inmate of the Tolbooth. The *Edinburgh Magazine* for the same month gives an account of his arrest, along with George White, tanner, and William Peacock, flesher, charged with being concerned in the murder of James M'Arthur, change-keeper in Halkerston's Wynd, during a quarrel in the latter's house—"alleged not to be one of very good repute"—in which M'Arthur was fatally assaulted with a bottle. The consequences of this regrettable incident were, so far as Brown was concerned, averted by the pardon aftermentioned. White, however, was brought to trial and found guilty of culpable homicide.

The law officers of the Crown were now busily preparing their case against Brodie, Smith, and Ainslie; and as, apart from the testimony to be borne by Brown, there was no direct evidence of the commission of the crime available, it was decided to accept Ainslie as King's evidence, and proceed only against Brodie and Smith upon the charge of breaking into and robbing the General Excise Office for Scotland. Accordingly, on 19th July, an indictment was served upon them, the trial being fixed to take place on 4th August. Owing, however, to some additional evidence having come to the knowledge of the Public Prosecutor, on 11th August, a new indictment had to be served, and the trial postponed until the 27th of that month.

Meanwhile, on 28th July, His Majesty's most gracious pardon had been obtained for John Brown *alias* Humphry Moore, which, in law, rendered that miscreant, as a witness, "habile and testable," notwithstanding the baseness of his character and his infamous record.

Deacon Brodie had, since his apprehension, been kept in close confinement in the Tolbooth. He was carefully watched day and night by two soldiers of the City Guard, and was not allowed either knife or fork with which to eat his victuals in case of dangerous consequences. On account of this inconvenient restriction, the Deacon, shortly before his trial, addressed the following remonstrance to a brother member of the Town Council and one of the magistrates of the city:—

"Edinburgh, 17th August, 1788.

"Dear Sir,

"The nails of my toes and fingers are not quite so long as Nebuchadnezzar's are said to have been, although long enough for a Mandarine, and much longer than I find convenient. I have tried several experiments to remove this evil without effect, which no doubt you'll think says little for your Ward's ingenuity; and I have the mortification to perceive the evil daily increasing.

"Dear Sir, as I intend seeing company abroad in a few days, I beg as soon as convenient you'll take this matter under consideration, and only, if necessary, consult my Guardian and Tutor *sine qua non*; and I doubt not but you'll devise some safe and easy method of operation that may give me a temporary relief. Perhaps the faculty may prescribe a more radical cure.

"Dear Sir, if not disagreeable to you, I'll be happy to see you. You'll be sure to find me at home, and all hours are equally convenient.

"Believe me to be, with great esteem,
"Your most affectionate Ward, and very humble servant,
"WILL. BRODIE.

"To Don. Smith Esq.
"Edinburgh."

This curious instance of a sense of humour retained in the most unfavourable circumstances throws an interesting sidelight on the Deacon's character.

On the Friday before the trial Smith, who appears to have abandoned all hope of an acquittal, wrote a letter to the Board of Excise, saying "that he was not to give them any trouble, for he would plead Guilty." He also prepared a written statement, which it was his intention to have read to the Court, but he was dissuaded from this course by his agent, Mr. Morrison, and finally decided to take his chance and plead not guilty. In this remarkable document—a copy of which is contained in the Appendix—Smith gives, *inter alia*, the following list of "such robberies as my accomplices and myself had determined to commit, had we not been timeously prevented:—

- "1. On Dalgleish & Dickie, watchmakers.

- 2. On White & Mitchell, lottery-office keepers.

- 3. On a rich baker near Brodie's Close—the name forgot.

- 4. The Council Chamber, for the mace.

- 5. The Chamberlain's Office, for money.

- 6. Forrester & Co.'s, jewellers.

- 7. Gilchrist & Co.'s, linen drapers.

Besides these, and as depredations of greater magnitude—

- 8. The Bank of Scotland (or Old Bank) was to have been broke into.

- 9. The Stirling stage coach, carrying a thousand pounds to pay the Carron workmen, was to have been stopped and robbed.

- 10. Mr. Latimer, Collector of Excise for the Dalkeith district, reported to have generally from one to two thousand pounds, was to have been robbed."

This comprehensive catalogue of the gang's prospective arrangements was, doubtless, perused with much interest by the intended victims, and the rich baker must have congratulated himself on escaping the attention of his respectable neighbour. The only one of these contemplated robberies, towards the accomplishment of which any steps would seem to have been taken, was that of the office of the City Chamberlain. We read in Smith's third declaration that "a false key was made by Brodie for the purpose of opening the door of the Chamberlain's cash-room of the city of Edinburgh; the declarant and Brodie had frequently been at the door of the Chamberlain's Office, in order to take the impression of the keyhole; that Brodie showed the declarant the said key after it was made; and Brodie told the declarant that it did not answer"—which was fortunate for the City Chamberlain. But the laudable intention which Smith, since his apprehension, had evinced "of making a clean breast" was not destined to gain for him any temporal advantage.

George Smith at the Bar.
(After Kay.)

The public interest in the approaching trial was intense, both on account of the magnitude of the late robberies and the prominent position which Deacon Brodie had so long occupied in Edinburgh. His escape and capture had further whetted the popular excitement, and at an early hour on the morning of Wednesday, 27th August, 1788, every part of the Justiciary Court was crowded to its utmost capacity. A detachment of the 7th Regiment of Foot from the Castle lined the Parliament Square for the purpose of securing an easy access for the members of the Court and jurymen, and to prevent any confusion that might arise from the great crowd assembled at the doors.

At a quarter to nine o'clock the prisoners were brought from the Tolbooth into Court. "They were conveyed, upon their request, in chairs, but each having a sentinel of the City Guard on the right and left, with naked bayonets, and a sergeant's guard behind, with muskets and fixed bayonets." A contemporary account informs us that "Mr. Brodie was genteelly dressed in a new dark-blue coat, a fashionable fancy waistcoat, black satin breeches, and white silk stockings, a cocked hat, and had his hair fully dressed and powdered." In contrast to the dashing appearance cut by his companion, Smith, we are told, was "but poorly clothed, having had no money since his confinement, which had already lasted six months." The Deacon affected an easy and confident demeanour; Smith, on the contrary, looked timid and dejected.

At nine o'clock the five judges, preceded by a macer bearing the Justiciary mace, and headed by the formidable Braxfield, took their seats, "and, the Court being fenced and the action called in the usual manner," the trial then commenced. As a *verbatim* report of the proceedings is contained in the following pages, and some account of the judges and counsel engaged therein will be found in the Appendix, it is only necessary here briefly to comment upon the more salient incidents which occurred in the course of the trial.

It is worthy of note that among those who served upon the jury were William Creech, the celebrated Edinburgh publisher and man of letters, and also Sir William Fettes, afterwards Lord Provost of Edinburgh, and James Donaldson, the well-known printer and pioneer of cheap literature, to whose munificence the city is indebted for the famous college and palatial hospital which bear the names of their respective founders.

The interest of the Deacon's friends had secured for him the services of Henry Erskine, then Dean of Faculty, and the chief ornament of the Scots bar, with whom were Alexander Wight, and Charles Hay, afterwards the jovial Lord Newton; while Smith's case was entrusted to the celebrated John Clerk of Eldin, at that time an inconsiderable junior, and Robert Hamilton, in later years the colleague of Sir Walter Scott. The Lord Advocate (Ilay Campbell) and the Solicitor-General (Robert Dundas), assisted by two Advocates-depute, conducted the prosecution.

Both prisoners pleaded not guilty; no objections were taken to the relevancy of the indictment; and it was stated for Brodie that he intended to prove an *alibi*. An objection taken by the Dean of Faculty to the specification of certain of the articles libelled on having been repelled, John Clerk attempted to make some observations on behalf of Smith, which resulted in the first of those passages of arms between him and Braxfield, whereby the dignified course of the proceedings was frequently enlivened. Clerk had then been at the bar less than three years; this was the most important case in which he had yet been employed; and it is said to have been his first appearance in the Justiciary Court. The remarkable and characteristic energy with which on that occasion he conducted his client's defence attracted the attention of the profession, and laid the foundations of his subsequent reputation and practice.

An interesting point of law arose in connection with the calling of Smith's wife as a witness for the prosecution against Brodie. Her proposed evidence was vigorously objected to by Clerk on account of the relation in which she stood to his client—both panels were included in one indictment, and it was impossible to criminate the one without the other. A sharp encounter with Braxfield ensued; but the Court admitted the witness. When Mrs. Smith entered the box, however, Alexander Wight, for Brodie, stated a fresh objection, viz., that the maiden name of the witness was wrongly given in the Crown list as "Mary Hubbart," whereas her real name was "Hibbutt," which, on her being requested by Braxfield to sign her name, turned out to be the fact. In view of this misnomer the objection was sustained and the witness dismissed.

Another legal point of interest arose when it was proposed to identify the five-pound bank-note libelled on, the Dean of Faculty objecting that it was not a "bank-note," as described in the indictment, having been issued by a private banking company in Glasgow. The Court sustained the objection, holding that nothing was to be deemed a bank-note but one issued from a bank established by Royal Charter.

The crucial question of the case, however, both for the prosecution and the defence, was whether or not Ainslie and Brown should be admitted as witnesses to prove the panels' guilt. So far the proof of their complicity in the robbery was mainly circumstantial. Although Smith, in his second declaration, had confessed his accession to the crime, yet, having pleaded not guilty, this was not in itself sufficient to convict him; while as regards the Deacon, apart from the statements of Smith, his guilt was only to be inferred from his flight and certain passages in his letters. It was, therefore, of vital importance to the prisoners that the direct evidence of their accomplices should be excluded, while the Crown case equally depended for a verdict upon its admission.

To the determining of this question each side accordingly addressed its strongest efforts, and the debate which followed will be found both lively and instructive. The authority of Sir George Mackenzie was quoted against the admission of the witnesses; but that venerable jurist was somewhat severely handled. The principal objection to Ainslie, as stated by the Dean of Faculty, was that he had been himself accused of the crime he was now to fasten upon another, and that the Sheriff of Edinburgh had offered him his life if he would criminate Brodie, of whose complicity he had hitherto said nothing. In the case of Brown, the battle was joined upon the precise effect of the pardon which had been obtained for that interesting criminal, and to what extent the pristine purity of his character was thereby restored. The Court, however, repelled the objections, and admitted both witnesses; and the evidence which they gave finally disposed of all chance of the panels' acquittal.

At the conclusion of Brown's evidence the Lord Justice-Clerk addressed that truculent scoundrel as follows:—"John Brown, you appear to be a clever fellow, and I hope you will now abandon your dissipated courses, and betake yourself to some honest employment." To which Brown suitably replied, "My Lord, be assured my future life shall make amends for my past conduct." He then left the box, and so passes out of the story, of which he was undoubtedly "the greater villain," and surely never did witness less merit judicial commendation than John Brown *alias* Humphry Moore.

The Crown case closed with the reading of the prisoners' declarations and the Deacon's letters, such portions of the former as related to matters unconnected with the trial being withheld from the jury. For the defence no witnesses were called for Smith, and an attempt to prove an *alibi* made on behalf of Brodie was entirely unsuccessful, the principal witnesses to it being his brother-in-law, Matthew Sheriff, and his mistress, Jean Watt, both obviously friendly to the Deacon's interests.

At one o'clock on the morning of Thursday, 28th August, the exculpatory proof was closed, and the Lord Advocate began his address to the jury. His Lordship's speech, while an able and convincing statement of the Crown case, was marred by one or two passages which would now be considered to exceed the limits of legitimate advocacy. Such are the references to facts "which would have been likewise sworn to by Smith's wife, if she had been allowed to be examined"; the assumption that the Deacon's foreman, Robert Smith, was convinced of his master's guilt; the use made of Ainslie's declaration, which that witness was told had been destroyed, and which was not before the Court; and the passage in the peroration referring to the "consequences to the inhabitants of this populous city" of the Deacon's acquittal.

At the conclusion of the evidence the Dean of Faculty and John Clerk had held a final consultation, when it was arranged that Clerk should speak first for Smith, and that Erskine should follow for Brodie, and strengthen or take up such points as he might think necessary. In order to put himself in fighting form, Clerk, we are told, drank a bottle of claret before commencing his address. This speech, the only extant example of his celebrated method of advocacy, was, in all the contemporary reports, reduced to a minimum for fear of offending the judges. Fortunately, however, a later writer, Peter Mackenzie, has preserved, in his "Reminiscences of Glasgow" (Glasgow, 1866), a full account of the suppressed passages, which he gives on the unquestionable authority of Æneas Morrison, the agent for Smith, who himself furnished the author with these particulars. They have accordingly been incorporated in the following report.

When Clerk, in the course of his address, came to deal with the evidence of Ainslie and Brown, a scene, almost incredible to us nowadays, occurred between the irrepressible young advocate and the overbearing judge. Clerk informed the jury that, in his opinion, these witnesses ought never to have been admitted, a statement which the bench naturally resented, and he went on to insist that, notwithstanding the ruling of the Court, the jury should discard their evidence entirely, as they (the jury) were to judge of the law as well as of the fact. In the course of the discussion which followed, the intervention of the Lord Advocate was met by a graceful allusion to His Majesty's Tory Administration as "villains" likely to contaminate the Crown.

A heated altercation between Clerk and Braxfield ensued, and, finally, the latter bade him go on with his speech at his peril. On Clerk refusing to proceed unless allowed to do so in his own way, Braxfield invited the Dean of Faculty to commence his address for Brodie, which that gentleman declined to do. Thereupon the Lord Justice-Clerk was about to charge the jury himself, when Clerk, starting to his feet and shaking his fist at the bench, cried out, "Hang my client if ye daur, my Lord, without hearing me in his defence!" These amazing words, the like of which had seldom echoed in judicial ears, caused the utmost sensation in Court, and, after an awful pause, the judges left the bench to hold a consultation. But, on their return, instead of anything tremendous taking place, his Lordship civilly requested Clerk to continue his address, and the incident terminated.

Thus was the redoubtable Braxfield forced to yield to the persistence of the fiery young counsel. On reading the discussion as reported, one cannot but think that Clerk was clearly in the wrong, and that his contention as to the jury being judges both of the fact and of the law was, as Braxfield roundly put it, "talking nonsense." Nor does it appear that the line which he saw fit to adopt could in any way benefit his unfortunate client, whose interests would have been better served by more temperate methods. Clerk, however, was thoroughly pleased with his performance, and subsequently observed that it was "the making of him" professionally.

It is said that Clerk's indignant repudiation of the prosecutor's argument that the King's pardon made Brown an honest man reached the ears of Robert Burns, and led him afterwards to write the famous lines—

A prince can mak' a belted knight,
A marquis, duke, an' a' that;
But an honest man's aboon his might,
Gude faith, he mauna fa' that!

At three o'clock in the morning the Dean of Faculty rose to address the jury on behalf of Deacon Brodie. In spite of the fact that he had been continuously engaged upon the case since nine o'clock the preceding morning, no signs of exhaustion appear in his eloquent and powerful speech. Every point telling in favour of the prisoner was given due prominence, and the utmost was made of the somewhat flimsy material of the *alibi*; the whole address forms a fine example of forensic oratory.

At half-past four o'clock the Lord Justice-Clerk—who is said never to have left the bench since the proceedings began—delivered his charge to the jury, which, one is glad to find, notwithstanding what had previously occurred, was a fair and impartial review of the evidence. His Lordship having concluded his charge at six o'clock on Thursday morning, the Court adjourned until one o'clock afternoon; the jury were inclosed; and the prisoners taken back to prison.

The *Edinburgh Advertiser* remarks—"Mr. Brodie's behaviour during the whole trial was perfectly collected. He was respectful to the Court, and when anything ludicrous occurred in the evidence he smiled as if he had been an indifferent spectator."

When the Court met again at one o'clock, the Chancellor of the jury handed in their written verdict, sealed with black wax, which unanimously found both panels guilty of the crime libelled, and the Lord Advocate formally moved for sentence.

A final effort was now made on behalf of the prisoners. Counsel for Brodie stated a plea in arrest of judgment, in respect that the verdict found the panels guilty "of breaking into *the* house in which the General Excise Office for Scotland was kept," whereas it appeared from the evidence that there were, in fact, two separate and distinct houses occupied as the Excise Office. This objection was, after argument, repelled by the Court, and the prisoners were sentenced to death, their execution being appointed to take place on Wednesday, 1st October.

When the sentence was pronounced, we are told "Mr. Brodie discovered some inclination to address himself to the Court, but was restrained by his counsel," and contented himself with bowing to the bench. The prisoners were then removed to the Tolbooth, escorted by the City Guard, amid a great concourse of spectators, and the proceedings terminated.

Æneas Morrison, the agent for Smith, adds the following particulars:—"The panels behaved in a manner different from each other, Smith appearing to be much dejected, especially at receiving his dreadful sentence, although in many instances he showed very great acuteness in his remarks upon the depositions of the witnesses and in the questions to them which he suggested. Mr. Brodie, on the other hand, affected coolness and determination in his behaviour. When the sentence of death was pronounced he put one hand in his breast and the other in his side and looked full around him. It is said that he accused his companion of pusillanimity, and even kicked him as they were leaving the Court. Thus ended a trial which had excited the public curiosity to an extraordinary degree, and in which their expectations were not disappointed. During the space of twenty-one hours— the time it lasted—circumstances continually followed each other to render it highly interesting, and more particularly to the gentlemen of the law, on account of the great variety and importance of the legal topics which were discussed and decided."

The prisoners were lodged in the condemned cell of the Tolbooth, along with two men, James Falconer and Peter Bruce, then under sentence of death for breaking into and robbing the office of the Dundee Banking Company. They were each chained by one foot to an iron bar, but a contemporary account records that "Brodie's chain is longer than the rest, as he can sit at a table and write by himself. They have behaved tolerable well, considering the small room they have on the goad, which goes across the room, very securely fixed from one end to the other in the wall, and hath four divisions or places on which the chains are fixed, with strong iron supporters fastened into the stone floor, and each has a mattress to lie on opposite to himself."

A terrible change this, for the unfortunate Deacon, from the comfortable chambers of his house in Brodie's Close and the social advantages which he had so long and undeservedly enjoyed. He seems, notwithstanding, to have kept up his spirits, and is said to have been as particular as ever in the matter of his dress. Having contrived to cut out the figure of a draughtboard on the stone floor of his dungeon, he amused himself by playing with any one who would join him, and in default of such, with his right hand against his left. The author of "Traditions of Edinburgh" states that this diagram remained in the room, where it was so strangely out of place, till the demolition of the Old Tolbooth in 1817. Many of his friends came to see him, for, until the time of his execution drew near, no restriction was placed upon their visits, and every effort was made by them to obtain a commutation of the death sentence to one of transportation for life.

In furtherance of this object Deacon Brodie, on 10th September, wrote letters to the Right Hon. Henry Dundas, afterwards Viscount Melville, and to the Duchess of Buccleuch, soliciting their influence in support of an application then being made to the Government on his behalf. Copies of these most interesting documents, which have never before been published, will be found in the Appendix—that addressed to the Duchess being also given in facsimile. This lady was Elizabeth, daughter of George, Duke of Montague, and wife of Henry, third Duke of Buccleuch, the friend of Sir Walter Scott, whose daughter-in-law, when Countess of Dalkeith, inspired "The Lay of the Last Minstrel." It is noteworthy that, in spite of his position and presumed education, the Deacon's spelling is more remarkable for originality than accuracy. His friends' "aplication above," however, proved unsuccessful, and the inevitable end had to be faced.

The Old Tolbooth of Edinburgh, showing the beam upon which criminals were executed.
(From a Drawing by D. Somerville.)

Deacon Brodie continued to bear up bravely, referring to his approaching exit as "a leap in the dark," and is said to have only once broken down, when he was visited by his eldest daughter, Cecil, on the Friday before his execution. On the Sunday preceding his death, the other two prisoners, Falconer and Bruce, who were to have been executed on the same day, were granted a respite of six weeks. Smith observed that six weeks was but a short time; whereupon the Deacon exclaimed, "George, what would you and I give for six weeks longer? Six weeks would be an age to us!" On the Tuesday he was visited by a friend, when, we are told, "the conversation turning upon the female sex, he began singing with the greatest cheerfulness from the 'Beggar's Opera' ' 'Tis woman that seduces all mankind,' &c."

The "Beggar's Opera," the well-known work of the poet and dramatist, John Gay, appears to have been a special favourite with the Deacon, for it will be remembered that he sang a stave from it on the night of the robbery of the Excise Office. The opera was frequently performed at the Old Theatre Royal, Edinburgh, at this period, and he had, no doubt, had many opportunities of hearing it. Commenting on this incident, the *Edinburgh Advertiser* remarks— "Brodie seemed to take the character of Captain Macheath as his model, and the day before his death was singing one of the songs from the 'Beggar's Opera.' This is another proof of the dangerous tendency of that play, which ought to be prohibited from being performed on the British stage. It is inconceivable how many highwaymen and robbers this opera has given birth to." The editor of the *Advertiser* was evidently less gifted with a sense of humour than the Deacon, and had never read Fergusson's lines "To Sir John Fielding, on his attempt to suppress the 'Beggar's Opera.'"

On the night before the execution, Deacon Brodie complained of the noise made by the workmen in effecting the alterations on the gibbet necessitated by the reprieve of the other prisoners, Falconer and Bruce; and it is stated in a contemporary report of the trial, published by Robertson on 2nd October, 1788, the day after the execution, that Brodie then said "he planned the model of the new place of execution, he purchased the wood, and gave his assistance in finishing it—but little did he imagine at the time that he himself would make his exit on it." The *Edinburgh Advertiser* of 3rd October, 1788, describing the execution, says—"It is not a little remarkable that Brodie was the planner, a few years since, of the new-invented gallows on which he suffered"; and Robert Chambers, in his "Minor Antiquities of Edinburgh," (1833, p. 168), remarks—"As the Earl of Morton was the first man executed by the 'Maiden,' so was Brodie the first who proved the excellence of an improvement he had formerly made on the apparatus of the gibbet. This was the substitution of what is called the 'drop' for the ancient practice of the double ladder. He inspected the thing with a professional air, and seemed to view the result of his ingenuity with a smile of satisfaction." William Chambers, however, in his "Book of Scotland" (1830, pp. 327-8), takes a different view, holding that the drop was first employed at Newgate in 1784, and had already been used in Edinburgh at an execution in 1785.

Popular tradition, with a fine sense of the requirements of poetic justice, has steadfastly held that Deacon Brodie was the first to test the efficacy of the drop which he himself invented, and was thus, in a double sense, the artificer of his own downfall. And although such a circumstance would be well in keeping with the Deacon's singularly dramatic career, it must unfortunately be dismissed as a picturesque improvement on the literal truth.

A careful examination of the Council records discloses the following facts, now for the first time published:—On 18th August, 1784, the Town Council remitted to Convener Jameson (mason), Deacon Hill (wright), and Deacon Brodie to inspect the west wall of the Tolbooth and consider in what manner a door or passage could be made in order that criminals might be executed there, and to report. Up till that time all public executions had taken place in the Grassmarket at the foot of the West Bow; and it was now proposed that criminals should be executed upon a platform to be erected on the low building which projected from the west gable of the Tolbooth. The report of the committee on the subject does not appear on the record; but in

September the new Council was elected for the ensuing year, and Deacon Brodie was not chosen a member of it.

On 24th November, 1784, "pursuant to a late remit to the Magistrates to consider as to fitting up a place adjoining to the Tolbooth of this city for the execution of criminals," estimates by Convener Jameson and Deacon Hill (who were members of the new Council) were accepted for the mason and wright work respectively. On 11th April, 1785, estimates by the same two Councillors were accepted for rebuilding the shops affected by the proposed alterations, "exclusive of the wright work for the platform and the machinery for an execution, conform to a former estimate." On the 13th of the same month, the Dean of Guild having inspected the work and reported favourably upon it, the magistrates passed an Act of Council appointing the west end of the Tolbooth to be the common place of execution in all time coming; and ordained Archibald Stewart, then under sentence of death for housebreaking, to be executed there in pursuance of his sentence. The execution was accordingly carried out on 20th April, 1785, but not, it would appear, upon the moveable platform or drop. On 7th September of that year, five months after Stewart's death, the Council for the first time authorised Deacon Hill "to make a *moveable* platform for the execution of criminals in terms of his estimate"; and among certain accounts ordered to be paid by the City Chamberlain on 13th September, 1786, we find one due "To Thomas Hill for erecting a *second* platform, west end of the Tolbooth, twenty-one pounds, seven shillings and elevenpence halfpenny"—his account for the former work being also mentioned.

This was, without doubt, the drop upon which, two years later, Deacon Brodie was to suffer the penalty of the law. It is possible, and indeed, from the contemporary evidence already quoted, probable that he himself designed the model, adopting the improvement recently introduced in England. He may even have sent in an estimate for the work, but, as he was not that year a member of Council, Deacon Hill had the better chance of securing the contract, and certainly obtained it.

It was, therefore, on the platform above referred to that the execution of William Brodie and George Smith took place, at half-past two o'clock on the afternoon of Wednesday, 1st October, 1788, in presence of an immense crowd of spectators, great numbers having come from all parts of the country to witness the event. The *Caledonian Mercury* observes—"The crowd on this occasion was the greatest ever known; the whole space from the prison to the Castle Hill being filled with spectators, pressed together in one compact and immoveable column." The proceedings were conducted with more than usual solemnity; the magistrates attended in their robes of office, "with white gloves and white staves"; ministers of divers denominations were present in their gowns and bands; and the City Guard formed a cordon round the place of execution. We read that "the great bell tolled during the ceremony, which had an awful and solemn effect." This is said to have been the first occasion of the kind on which the bell of St. Giles' Church was tolled. It is characteristic of the man that, on his last public appearance, we are informed, "Mr. Brodie appeared in a handsome suit of black clothes, and had his hair powdered and dressed with taste." Twice, owing to some defect in the adjustment of the ropes, did the Deacon descend from the platform and enter into conversation with his friends; but, notwithstanding this dreadful delay, his fortitude remained unshaken, and he met his fate with a courage and equanimity worthy of a better cause:

Nothing in his life
Became him like the leaving it.

With his hand thrust carelessly into the open front of his vest, as we see him in his portrait, the Deacon calmly took that step out of the world which his own ingenuity is said to have shortened.

The *Edinburgh Evening Courant* of 2nd October, 1788, voices the popular sentiment of the time as follows:—"Thus ended the life of William Brodie, whose conduct, when we consider his situation in life, is equally singular and contradictory. By the low and vicious connections he formed he had everything to lose—he could gain little even if successful; for, from the moment he embarked in the enterprises of his desperate associates, his property, his life, was at their mercy. Indeed, his crimes appear to be rather the result of infatuation than depravity; and he seemed to be more attracted by the dexterity of thieving than the profit arising from it. To excel in the performance of some paltry legerdemain or slight-of-hand tricks, to be able to converse in the cant or flash language of thieves, or to chant with spirit a song from the 'Beggar's Opera,' was to him the highest ambition. Those who knew him best agree that his

**Deacon Brodie.
(After Kay.)**

disposition was friendly and generous, and that he had infinitely more of the dupe than the knave in his composition; and was, indeed, admirably fitted for designing and wicked men to work upon." The Deacon, even in his own day, did not lack apologists. And though there may be some diversity of opinion regarding the precise shade which that unhappy gentleman had stained a character in other respects not without redeeming traits, there can be none as to the monstrous injustice of the penalty exacted by the law for his offence. In these more merciful times, when conscientious juries hesitate to convict the guilty upon a capital charge, and rather than deliver a fellow-being to an irrevocable doom will sometimes evade responsibility by the *via media* of "not proven," it is difficult to realise the callous indifference to human life for which our criminal code was formerly notorious. At that period a man might, literally, as well be hanged for a sheep as for a lamb; and that the Deacon should suffer a punishment so disproportionate to his deserts would, however repugnant to modern feeling, seem natural enough to his stoical contemporaries.

In explanation of the singular degree of coolness exhibited to the last by Deacon Brodie, a curious story became current. Much anxiety had undoubtedly been shown both by himself and others that his body might not be detained in prison, but should be delivered to his friends so soon as the execution had taken place. With this view the Deacon, on the forenoon of the fatal day, addressed to the Lord Provost the following remarkable letter:—

"Edinburgh Tolbooth,
"Oct. 1, 1788, Eleven o'clock.

"My Lord,

"As none of my relations can stand being present at my dissolution, I humbly request that your Lordship will permit —— to attend, it will be some consolation in my last hour; and that your Lordship will please give orders that my body after be delivered to and by no means to remain in gaol; that he and my friends may have it decently dressed and interred. This is the last request of

"Your most obedient
but most unfortunate,
WILL. BRODIE."

"Both of which requests," we are told, "his Lordship most readily granted." It is said, by the author of the letterpress in "Kay's Portraits" (1877, vol. 1., pp. 262-3), on the authority of an eye-witness of the execution, that Brodie had been visited in prison by a French quack, Dr. Peter Degravers, who undertook to restore him to life after he had hung the usual time; that, on the day preceding the execution, this individual had marked the Deacon's temples and arms with a pencil, in order to know the more readily where to apply his lancet; and that with this view the hangman had been bargained with for a short fall. "The excess of caution, however, exercised by the executioner in the first instance in shortening the rope proved fatal by his inadvertency in making it latterly too long. After he was cut down his body was immediately given to two of his own workmen, who, by order of the guard, placed it in a cart and drove at a furious rate round the back of the Castle. The object of this order was probably an idea that the jolting motion of the cart might be the means of resuscitation, as had once actually happened in the case of the celebrated 'half-hangit Maggie Dickson.' The body was afterwards conveyed to one of Brodie's own workshops in the Lawnmarket, where Degravers was in attendance. He attempted bleeding, &c., but all would not do. Brodie was fairly gone."

The irregular practitioner above mentioned was certainly in Edinburgh about that time, for we read in the newspapers of the day advertisements, which he issued from his rooms in Charles Street, offering his professional services to the public at the moderate fee of half-a-crown "in all cases." Judging by the testimonials from grateful patients which he also published, the doctor must have given wonderful value for the money; but in the somewhat exceptional circumstances of the Deacon's case he would, if successful, have surely been entitled to a larger fee.

A more picturesque, if less probable version of the same story is given by the author of "Reminiscences of Glasgow," on the authority of Æneas Morrison. It is there stated that any attempt to effect the Deacon's rescue by overpowering the City Guard or breaking into the Tolbooth having, after due consideration, been abandoned by his friends as hopeless, the following elaborate scheme was to be attempted to save his life. Shortly before the hour of his execution, the Deacon was to beg that he might speak to certain of his friends alone for a few moments upon his private affairs. This request being complied with, the opportunity should be seized for introducing into his throat and mouth a small silver tube made for the purpose, with the view of preventing suffocation, and wires were to be carried down his sides from head to foot to save the jerk from the scaffold. The executioner was to be induced to give him a short drop, and other liberties were to be taken with the fatal rope. A surgeon—doubtless the philanthropic Degravers—was to be in attendance to bleed him as soon as the body was cut down; and, if this succeeded, the Deacon was to lie quiet in his coffin, exhibiting no symptom of life, till such time as it could be safely removed to his own house for presumed interment by his relatives. Whether or not this remarkable programme was ever carried out is not recorded.

It would appear from these reports that an attempt of some kind was made with a view to resuscitate the Deacon; and there is no doubt that many people believed at the time that he had "cheated the wuddy" after all. It was said that he had actually revived and made good his escape from Scotland; that he was afterwards seen and conversed with in Paris. His coffin was certainly interred in the north-east corner of the burying-ground of St. Cuthbert's Chapel of Ease—now Buccleuch Parish Church; but there is a tradition that, on a subsequent occasion, the grave was opened, when no trace of his body could be found.

These stories are probably apocryphal; but they are curious as showing the exceptional interest which the Deacon's strange career aroused in the minds of his fellow-townsmen. And although his mortal remains, wheresoever situated, must long since have crumbled into dust, the name and doings of Deacon Brodie are indissolubly associated with the annals of that ancient city in which, to a conclusion so disastrous, he played his double part.

THE TRIAL

―――

WEDNESDAY, 27TH AUGUST, 1788.

―――

The Court met at Nine o'clock.

―――

Judges Present―

THE LORD JUSTICE-CLERK (*Lord Braxfield*). LORD HAILES. LORD ESKGROVE.	LORD STONEFIELD. LORD SWINTON.

―――

Counsel for the Crown―

THE LORD ADVOCATE (*Ilay Campbell*).
THE SOLICITOR-GENERAL (*Robert Dundas*).
WILLIAM TAIT and JAMES WOLFE MURRAY, Esqs.,
Advocates-Depute.

―――

Agent―

Mr. ROBERT DUNDAS, Clerk to the Signet.

―――

Counsel for the Pannel William Brodie―

THE DEAN OF FACULTY (*Hon. Henry Erskine*).
ALEXANDER WIGHT and CHARLES HAY, Esqs., *Advocates*.

―――

Agents―

Mr. ROBERT DONALDSON, W.S., and Mr. ALEXANDER PATERSON,
Writer, Edinburgh.

―――

Counsel for the Pannel George Smith―
JOHN CLERK and ROBERT HAMILTON, Esqs., *Advocates*.

―――

Agent―
Mr. ÆNEAS MORRISON, Writer, Edinburgh.

CURIA JUSTICIARIA S. D. N. REGIS, Tenta in Nova Sessionis domo de Edinburgh, Vicesimo Septimo die Augusti millesimo septingentesimo

Octogesimo octavo, Per Honorabiles Viros; ROBERTUM M'QUEEN de Braxfield, Dominum Justiciarium Clericum; Dominum DAVIDEM DALRYMPLE de Hailes, Baronetum; DAVIDEM RAE de Eskgrove; JOANNEM CAMPBELL de Stonefield; et JOANNEM SWINTON de Swinton, Dominos Commissionarios Justiciariae dict. S. D. N. Regis.

Curia Legitime Affirmata.

INTRAN. William Brodie, sometime Wright and Cabinetmaker in Edinburgh, and George Smith, sometime Grocer there, both prisoners in the Tolbooth of Edinburgh,

PANNELS.

INDICTED and ACCUSED at the instance of Ilay Campbell, Esq., His Majesty's Advocate for His Majesty's Interest, for the Crime of Theft attended with House-breaking, in manner mentioned in the Criminal Indictment raised against them thereanent, bearing as follows:—

WILLIAM BRODIE, sometime Wright and Cabinetmaker in Edinburgh, and GEORGE SMITH, sometime Grocer there, both prisoners in the Tolbooth of Edinburgh, You are indicted and accused at the instance of Ilay Campbell, Esq., His Majesty's Advocate, for His Majesty's interest: THAT ALBEIT, by the laws of this, and of every well-governed realm, THEFT, more especially when attended with house-breaking, and when committed by breaking into a house used or kept as an Excise Office, or other public office, under cloud of night, and from thence abstracting and stealing money, is a crime of an heinous nature, and severely punishable: YET TRUE IT IS, AND OF VERITY, That You, the said William Brodie, and George Smith, are both, and each, or one or other of You, guilty actors, or art and part, of the said crime, aggravated as aforesaid: IN SO FAR AS, upon the night of the 5th day of March, last, in this present year of our Lord 1788, or upon one or other of the days or nights of that month, or of February immediately preceding, or of April immediately following, You, the said William Brodie, and George Smith, did, by means of false keys, or other instruments, wickedly and feloniously break into the house in which the General Excise Office for Scotland was then kept, in Chessels's buildings, on the south side of the High-street of Canongate of Edinburgh, within the royalty or liberties of the city of Edinburgh, and county of Edinburgh, and did thence feloniously abstract and steal money, to the amount of Sixteen pounds Sterling, or thereby, consisting partly of Bank-notes, and partly of silver and halfpence. And You, the said George Smith, having been afterwards apprehended, and brought before Archibald Cockburn, Esq., Sheriff-depute of the county of Edinburgh, did, in his presence, emit three several declarations; the first of date the 8th day of March, the second of date the 10th day of March, and the third of date the 19th day of March, all in this present year of our Lord 1788:

And having afterwards been brought before John Stewart, Esq., Sheriff-substitute of the said county, You did, in his presence, emit a fourth declaration, of date the 17th day of July, likewise in this present year 1788: The first of which declarations was signed by the said Archibald Cockburn, the second and third by you, the said George Smith, and the said Archibald Cockburn, and the fourth by you, the said George Smith, and the said John Stewart. AND FURTHER, You, the said William Brodie, having, in the month of March last, when the said George Smith was committed to prison, left Edinburgh, and fled from this country; and having afterwards been brought back, and taken into custody, did, upon the 17th day of July, in this present year 1788, in presence of the said Archibald Cockburn, Esq., emit a declaration, which was signed by you, the said William Brodie, and the said Archibald Cockburn; the whole of which declarations, together with a letter written by You, the said William Brodie, and signed John Dixon, dated at Flushing, Tuesday, 8th April, 1788, twelve o'clock forenoon, and addressed to Mr. Matthew Sheriff, upholsterer, Edinburgh; another letter, or two letters, on one sheet of paper, written by You the said William Brodie, and signed with your initials, dated Thursday, 10th April, 1788, and addressed to Mr. Michael Henderson, Grass-market, stabler, Edinburgh; an unsigned scroll, or copy of a letter, in the hand-writing of You, the said William Brodie, marked No. 1. without date or address; another unsigned scroll, or copy of a letter, in the hand-writing of You, the said William Brodie, marked No. 2. without date or address; an account, or state, in the hand-writing of You, the said William Brodie, entitled, "A state of my affairs, as near as I can make out at present from memory, having no other assistance"; a letter, dated London, 1st May, 1788, signed Lee, Strachan, and Co. and addressed to Mess. Eml. Walker and Co., merchants, Philadelphia; a gold watch, with a chain, seal, and key; a chest, or trunk, containing various articles; a five-pound bank-note; an iron coulter of a plough; two iron wedges; an iron crow; a pair of curling irons or toupee tongs; a spur; a dark lanthorn; a pair of pistols; several false keys and pick-locks; and two spring-saws; are all to be used in evidence against You the said William Brodie and George Smith; and, for that purpose, will be lodged in the hands of the clerk of the High Court of Justiciary, before which You are to be tried, in order that You may have an opportunity of seeing the same: AT LEAST, time and place foresaid, the said house in which the General Excise Office for Scotland was then kept as aforesaid, was feloniously broke and entered into, and a sum of money feloniously and theftuously taken and stolen therefrom as aforesaid; and You the said William Brodie, and George Smith, above complained upon, are both, and each, or one or other of You, guilty thereof, actor or actors, or art and part. ALL WHICH, or part thereof, being found proven by the verdict of an assize, before the Lord Justice-General, Lord Justice-Clerk, and Lords Commissioners of Justiciary, You, the said William Brodie, and George

Smith, OUGHT to be punished with the pains of law, to deter others from committing the like crimes in all time coming.

ILAY CAMPBELL.

LIST OF WITNESSES TO BE ADDUCED IN THE TRIAL FOR THE PROSECUTOR.

1. John Brown *alias* Humphry Moore, sometime residing in Edinburgh, present prisoner in the Tolbooth of Canongate of Edinburgh.

2. Andrew Ainslie, sometime shoemaker, present prisoner in the Tolbooth of Canongate of Edinburgh.

3. Mary Hubbart or Hubburt, spouse of the said George Smith.

4. Grahame Campbell, sometime servant to the said George Smith.

5. Alexander Thomson, accountant of Excise in Edinburgh.

6. Peter M'Farlane, clerk in the office of the cashier of Excise there.

7. Adam Pearson, assistant secretary of Excise in Edinburgh.

8. Janet Baxter, servant to the said Adam Pearson.

9. William M'Kay, porter in the Canongate of Edinburgh.

10. John Duncan, doorkeeper to the Excise Office, Edinburgh.

11. Laurence Dundas, housekeeper of the said Excise Office.

12. Margaret Black, late servant to the said Laurence Dundas.

13. Margaret Bain, late servant to the said Laurence Dundas.

14. James Bonar, deputy-solicitor of the Excise, Edinburgh.

15. Robert Smith, wright in Edinburgh, late foreman to the said William Brodie.

16. Isobel Gilmour, spouse of John Gilmour, ropemaker in West Bow, Edinburgh.

17. Daniel M'Lean, waiter to William Drysdale, innkeeper in the New Town of Edinburgh.

18. Patrick Taylor, smith in Edinburgh.

19. Charles M'Leod, apprentice to the said Patrick Taylor.

20. Jacobina Pearson, spouse of Hugh Macpherson, shoemaker in Duddingston, near Edinburgh.

21. John Kinnear, servant to the Earl of Abercorn at Duddingston.

22. Robert Tait, servant to the Earl of Abercorn there.

23. Isobel Wilson, spouse of Adam Robertson, wright in Duddingston.

24. John Clerk, book-keeper to William Drysdale, innkeeper in the New Town of Edinburgh.

25. David Robertson, merchant in Edinburgh.

26. John Geddes, tobacconist in Mid-Calder and county of Edinburgh.

27. Margaret Tweddle *alias* Geddes, spouse to the said John Geddes.

28. James Laing, writer in Edinburgh.

29. John M'Leish, clerk to Mr. Hugh Buchan, City Chamberlain of Edinburgh.

30. George Williamson, messenger-at-arms in Edinburgh.

31. William Middleton, indweller in Edinburgh.

32. James Murray, sheriff-officer there.

33. Alexander Williamson, sheriff-officer there.

34. James Fraser, sheriff-officer there.

35. Archibald Cockburn, Esq., Sheriff-depute of the county of Edinburgh.

36. John Stewart, Sheriff-Substitute of the said county.

37. William Scott, Procurator-Fiscal of the county of Edinburgh.

38. William Augustus Wishart, clerk to the said William Scott.

39. Joseph Mack, writer in the Sheriff-Clerk's Office, Edinburgh.

40. Alexander Fraser, grocer and change-keeper in the New Town, Edinburgh.

41. Laurence Blair, servant to Mr. Charles Hope, advocate.

42. Thomas Longlands, solicitor-at-law in London.

ILAY CAMPBELL.

LIST OF ASSIZE.

1. Andrew Bonar, banker in Edinburgh.

2. Alexander Houston, banker there.

3. Robert Forrester, banker there.

4. Robert Allan, banker there.

5. Henry Jamieson, banker there.

6. John Hay, banker there.

7. William Creech, bookseller there.

8. James Carfrae, merchant there.

9. William Gillespie, merchant there.

10. William Simpson, banker there.

11. George Kinnear, banker there.

12. John Black, merchant there.

13. Francis Blair, merchant there.

14. Elphingston Balfour, bookseller there.

15. Peter Forrester, merchant there.

16. John Thomson, insurance-broker there.

17. Thomas Elder, merchant there.

18. Edward Innes, confectioner there.

19. John Balfour, merchant there.

20. William Fettes, merchant there.

21. John Milne, founder there.

22. Dunbar Pringle, tanner there.

23. Peter Robertson, goldsmith there.

24. Thomas Campbell, merchant there.

25. William Turnbull, merchant there.

26. Alexander Brown, merchant there.

27. Charles Cowan, merchant there.

28. David Paterson, insurance-broker there.

29. Francis Sharp, merchant there.

30. James Donaldson, printer there.

31. John Hutton, stationer there.

32. John Balfour, papermaker there.

33. Robert Young, upholsterer there.

34. John Learmonth, junior, tanner there.

35. Thomas Cleghorn, coachmaker there.

36. Thomas Hutcheson, merchant there.

37. James Craig, corn merchant there.

38. Alexander Bruce, merchant there.

39. Benjamin Yule, baker there.

40. William Smellie, printer there.

41. Orlando Hart, shoemaker there.

42. James Ranken, merchant there.

43. William Young, baker there.

44. William Brown, grocer there.

45. Alexander Weir, painter there.

ROB. M'QUEEN.
DAV. DALRYMPLE.
DAV. RAE.

LIST OF WITNESSES TO BE ADDUCED IN EXCULPATION OF WILLIAM BRODIE.

1. Robert Smith, wright in Edinburgh, late foreman to the said William Brodie.

2. George M'Intosh, also wright, and late journeyman to the said William Brodie.

3. John Niel, also wright, and late journeyman to the said William Brodie.

4. Arthur Giles, wright in Edinburgh.

5. William Watson, wright in Canongate.

6. William Retson, or Reston, nailer, Portsburgh.

7. James Cargill, ironmonger, Edinburgh.

8. Alexander Miller, ironmonger there.

9. George Burton, ironmonger there.

10. James Goldie, ironmonger there.

11. Daniel MacLean, waiter to William Drysdale, vintner in Edinburgh.

12. George Lees, coachmaker there.

13. Alexander Fergusson, dyer there.

14. Patrick Taylor, smith there.

15. Charles MacLeod, apprentice to Patrick Taylor.

16. Agnes Finlay, spouse to Michael Henderson, stabler, Grassmarket.

17. Alexander MacKay, inner turnkey in the Tolbooth of Edinburgh.

18. James Reid, indweller in Edinburgh, and present prisoner in the Tolbooth.

19. Alexander Brodie, baker, Nether Bow.

20. James Murray, sheriff-officer.

21. Helen Alison, spouse to William Wallace, mason, Libberton's Wynd.

22. Jane Watt, residenter there.

23. Peggy Giles, servant to—Grahame, publican at Mutton-hole, near Edinburgh.

24. Matthew Sheriff, upholsterer in Edinburgh.

Under protestation to add and eik.

ALEXANDER WIGHT, for the pannel.

The diet having been called "at the instance of Ilay Campbell, Esquire, His Majesty's Advocate, for His Majesty's interest, against William Brodie, sometime wright and cabinetmaker in Edinburgh, and George Smith, sometime grocer there," the Lord Justice-Clerk desired the pannels to attend to the indictment then to be read.

Mr. NORRIS, Depute-Clerk of Court, then read aloud the indictment, after which,

The pannels having been asked to stand up,

The LORD JUSTICE-CLERK—William Brodie, you have heard the indictment raised against you by His Majesty's Advocate—are you guilty of the crime therein charged, or not guilty?

WILLIAM BRODIE—My Lord, I am not guilty.

The LORD JUSTICE-CLERK—George Smith, you have heard the indictment raised against you by His Majesty's Advocate for His Majesty's interest—are you guilty of the crime therein charged, or not guilty?

GEORGE SMITH—Not guilty, my Lord.

The LORD JUSTICE-CLERK then asked the counsel for the pannels if they had any objection why the said indictment should not be remitted to the knowledge of the assize.

Mr. CHARLES HAY—My Lords, I appear as counsel for William Brodie, the prisoner at the bar. I do not observe anything in this indictment upon which I can found an objection to the relevancy of it, and therefore I will at present confine myself to a simple denial of the charge against Mr. Brodie, and your Lordships will fall to pronounce the usual interlocutor on the relevancy, in which the prisoner will be allowed a proof of all facts and circumstances tending to his exculpation.

The SOLICITOR-GENERAL—My Lords, I desire to know the nature and tendency of the exculpatory evidence proposed to be adduced, in order that, in the course of leading the proof upon the part of the prosecutor, we may be prepared to meet it.

The LORD JUSTICE-CLERK—It is not sufficient for the prisoner to deny the charge if he intends to prove any facts in exculpation; it is but fair to the public prosecutor and to the gentlemen of the jury that these should now be mentioned that they may have them in their view in the course of the trial.

The DEAN OF FACULTY—My Lords, I likewise appear as counsel for William Brodie, the prisoner at the bar. I admit that it is fair to mention the facts which are to be insisted on in his defence; and therefore, adhering to the general denial of the crime charged, we undertake to prove that Mr. Brodie went, before eight o'clock of that night in which the Excise Office is said to have been broken into, to the house of Janet Watt, a person residing in Libberton's Wynd, with whom he had a particular connection, and that he remained in that house from the said hour until about nine o'clock the next morning. This will be instructed by the woman herself and by other unexceptionable witnesses.

Mr. ROBERT HAMILTON—My Lords, I appear as counsel for the prisoner George Smith. No objection appears to me upon the relevancy of the indictment, and the prisoner rests his defence upon a general denial of the facts charged, having no exculpatory proof to offer.

The Court then pronounced the following interlocutor:—

The Lord Justice-Clerk and Lords Commissioners of Justiciary, having considered the criminal indictment raised and pursued at the instance of Ilay Campbell, Esq., His Majesty's Advocate, for His Majesty's interest, against the said William Brodie and George Smith, pannels, they find the indictment relevant to infer the pains of law, but allow the pannels and each of them to prove all facts and circumstances that may tend to exculpate them or alleviate their guilt, and remit the pannels with the indictment as found relevant to the knowledge of an assize.

ROBERT M'QUEEN, I.P.D.

The Court were proceeding to select fifteen from amongst the forty-five gentlemen summoned as jurymen, when it was discovered that some of the witnesses had not come forward. In about half-an-hour they all arrived. The Lord Advocate then moved the Court to inflict some fine on those witnesses by whom the delay had been occasioned; but it being found upon inquiry that the hour of cause, but no particular hour, was specified in the citations given them, his Lordship, in respect that the hour of cause was understood to mean ten o'clock, withdrew his motion, and the Lord Justice-Clerk, to prevent similar delays, gave directions that in time coming the citations given to jurymen and witnesses should bear a specified hour at which their attendance is to be required.

Out of the above forty-five jurymen the following fifteen persons were named to pass upon the assize of the pannels; and the pannels being asked if they had any objections why they should not pass upon this assize, and no objections being made on the contrary, they were all lawfully sworn in by the following oath, five at a time:—

You swear by Almighty God, and as you shall answer to God at the great day of judgment, that you will truth say, and no truth conceal, so far as you are to pass upon this assize.

> 1. Robert Forrester, banker.
> 2. Robert Allan, banker.
> 3. Henry Jamieson, banker.
> 4. John Hay, banker.
> 5. William Creech, bookseller.
> 6. James Carfrae, merchant.
> 7. John Kinnear, banker.
> 8. William Fettes, merchant.
> 9. John Milne, founder.
> 10. Dunbar Pringle, tanner.
> 11. Thomas Campbell, merchant.
> 12. Francis Sharp, merchant.
> 13. James Donaldson, printer.
> 14. John Hutton, stationer.
> 15. Thomas Cleghorn, coachmaker.

The jury being impanelled and furnished with pen, ink, and paper, and copies of the indictment being laid before them, the Court ordered the counsel for the prosecutor to proceed to the evidence.

At this stage, before the evidence was led,

Mr. WIGHT—My Lords, I likewise attend your Lordships on the part of Mr. Brodie, and although there does not appear upon the face of this indictment any sufficient ground for an objection to the relevancy of it, yet there are some particulars of which I consider it my duty to take notice; and, in order to save time and trouble to the Court, I propose to do it now rather than hereafter.

The law of this country has been very careful to give unhappy men in the situation of the prisoners every opportunity of preparing for their trials; they are allowed fifteen days after being served with their indictments; they are furnished with a list of the witnesses' names and designations who are to be adduced against them; and the declarations, writings, and articles to be used in evidence in the course of the trial are particularly specified. The present indictment, though not irrelevant, is perhaps laid in the most vague and general manner I have ever seen. Here there are certain letters and declarations founded on, and other articles, such as a gold watch with a chain, and seal, and key, a chest or trunk containing various articles, a five-pound bank-note, an iron coulter of a plough, &c. These are mentioned in so vague a manner as not to distinguish them from other articles of the same kind, consequently in such a manner as not to give the pannels proper opportunity of preparing for their defence. This is the more inexcusable that all of these articles admitted of a more accurate description.

[Here Mr. Wight was interrupted by the Court.]

The LORD JUSTICE-CLERK—Mr. Wight, these objections are out of place; they ought to be stated when the articles you mention come to be produced by the prosecutor.

The DEAN OF FACULTY—It is no doubt true that the objection to each of these articles falls properly to be stated when they are founded upon by my Lord Advocate; but it was thought proper and respectful to the Court to state the general objection at this stage of the business in order to save time.

The SOLICITOR-GENERAL—My Lords, I wish that Mr. Wight may be allowed to proceed.

The LORD JUSTICE-CLERK—Mr. Wight, go on.

Mr. WIGHT—I say, my Lords, that the articles mentioned in the indictment admitted of a more accurate description than that which my Lord Advocate has given them. The maker's name and number of the watch might have been mentioned, the device on the seal, too, ought to have been specified, also the number of the note and by whom it was issued; and as to the chest or trunk, which is only described by saying that it contained sundry articles, there is no particular description of it, or of any of the articles it contained. It is not said that it is a hair trunk, or the size or shape of it, or any other

The Solicitor-General (Robert Dundas).
(After Kay.)

mark condescended upon, whereby it could be distinguished. It might have been mentioned what sort of a trunk it was, whether made of fir, of oak, or of ash; to whom it belonged, and where and in whose possession it was found.

To show your Lordships that this is no immaterial objection, I must beg leave to mention a circumstance that occurred in the present case. Some days ago, Mr. Brodie's agent went to the Justiciary Office to examine the articles founded on in the indictment; and upon inquiring for the trunk, he was shown a black trunk, a trunk different from the one now to be used in evidence. Thereafter the counsel for the Crown discovered they had committed a mistake; they were so much misled by this want of description that they had sent the trunk referred to, or meant to be referred, in the libel to the prison to Mr. Brodie, and had lodged a wrong trunk with the Clerk of Court. They did not discover this mistake till yesterday morning, and they then applied to the Sheriff for a warrant to recover the trunk, which is now in Court, out of the possession of Mr. Brodie, and which was only lodged in the Justiciary Office yesterday.

Although I have thrown out this general objection, I do not mean to plead it to the effect of setting aside the libel altogether; yet, when the prosecutor attempts to apply his evidence to these articles, I reserve to myself the liberty of making special objections to each article, as it shall be referred to.

The SOLICITOR-GENERAL—My Lords, I will not take up the time of the Court in making any answer to the objection stated, as to the manner in which the watch and the other articles are described in the indictment, as I have no hesitation to say that it does not deserve one. All these articles, as well as the other articles libelled on, have been for weeks past lying in the hands of the Clerks of Court, where the counsel and agents for the pannels have had full opportunity of examining and taking from them whatever description they might think proper.

As to the story of the trunk, it is shortly this: there were two trunks the property of Mr. Brodie; and one of them, containing linens and other articles, was, from motives of humanity, allowed to remain in his possession. This was the trunk referred to in the indictment; the other was, however, sent by mistake to the Justiciary Office, but as soon as the error was discovered, Mr. Brodie was applied to to deliver up the proper trunk. This he refused to do, and therefore it became necessary to apply to the Sheriff, who granted a warrant; in consequence of which it was recovered from the prisoner and lodged in the Justiciary Office. This is the plain state of the fact, and, having laid it before your Lordships, I do not consider it necessary to add one word more to the subject.

The LORD ADVOCATE—My Lords, if it had been intended to charge the prisoners with stealing the watch, or any of the other articles, a more accurate description might have been necessary, but here there is no such intention— the crime of which the prisoners are accused is breaking into the Excise Office.

From the nature of the thing, my Lords, as well as from the tenor of the indictment, it must be evident to every one that it is only meant to produce these articles in evidence, to refer to them when the witnesses are examined. It may be necessary, for example, to prove that certain letters were found in the chest, and to whom the chest belonged; it is no matter of what form the chest is, and not of the smallest consequence whether it is identified or not; nay, more, my Lords, there was no necessity for producing it at all. If every nail of a trunk or every trinket of a watch, or other articles which it might be necessary to found upon in trials of this kind, were to be so particularly described as Mr. Wight has contended for, it would swell indictments to a very inconvenient and unnecessary length.

The objection that the proper trunk was not produced in sufficient time to give the prisoner an opportunity of examining it is certainly a very uncommon one, when it is considered that it was allowed to remain in his own possession until yesterday; and with regard to the watch, all the use I mean to make of it is to identify some letters from Mr. Brodie, which are sealed with the seal appended to it.

The DEAN OF FACULTY—My Lords, what may be the consequence to the prisoners at the bar of your Lordships repelling the present objection I do not know. The gentlemen on the other side of the table have taken care to lay their indictment in such a manner as to leave the counsel for the prisoners altogether in the dark as to the nature of the proof they mean to lead and the manner in which these articles are to be used in evidence; but, my Lords, sure I am of this, that the decision of the present question is of the greatest importance to the law of this country. I am not surprised that the Solicitor-General should say that he will make no answer to the objection, because I am convinced that it admits of none.

It is no light matter the framing of an indictment; the specification of the proofs by which it is to be supported is of the utmost consequence. I am persuaded, my Lords, that I would have no difficulty to satisfy your Lordships, from the nature of the thing itself, that this objection is well founded. But I resort to better evidence. I appeal to the Books of Adjournal on your Lordships' table, and I call upon the counsel for the Crown to point out one single instance recorded in them where articles have been founded on in an indictment and produced in evidence without being specially described. Having so respectable an authority as the uniform practice of your Lordships and your predecessors to support the objection now stated, you will think well before you introduce an innovation that may be attended with the most dangerous consequences.

We are told that some of the articles in question are of no consequence; if so, why are they here? I will not enter into the question whether the trunk was really produced in the Justiciary Office in proper time or not, as all the indictment says is, that "it will be produced."

My Lords, there are two kinds of articles produced in criminal trials, first the *corpora delicti*, to prove that the crime was actually committed; and, secondly, articles from which the leading circumstances are to be inferred. The Lord Advocate admits that the first of these must be particularly described, but denies the necessity of describing the second. This is a distinction not known in the law of this country, and directly contrary to the established forms of criminal procedure. What would be the consequence were it recognised? Suppose, for instance, that a person breaks into a house and leaves his hat behind him; nothing could establish his guilt more clearly than to prove that this hat was his. But although this is only a leading circumstance, would it be enough to say that a hat was to be produced in evidence, without specifying where it was found, or any circumstances attending it, so as to give the accused an opportunity of proving that it belonged to another, and not to him?

I will appeal, my Lords, to the practice of the public prosecutor himself, to show that no such distinction exists. A declaration is an article used in evidence as well as a gold watch, yet his Lordship does not think it sufficient to say "a declaration," without specifying any other circumstances, such as before whom, and of what date, it was emitted. On the contrary, there are several declarations referred to in this indictment, and they are all particularly described. It is the duty of the public prosecutor to specify every particular, and to say what is meant to be proved by each article, or in what manner it has been used in the commission of the crime charged. In the case of Gordon, the sheep-stealer, a man for whom I was counsel at this bar several years ago, and who still languishes in prison, notwithstanding his having received His Majesty's pardon[1]—your Lordships refused to allow an article to be produced in evidence which had not been libelled on: and the articles objected to might as well not have been libelled on at all, as in the general and vague manner in which they are mentioned in the indictment.

My Lords, there is another circumstance to which I beg to draw your Lordships' particular attention. It is our good fortune to live under a mild Government; to live in days when there is no danger to be apprehended from the conduct of the public prosecutor; but worse times may arrive, and it is for your Lordships to reflect upon what use might then be made of the present practice if your Lordships were to allow it to be now introduced. The public prosecutor may, for example, libel upon a watch, and the Clerk of Court may show one watch in the Justiciary Office to the prisoner's counsel or agent, and against the day of trial may produce another in Court. The principal reason why articles such as the present are mentioned in the indictment is that the prisoner may be certain that these articles, and these articles alone, are to be used in evidence against him; and it is clear that this certainty must be withdrawn from the prisoner if a vague description is permitted to be given of them, because, as I have already mentioned, others may be substituted in their place. If an article of evidence be not particularly described so as to prevent the possibility of doubt with regard to the identity of it, the dearest rights of mankind might be endangered and at the mercy of corrupt men, and no one could say how fatal the consequences might be.

The LORD ADVOCATE—My Lords, I admit the justice of what the Dean of Faculty has stated if such an objection as the present were made to the description of the *corpora delicti*. If the prisoners were charged with having stolen the watch or trunk mentioned in the indictment, the description there given of them would not be sufficient; but, as they are not the *corpora delicti*, and are only referred to as circumstances of evidence, I contend that the description is sufficient; but, rather than detain the Court longer with an objection of this kind, I will give up the trunk altogether, as I do not suppose that I shall stand in need of it; I, however, submit the matter to the Court.

The LORD JUSTICE-CLERK—Your Lordships have heard the objection and answers on this point. What is your opinion?

Lord HAILES—My Lords, there is no objection made to the production of the different papers founded on in the indictment, and I do not perceive that there is any force in the objection as to the gold watch; because, although the pannel's counsel cannot know, from the manner in which it is described in the indictment, what is meant to be proved by it, neither do they know what is intended to be proved by the different witnesses who are cited.

The objection with regard to the trunk appears to me to be much more strong; and I confess that I never saw any article so vaguely stated in an indictment as it is in the present case, viz., "a trunk containing various articles." It is no good answer to the objection that the proper trunk was not timeously produced, that it was allowed to remain in Brodie's possession, because that article is founded on in the libel against Smith as well as against him. I am therefore inclined to sustain the objection as to the trunk, but no further.

Lord ESKGROVE—My Lords, I am not disposed to abridge in the smallest degree the security of the subjects of this country, although the law is here more attentive to the safety of persons accused than in any other country whatever. Here the pannel must not only be furnished with the names and designations of the witnesses, but he must also be made acquainted with every document and article to be used in evidence against him.

In the present case there are a number of writings, and likewise a variety of articles, founded on in the indictment; there is no objection to the production of the papers, but it is objected on the part of the pannel that the other articles are not particularly described. I do not think, my Lords, that this objection is much aided by the argument founded on the declarations and other parts of the libel being more particularly described than these articles.

The Dean of Faculty has referred your Lordships to the Books of Adjournal, from which he says that it appears to have been the practice to describe such articles more minutely; but I have no doubt that a perusal of these books would furnish many instances where articles have been described as loosely as they are said to be in the present libel; and, my Lords, as the pannel's counsel have neither produced, nor offered to produce, any decision of this Court finding libels irrelevant from the articles referred to in them being thus described, I am bound to hold the objection to be of no force.

My Lords, I can see no injury that will be sustained by the prisoners by the repelling of the present objection; all the articles were lodged in the hands of the Clerk of Court, and their agent and counsel had an opportunity of examining them. The trunk is no doubt vaguely described, but that appears to me not to be material, because it will not be sufficient for a witness to say that he found papers or other articles in a trunk; he must say that he found them in the trunk shown to him in Court, otherwise his evidence in that particular will be of no consequence. If the pannels should say that this is a different trunk, and that they never saw it before, I would listen to the objection; but as they cannot, and as I can figure no injury to the prisoners in repelling this objection, I am for over-ruling it.

Lord STONEFIELD—My Lords, I think the description in this case is sufficiently full; therefore I am for repelling the objection.

Lord SWINTON—My Lords, the present objection is made in the wrong place; and I cannot so well judge of it in this general shape as I could have done had it been stated when the particular articles came to be used in evidence; but I must judge of it in the form in which it has been brought before the Court.

I think, my Lords, that it ought to be repelled for the reasons your Lordships have already heard, and because no injury can be done to the pannels from these articles not having been more particularly described, as they will have an opportunity of traversing the evidence that may be brought relating to them. There are many of the articles, such as two iron wedges, an iron crow, &c., that would not admit of a more particular description than has been given. Upon the whole, my Lords, I am for repelling the objection.

The LORD JUSTICE-CLERK—My Lords, the present question is of great importance to the law of this country. I am one of those who are always for giving fair-play to pannels, and will never allow any advantage to be taken of them; but I am likewise for giving fair-play to evidence. It is frequently necessary, my Lords, that the testimony of witnesses should be elucidated by articles referred to being produced; but if the present objections were sustained, I am afraid it would strike against the admissibility of this kind of evidence altogether; because, let a public prosecutor describe such articles with the greatest attention, it still may be contended that they admitted of a more accurate description than the one given.

By the former state of our law the prosecutor was not allowed to prove anything that was not particularly specified in the libel; but the Act 153, Parliament 11th, James VI., was introduced to obviate this defect in our law, and by that Act the prosecutor is allowed to prove every circumstance to substantiate the charge, or in general art and part of the charge. It is very true, my Lords, that the humanity of public prosecutors of late years has induced them to be more special than they had any occasion to be, but surely they are not cut off from the generality allowed them by law, although such generality may have been deviated from through lenity in practice. Apply this to the present case. It is true that the Lord Advocate, as public prosecutor, has been induced to state particular circumstances, and to specify the articles to be founded on; yet that does not alter the law, nor deprive him of the generality which he is allowed by law. As the names of witnesses are given, without specifying what they are to say, in the same way it is only necessary to state that such articles are to be produced in evidence, but not necessary to specify a description of them; and it is the duty of the prisoner himself, or those who act for him, to survey them when lodged in the Justiciary Office. As there is no precise time against which articles to be founded on are required to be lodged in the Justiciary Office, there appears to be no undue delay in lodging this trunk. Had it been pled that it was not lodged *debito tempore*, and that the pannel had been injured thereby, then a delay of the trial must have taken place.

I remember it once happened on a circuit that the articles founded on in the libel were only lodged the very morning of the trial in the Clerk's hands; but I then refused to allow them to be founded on, because the pannel had not a reasonable time to prepare himself against evidence that might arise from the production of these articles; but the present case is very different, and therefore, upon the whole, I am for repelling the objection.

Mr. JOHN CLERK—My Lord Justice-Clerk, before the interlocutor is written out, I beg leave to make one objection in behalf of the pannel, George Smith.

The LORD JUSTICE-CLERK—What! After the Court have delivered their opinions, it is not decent in you to propose to say anything, and I apprehend the prisoners are in no danger of suffering anything by your not being allowed to supply the defects of the Dean of Faculty.

Mr. JOHN CLERK—My Lord, the Dean of Faculty has no authority to plead for my client.

The DEAN OF FACULTY then moved the Court to allow the general objection to be entered upon record, and proposed to repeat it and refer to it as often as any of the particular articles came to be produced in evidence, which was accordingly agreed to, and the following interlocutor was pronounced repelling the objection:—

The Lord Justice-Clerk and Lords Commissioners of Justiciary having considered the foregoing debate, they repel the objection stated to producing and founding on the articles specified in the objection and mentioned in the indictment, and allow them to be adduced in the course of the trial.

ROBT. M'QUEEN, I.P.D.

The prosecutor, for proof of the indictment, then proceeded to adduce the following witnesses, who were all lawfully sworn, purged of malice and partial counsel, and emitted their depositions *viva voce* in presence of the Court and jury, without being reduced in writing, in terms of the late statute.

Evidence for Prosecution.

William Scott

1. WILLIAM SCOTT, Procurator-Fiscal of the county of Edinburgh, called in and sworn.

Examined by Mr. MURRAY—Mr. Scott, you know the prisoners at the bar? Were you present when they emitted certain declarations before the Sheriff-depute of Edinburgh and his substitute?

WITNESS—I was.

Mr. MURRAY—Look at these declarations, and tell the Court and the gentlemen of the jury if they were emitted in your presence by the pannel, George Smith, freely and voluntarily.

WITNESS—They were; and the prisoner appeared to me at the time cool and recollected.

Mr. MURRAY—Look at this declaration. Was it emitted in your presence by the other pannel, William Brodie, freely and voluntarily, and he was cool and recollected?

WITNESS—It was emitted in my presence freely and voluntarily, and he was cool and recollected.

Mr. MURRAY—Do you know anything concerning a warrant that was applied for against William Brodie in the month of March last? If you do, tell the Court and the gentlemen of the jury what happened in consequence of it?

WITNESS—Upon the afternoon of Monday, the 10th of March last, I, as Procurator-Fiscal, gave in a petition in my own name to the Sheriff of Edinburgh, charging Mr. Brodie with breaking into the Excise Office, and praying for a warrant to apprehend him. A warrant was accordingly granted, and search diligently made for him that night, but he was not found, and I afterwards learned that he had gone off for London on the day preceding.

Cross-examined by Mr. JOHN CLERK, for George Smith—Mr. Scott, you say you were present when George Smith emitted the declarations which have been shown you; did Smith, in the course of his different examinations, say anything more than is contained in these declarations?

WITNESS—I do not think he did; everything material was taken down. No compulsion or undue means was used to induce the prisoners to sign these declarations.

2. JOSEPH MACK, writer in the Sheriff-Clerk's Office of Edinburgh, called in and sworn, and shown the declarations above mentioned.

WITNESS—These declarations were written by me, to the dictation of the Sheriff, and were emitted by the pannels freely and voluntarily, and the pannels appeared to me to be cool and recollected when emitting them.

Cross-examined by Mr. JOHN CLERK—Was everything which Smith declared when examined taken down?

WITNESS—Everything that was material. With regard to the robbery of Bruce's shop—[Here the Court stopped the witness, as that was a matter which was not before them.]

The LORD JUSTICE-CLERK—Did he desire anything to be taken down that was not?

WITNESS—No.

3. THOMAS LONGLANDS, solicitor-at-law in London, called in and sworn.

Examined by MR. WILLIAM TAIT—Mr. Longlands, did you hear of William Brodie, the prisoner at the bar, having fled from this country in March last, and of his having been brought back? Tell the Court and the gentlemen of the jury what you know of the matter?

WITNESS—In the month of June or July last I was employed by the officers of the Crown for Scotland to take such steps as appeared to me to be proper for the discovery of Mr. Brodie. In consequence of this employment I called frequently at the Secretary of State's Office, and had several conversations with Mr. Fraser, Under-Secretary in the office of Lord Carmarthen, and gave them the information I had received from Scotland. I likewise waited upon Sir Sampson Wright, of the Public Office, Bow Street, whose assistance I judged necessary to call in as to the proper measures to be pursued. As the information received gave reason to suspect that Mr. Brodie was at Flushing, Ostend, or some place in Holland, it was agreed upon to send a messenger immediately in search of him. Sir Sampson Wright recommended to me a Mr. Groves from his office as a proper person to send to the Continent in search of Mr. Brodie, and I accordingly despatched him with proper instructions. Mr. Groves traced Mr. Brodie to Ostend, and learned that he had been there upon the 4th of June, His Majesty's birthday, and he was afterwards traced to Amsterdam, where he was apprehended, identified, and committed to prison. Upon proper application, he was delivered up to Mr. Groves, and was brought from thence to London by him. Immediately upon his arrival at London he was examined before Sir Sampson Wright, and committed to Tothilfields Bridewell; some time afterwards he was sent to this country. I was present at the examination of the person brought back from Amsterdam, and I know the prisoner at the bar to be him. There was a trunk containing linens and a variety of other articles, belonging to Mr. Brodie, brought with him from Amsterdam; and I received from Mr. Cartmeal, one of the persons who came along with him, two watches, twenty crowns, and some other articles, which he said were found upon Mr. Brodie; and the watch now upon the table I know to be one of them, having taken particular notice of the maker's name and number. [The counsel for the pannels here repeated the objection against adducing the watch, as mentioned in the general objection and interlocutor before taken down.] There was likewise another trunk belonging to Mr. Brodie, which was sent over from Ostend by Sir John Potter, in consequence of a letter written to him in my presence by Mr. Groves, after Brodie's return to London. This trunk, upon its being brought to London, was opened by Sir Sampson Wright in my presence, and in the course of examining the contents of it I discovered a wrapper with some papers, which I opened, and some of the papers appearing to me to be important, I transmitted them to the Lord Advocate. [Here the unsigned scrolls were shown to the witness.] Both Sir Sampson Wright and I put our initials to them, and I am sure that these are the same, as well from seeing my initials as from the strength of some of the expressions, which made a great impression upon me at the time. [The state of affairs and letters of credit were likewise shown to the witness.] I have seen these before; they came in a packet to Sir Sampson Wright from Mr. Rich, the English resident at Amsterdam, and Sir Sampson Wright delivered to me the letter in which they came with them inclosed.

Cross-examined by the DEAN OF FACULTY—Mr. Longlands, have you any other cause of knowledge concerning the trunks and other articles being the property of Mr. Brodie, and the same which were brought from Ostend and Amsterdam, than the information of Sir Sampson Wright and Mr. Groves?

WITNESS—No other cause of knowledge than what I have already mentioned, namely, the letters accompanying the same, which I saw, and my being present when the trunks were opened.

John Geddes

4. JOHN GEDDES, tobacconist in Mid-Calder, called in and sworn.

Examined by the SOLICITOR-GENERAL—Were you lately in London? Do you know the prisoner? Tell the jury what you know about him?

WITNESS—I was in London in the month of March last, and my wife and I took our passage in the "Endeavour," of Carron, Captain Dent, bound for Leith. We went on board on a Saturday, and the next day, Sunday, the vessel fell two or three miles down the river, and then we cast anchor at Blackwall. In the evening the master went on shore to get hands to man her, leaving me and my wife on board. About twelve at night a passenger, who appeared sickly, came on board, in company with Mr. Hamilton and Mr. Pinkerton, two of the owners of the vessel, and another gentleman I did not know. These gentlemen remained about half an hour, and then all went ashore, except the passenger, who remained on board. He was dressed in a blue great-coat, with a red collar, round wig, black vest, breeches, and boots. He was allotted a bed in the state-room, near the fire, as he was sick. The next morning the vessel set sail, but afterwards ran aground opposite to Tilbury Point, where she remained about eight or ten days, and we did not get clear of the Thames for a fortnight. During all that time the passenger remained on board, except one day that he, along with the master of the vessel and my wife and I, went on shore, and dined at a neighbouring village, and another day that he went ashore by himself to get a bottle of milk. For the first two or three days after the passenger came on board we called him "the gentleman," as we did not know his name, but, upon my inquiring of him what his name was, he told me it was John Dixon.

The SOLICITOR-GENERAL—Would you know that person again?

WITNESS—I would.

The SOLICITOR-GENERAL—Look at the prisoners at the bar and say if you know either of them?

[Here the witness pointed out Mr. Brodie to be the same person that had called himself John Dixon.]—On getting out to sea Mr. Dixon delivered to the captain a letter from Mr. Hamilton or Mr. Pinkerton, but, although I desired him to let me read it, I did not see it. In consequence of this, the captain altered his course and steered for Holland, and the vessel, although bound for Leith, sailed to Flushing. I do not think she was driven there by contrary winds, as the wind was south-west, and fairer for Newcastle or Leith than for Holland. During the voyage, Mr. Dixon complained much of a sore throat. When we arrived at Flushing we cleaned ourselves and went ashore, and Mr. Dixon set off for Ostend in a skiff which he hired for that purpose. On shore, before he left, Mr. Dixon gave me a packet containing two letters, one of which had another within it, to carry to Scotland to be delivered in

Edinburgh. One of the letters was directed to Mr. Michael Henderson, stabler in the Grassmarket, in which there was one inclosed to Mrs. Anne Grant, Cant's Close, and the other to Mr. Matthew Sheriff, upholsterer in Edinburgh, signed and dated as mentioned in the indictment. We did no business at Flushing, and I am of opinion that the ship did not come there with that intention. After landing Mr. Dixon we sailed for Leith. When I arrived in Leith, from the accounts I heard about Brodie, I was convinced that Dixon and Brodie were the same person. Next day I went to Mid-Calder, and about three weeks afterwards was at Dalkeith, where I had occasion to see the newspapers, and the description of Brodie therein given confirmed me in the above suspicion. I then delivered the letters to Sheriff Cockburn. I had previously opened the packet and read them. [The witness was here shown the letters libelled on.] I know that these are the letters I received from the prisoner and delivered to the Sheriff.

The SOLICITOR-GENERAL—Did Brodie say that he had any business at Flushing?

WITNESS—He mentioned that he had business at Ostend, and Captain Dent said he was to wait till he returned, and that he supposed he belonged to the Carron Company; but when the wind came fair, Captain Dent said he would not wait for him, and the devil a bit of business he supposed he had.

Cross-examined by the DEAN OF FACULTY—You have told us that you went ashore when you arrived at Flushing. Pray, sir, did you make any purchases there?

WITNESS—None, except a piece or two of nankeen for breeches to myself.

The DEAN OF FACULTY—Did you purchase nothing else?

WITNESS—Nothing, except two or three handkerchiefs for my own use.

The DEAN OF FACULTY—You will remember, sir, that you are upon your great oath, and that it is your duty to tell the whole truth.

Lord HAILES—My Lords, the witness should be informed that if he purchased any contraband goods he has nothing to fear from acknowledging that he did so.

The LORD JUSTICE-CLERK—It is certainly very proper. [To witness]—John Geddes, if you made any purchases of contraband goods when you was at Flushing, it is your duty to inform the Court and the gentlemen of the jury that you did so, and you have nothing to fear from such an acknowledgment, because whatever you say here will be no evidence against you afterwards in the Court of Exchequer or elsewhere.

The DEAN OF FACULTY—Did you purchase no lace, sir, when you was at Flushing?

WITNESS—A few yards.

The DEAN OF FACULTY—Why, then, did you say that you purchased nothing except the nankeen and the handkerchiefs?

WITNESS—It was my wife and not me that purchased it.

The DEAN OF FACULTY—Did you offer the lace for sale?

WITNESS—No; there is part of it about a cloak which my wife has here with her, and I believe part of it about her sister's.

The DEAN OF FACULTY—And what became of the rest of it? Remember, sir, you are upon your great oath.

WITNESS—That was it all, except a few yards I sold at Bathgate for twenty-two shillings.

The DEAN OF FACULTY—Did you not say even now that you had offered none of it for sale?

WITNESS—I said that I offered none of it for sale in this place.

The DEAN OF FACULTY—Did you purchase no tobacco in Flushing?

WITNESS—I did not, except a little for chewing.

The DEAN OF FACULTY—Did you purchase any gin?

WITNESS—None, except a little for sea store.

The DEAN OF FACULTY—Pray, sir, when did you open these letters you have told us of? Was it before or after you came to Leith?

WITNESS—It was after.

The DEAN OF FACULTY—You told us, sir, that upon reading the newspapers you discovered that Dixon and Brodie were one and the same person. Pray, sir, when or where did you first read the newspapers?

WITNESS—At Dalkeith.

The DEAN OF FACULTY—How long was that after your arrival?

WITNESS—Three weeks.

The DEAN OF FACULTY—And pray, sir, what was the reason that in all that time you did not deliver these letters to the persons to whom they were directed?

WITNESS—I did not remember that I had such letters when I was in Edinburgh myself, and I afterwards wished my brother-in-law to deliver them.

The DEAN OF FACULTY—Did you open the letters?

WITNESS—I did.

The DEAN OF FACULTY—And what was your reason for doing so?

WITNESS—I opened them and delivered them to the Sheriff for the good of my country.

The DEAN OF FACULTY—And would it not have been as much for the good of the country to have delivered them without opening them?

WITNESS—I just opened them, and that's all; I can give no other reason.

The DEAN OF FACULTY—Did you inform any person that you had such letters?

WITNESS—I did; I informed John Tweddle, my brother-in-law, who advised me to deliver them to the persons for whom they were intended. I afterwards showed them to a gentleman named Mr. Learmonth in Linlithgow, who wrote a letter by me to a gentleman of this place.[2] By him I was carried to Mr. Erskine, but he would give me no advice, and therefore I returned home to Mid-Calder. That same evening, or early next morning, Mr. Scott, Procurator-Fiscal, and Mr. Williamson, messenger, called upon me, and I accompanied them to Edinburgh and delivered the letters to the Sheriff.

The DEAN OF FACULTY—My Lords, as the witness has mentioned his having called upon me, I beg leave to state to the Court what passed upon the occasion. He was brought to my house by a gentleman, and he showed me the letters. I informed him that I was counsel for Mr. Brodie; that he himself knew best the directions that he had received from the person who committed these letters to his charge; and that I could give him no other advice than this, that he ought to do in the matter that which his own conscience should point out to him as most proper.

The LORD JUSTICE-CLERK—That was a very proper advice, and was just what I would have expected from the Dean of Faculty.

The LORD ADVOCATE—My Lords, you will have observed that there were three letters from the prisoner delivered up. It was only judged necessary to libel on two of them; but if the prisoner thinks that the other letter, or any of his other papers in my possession, will be of the least service to him in supporting his defence, I have no objection to produce them.

5. MARGARET TWEDDLE, spouse of the said John Geddes, called in and sworn.

WITNESS—I was in London with my husband in the month of March last, and went with him on board of a vessel bound for Leith. One night, when it was dark, a person, whom I now see a prisoner at the bar, and some others with him, came on board. The prisoner remained on board, but the others went ashore in about half-an-hour afterwards. I think the person had a wig on when he came on board, and he appeared to be in bad health. He passed by the name of John Dixon. The vessel sailed for the coast of Holland, and when she arrived there the prisoner went on shore. I saw my husband receive a packet of letters from Mr. Dixon; but I know nothing more of them. I never saw these letters afterwards.

Cross-examined by the DEAN OF FACULTY—Did you or your husband make any purchases while in Flushing?

The LORD JUSTICE-CLERK—Margaret, if you or your husband purchased any contraband goods when you were at Flushing you will inform the Court and the gentlemen of the jury that you did so, and you have nothing to fear from such an acknowledgment, because whatever you say here will be no evidence against you afterwards in the Court of Exchequer or elsewhere.

WITNESS—We purchased some pieces of nankeen, some handkerchiefs, and some yards of lace.

6. ROBERT SMITH, wright in Edinburgh, called in and sworn.

WITNESS—I was some time ago foreman to the pannel, Mr. Brodie, and I remember to have been sent for by him upon the Sunday morning, the 9th of March, at eight o'clock, after it was reported that the Excise Office had been broke into. The message was not particular, but such a one as I usually received from him when he wanted to give me orders about some work, as he frequently sent for me for that purpose, especially if he was going to the country. When I came to him he asked me if there were any news about the people who had broke into the Excise. I answered that I had been informed that George Smith was committed to prison, and that Brown had been sent into England in search of Inglis & Horner's goods. I added that I hoped he, Mr. Brodie, had no concern in these depredations; but he returned to me no answer. The reason I asked this question was that I had often seen my master in their company, and knew him to be intimate with them. Mr. Brodie told me he was going out of town for a few days, and sent me a message for a waistcoat and pair of breeches; but before my return he was gone, and I did not see him again till after he was brought back to this country. On the Monday evening following, the 10th of March, a search was made for him, and several doors of his house were broken open, in virtue of a warrant from the Sheriff, as I was informed. [Here the witness was shown the two letters founded on in the indictment, and desired to say whether or not they were in the handwriting of Mr. Brodie.] I have seen the handwriting of Mr. Brodie, and I think the writing of these letters very like his, but I never saw Mr. Brodie subscribe with initials; and as I am no judge of writing, I cannot say whether I believe these letters to be written by Mr. Brodie or not. [Here the witness was shown the unsigned scrolls, and desired to say whether or not he believed they were in the handwriting of Mr. Brodie.] I never saw Mr. Brodie write so bad a hand as these letters are written in, nor after the manner in which they are written, and I do not think that they have been wrote by Mr. Brodie. [Here the state of affairs referred to in the indictment was shown to the witness.] I think this is very like the handwriting of Mr. Brodie, much more so than any of the others.

James Laing

---

7. JAMES LAING, writer in Edinburgh, called in and sworn.

WITNESS—I am assistant clerk in the Council Chamber. I know Mr. Brodie, the prisoner at the bar. I have seen him write, and I am a little acquainted with his handwriting. [Here the two letters were shown to the witness.] The writing of these letters is very like Mr. Brodie's handwriting. I think they have been wrote by him. [Here the unsigned scrolls were shown to the witness.] I think these are of Mr. Brodie's handwriting too, though worse written. [State of affairs shown to the witness.] I think this also is written by Mr. Brodie.

John Macleish

---

8. JOHN MACLEISH, clerk to Hugh Buchan, City Chamberlain of Edinburgh, called in and sworn.

WITNESS—I know Mr. Brodie, the prisoner at the bar, and have had some opportunity of knowing his handwriting. I have got receipts from him in the Chamberlain's office, and have received cards from him. I have likewise seen him write in his own shop. [Here the witness was shown the two letters.] I think these letters are of his handwriting. [Shown the scrolls.] I never saw Mr. Brodie write in so crowded a way, or interline so much, but, notwithstanding,

I think that these are of his handwriting. [State of affairs shown the witness.] I think that this also is of Mr. Brodie's handwriting.

Cross-examined by the DEAN OF FACULTY—How do you come to know Mr. Brodie's writing so exactly?

WITNESS—From many accounts and receipts, of his writing, which I have in my custody belonging to the office.

John Duncan

---

9. JOHN DUNCAN, door-keeper to the Excise Office, Edinburgh, called in and sworn.

WITNESS—I have been in that office for thirty-seven years. The doors of the Excise Office, when it was kept in the Canongate, were usually locked by me about eight o'clock at night, and I carried the key immediately thereafter to the housekeeper. A watch was set to guard it about ten o'clock, and the night watchman went away about five in the morning. I remember to have locked the door on Wednesday, the 5th of March last, about a quarter after eight o'clock in the evening, and I gave the key to one of Mr. Dundas, the housekeeper's, maid-servants. The cashier's room lay within the outer door, which I had locked, as before mentioned, and it had a double door.

Cross-examined by Mr. CLERK, for George Smith—Pray, sir, was the Excise Office kept in one or in two houses?

WITNESS—The Excise Office was kept in a large house; but there was likewise a small house fronting and adjoining the great one, in which Mr. Broughton's office and the Register of Seizures were kept. There was no communication from the one to the other without going out to the open air, and the whole were in one court, inclosed by a parapet wall and iron rail.

William Mackay

---

10. WILLIAM MACKAY, porter in the Canongate of Edinburgh, called in and sworn.

WITNESS—I was employed as a watch to guard the Excise Office when it was kept in Chessels's Buildings, and upon Wednesday, the 5th day of March last, I went to the office at the usual hour, which was a little before ten o'clock at night. I found one of the leaves of the outer door open, and the passage door and the door of the cashier's room also open; and upon making this discovery I went to Mr. Dundas, the housekeeper's, and inquired of the maid who had been last at the office, as the doors were open. The maid answered

John Duncan, the last witness, had left it about a quarter after eight o'clock. Mr. Dundas's son, hearing me make this inquiry, asked what was the matter. When I told him that the door was broke open, he said, "Then, something worse is done." Immediately Mr. and Mrs. Dundas and the whole family went into the office with me and examined the cashier's room; we found all the desks and presses broke open, and the coulter of a plough, and two iron wedges, lying in the room; and we likewise found a spur in the hall, with part of the leather of it torn. Mr. Dundas immediately sent me for Mr. Alexander Thomson, the accountant. I found Mr. Thomson, and he returned with me to the Excise Office. [Here the witness was shown the coulter of the plough, the two iron wedges, and the spur.] These are the same articles which I saw in the Excise Office. [The counsel for the pannels here repeated the objection against adducing the coulter and two wedges, as mentioned in the general objection and interlocutor before taken down.]

Alexander Thomson

11. ALEXANDER THOMSON, accountant of Excise, called in and sworn.

WITNESS—I remember that the Excise Office was broke into on Wednesday, the 5th of March last. When I left the office at the usual hour that night, about eight o'clock, I locked the door of the cashier's room before I left, and carried the key away with me. I saw John Duncan, the door-keeper, in the hall as I came out. I left in two concealed drawers below the desk about £600 sterling, and in the desk itself £15 16s. 3½d., being two-thirds of the proceeds of a seizure sent from Greenock, to be divided amongst three people. About ten o'clock the same evening the office porter, or watchman, came to me and informed me that the Excise Office had been broken into. I immediately repaired to the office, and found Mr. Dundas, the housekeeper, and Mr. Pearson, the secretary, there; and, along with them, I examined the premises. The outer door and the passage door appeared to have been opened without violence, but the door of the cashier's room seemed to have been forced with a lever or other instrument; the door of a small press in the room appeared likewise to have been forced open, and a few shillings, and some stamps for receipts that were in it, carried off. The key of my desk, which I usually kept in this place, had likewise been taken out, and the desk opened with it. The £15 odds, which I had left in the desk, were gone, and also a receipt for £7 18s. 2d., but the concealed drawers, in which the £600 was contained, were untouched. These drawers cannot be opened without first opening the desk, and the keyhole is concealed by a slip of wood, which might escape a slight observer. Accordingly it had remained untouched, although the key of it lay in the desk. Behind the door there was left the coulter of a plough and two iron wedges—[Here these articles were shown to the witness]—the same as these now on the table.

Cross-examined by Mr. JOHN CLERK for George Smith—Pray, Mr. Thomson, was the Excise Office, when in the Canongate, kept in one house or in two houses?

WITNESS—It was kept in three houses, or in one large house, consisting of a front and two wings, and, besides this principal house, there was a small one fronting, and nearly adjoining to it, in which Mr. Broughton's office, Mr. Dick's office, and the Register of Seizures were kept.

: Laurence Dundas

---

12. LAURENCE DUNDAS, housekeeper of the Excise Office, called in and sworn.

WITNESS—There was a practice, previous to the time when the Excise Office was broke into, of locking the door betwixt eight and nine o'clock at night, and lodging the key in my house, and of putting a watch upon it at ten o'clock. I remember that upon Wednesday, the 5th of March last, the door was locked at the usual hour, and the key left by John Duncan at my house. A little before ten o'clock that night, William Mackay, the porter employed to watch the office, came to my house and gave information that the office had been broke open. I immediately went to the office, and found the outer door, the passage door, and the door of the cashier's room, all open. This last-mentioned door seemed to have been forced with some instrument. Within the room I found the coulter of a plough and two iron wedges, all of which I now observe upon the table. Every drawer in the room, except the money drawers, seemed to have been forced open. I immediately sent for Mr. Thomson, the accountant, and Mr. Pearson, the secretary, and both of them immediately came to the office. Mr. Thomson told me that he had about £17 in his desk, which he supposed was all gone, but he hoped that the money drawers were safe. The key of the money drawers was found amongst others lying in the desk.

Cross-examined by Mr. JOHN CLERK, for George Smith—Mr. Dundas, was the Excise Office, when in Chessel's Buildings, kept in one house or in two houses?

WITNESS—Principally in one house, but there was likewise another small house in which Mr. Broughton's office, Mr. Dick's office, and the Register of Seizures were kept; both houses were inclosed with an iron rail.

: Janet Baxter

---

13. JANET BAXTER, servant to Adam Pearson, assistant secretary of the Excise, called in and sworn.

WITNESS—I was out upon a message about eight o'clock at night on Wednesday, the 5th of March last, and, returning homewards, I met with an acquaintance, with whom I conversed for a little in the entry to Chessels's Buildings, in which my master lived. I then went down the close, and on my way down I saw a man, dressed in a whitish great-coat and slouch hat, leaning over the rails at the entry to the court, and, judging him to be a light or suspicious person, I was afraid of him, and ran into my master's house.

James Bonar

14. JAMES BONAR, deputy-solicitor of Excise, Edinburgh, called in and sworn.

WITNESS—I recollect having occasion to call at the Excise Office upon Wednesday, the 5th of March last, about half-past eight in the evening, and as I thought it was probable that there might be still some person in the office, I went straight forward to the door without calling for the key, and finding the door on the latch, I opened it and went in. Just as I entered, a man, who appeared to be dressed in a black coat and cocked hat, stepped out. He seemed to be in a hurry, and I stepped aside to give way to him. He was a square-built man, and was rather taller than me. I took no suspicion, thinking it was some of the people belonging to the office, detained later than usual. I went upstairs to the solicitor's office, and into the room in which I usually write. I remained there about ten minutes, came down again, and then went away. I saw no person either in the entry or the court as I came out.

Isobel Wilson

15. ISOBEL WILSON, spouse of Adam Robertson, wright in Duddingston, called in and sworn.

Examined by the SOLICITOR-GENERAL—Pray, madam, do you remember anything of two persons coming to your house in the month of March last?

WITNESS—I did not remember, at first, anything of the matter, but having afterwards seen John Brown [a succeeding witness] in the Sheriff-Clerk's Office, he mentioned some circumstances which passed upon the occasion, which brought to my recollection that there were two persons in my house at the time you mentioned, and I think that Brown was one of them. They called for a bottle of porter, which they drank and paid for, but I do not recollect anything else that passed upon the occasion.

16. JOHN KINNEAR, servant to the Earl of Abercorn at Duddingston, called in and sworn.

WITNESS—I recollect that the coulter of a plough with which I had been at work and two iron wedges were stolen from a field some time last spring, but whether in February or March I cannot say, only I recollect that there was then snow upon the ground. I loosed from work between two and three o'clock on the day on which the articles were stolen, and went to Edinburgh, and on my way thither, about four o'clock, I observed two men in blackish clothes standing upon the ploughed land by the plough to which the coulter belonged, and there was a black dog at some distance from them.[3] When I came to work next morning I found the coulter of the plough and the wedges had been taken away. [Here the coulter and the wedges referred to in the indictment were shown to the witness.] These are the coulter and wedges that were stolen from my plough.

Cross-examined by Mr. JOHN CLERK, for George Smith—How do you come to know that?

WITNESS—I know this to be the same coulter, my attention being called to it from this circumstance particularly, that a short time before it was stolen it was sent to a smith, with instructions to sharpen it the whole length, that it might be fit for cutting the turf which was to be ploughed up. He did not observe these instructions, but returned it in the situation it is now in.

17. GRAHAME CAMPBELL, sometime servant to the pannel, George Smith, called in and sworn.

WITNESS—I was servant to the prisoner, George Smith, and I know the other prisoner, Mr. Brodie. I never heard of the Excise Office being broke until I was apprehended, along with my mistress and Andrew Ainslie, and committed to prison in the beginning of last spring. I have seen Mr. Brodie, and likewise Andrew Ainslie and John Brown, often in Mr. Smith's house, and they were all very frequently there in company together. In particular I remember their being all there one night about the dusk of the evening, not long before I was apprehended, but as they were so frequently at my master's house I cannot distinguish that night from any other, nor can I say at what hour they came, only I remember they were in a room above-stairs, and that Mr. Brodie passed through the shop and asked my mistress how she did to-night. Mr. Brodie was at this time in an old-fashioned black coat, and, to the best of my knowledge, I never saw him in the same dress before. I have seen him in other black clothes, but they were always of a newer fashion. My master, Smith, was upstairs with Brown and Ainslie, when Mr. Brodie came in and joined them. I do not know when they went out, as I was employed below-stairs in the back cellar; but I think they remained together a considerable time before they went out. I believe they all went out together, for when I went into the kitchen my mistress desired me to go upstairs to put the room in order and wipe down the table, which I did, and at that time all of them were gone. My master returned in something more than an hour, and said he had been seeing Mr. Maclean, who is Mr. Drysdale's waiter. Mr. Ainslie had been in before him, but had gone out again, and Brown came in in quest of him, and also went out again. They both returned about ten or eleven o'clock, and Mr. Brodie then came back likewise. Mr. Brodie had on at this time the whitish clothes which he usually wore, and as he passed through the shop he again asked my mistress how she did to-night. I expressed my surprise to my mistress that Mr. Brodie should wear such a strange dress when he came in the first time in his old black clothes, and she answered that it was his frolick; but I took no notice to her afterwards of his having changed his dress. They all supped in the kitchen, except Mr. Brodie, who would not sit down, but walked up and down the room. Brown and Ainslie usually supped at my master's. They remained together about two hours. Mr. Brodie went out first, and Mr. Brown and Mr. Ainslie soon thereafter, with an intention, as they first said, to go to bed. I think they said afterwards that they were going to play cards with Mr. Maclean. My master, George Smith, did not go out again that night.

Cross-examined by the DEAN OF FACULTY, for Brodie—You have mentioned that Brown and Ainslie and the prisoners at the bar, when they first met, were a considerable while together. In what manner were they employed?

WITNESS—I was for the most part down below in the back cellar; but they had some bottles of porter together, and either a cold fowl or some herrings to eat.

The DEAN OF FACULTY—You have said that Mr. Brodie and Brown and Ainslie were frequently in your master's house. What did they do when together; did you ever see them play at any game—at cards or at dice?

WITNESS—I have often seen them play both at cards and at dice, sometimes in the kitchen and at others in the room above-stairs, but chiefly at dice, when Mr. Brodie was present.

The LORD JUSTICE-CLERK—My Lord Advocate, is the witness now at liberty? I understand she has been detained in prison for some time past?

The LORD ADVOCATE—There is no reason for detaining her any longer; she was only confined until her evidence should be given in this trial.

The LORD JUSTICE-CLERK—Grahame Campbell, you are now at your liberty.

Mary Hubbart or Hubburt

---

18. MARY HUBBART or HUBBURT was then called.

Mr. JOHN CLERK, for Smith—My Lords, the witness now called is the wife of George Smith, the pannel at the bar, and therefore I object to her evidence being taken in this trial.

The LORD ADVOCATE—My Lords, I certainly do not intend to examine this witness as to any particular that relates to the conduct of her husband, but I conceive that she is an unexceptionable witness against the other pannel, Mr. Brodie, and that I am entitled to examine her as to him, if I keep clear of any question that has a tendency to bring out the guilt of her husband.

Mr. JOHN CLERK—My Lords, I desire your particular attention to this, that the two pannels are joined together in one indictment, that they are charged with being guilty of the same crime; and that they are in every respect in the same circumstances. I have no conception, my Lords, of any question tending to the crimination of Mr. Brodie that will not at the same time bring out the guilt of Mr. Smith.

The LORD ADVOCATE—My Lords, that I may remove all apprehensions concerning the questions I mean to put, I shall only ask the witness whether Mr. Brodie was in her house on Wednesday, the 5th of March last; when he came there; and in what manner he was then dressed?

Lord HAILES—My Lords, it is clear that this woman cannot be examined as a witness against her husband; but at the same time, although her husband and Brodie are here tried upon one indictment, I see nothing to prevent my Lord Advocate from putting such questions to her as do not affect her own husband, but only the other pannel.

Lord ESKGROVE—My Lords, I am of the opinion which has been delivered by my Lord Hailes.

Lord STONEFIELD—My Lords, I am of the same opinion.

Lord SWINTON—My Lords, I agree with the opinion given.

The LORD JUSTICE-CLERK—My Lords, there is no doubt that a wife cannot be received as a witness whether for or against her husband, and her situation is different by our law from that of all other near relations. If a son, for instance, is brought forward as a witness against his father, he may no doubt decline to bear testimony, and no Court of law can compel him to do so; but if he is willing to give his evidence it may be received. A wife, on the contrary, cannot be received as a witness, even though she be willing; a judge can pay no regard to what she says either for or against her husband; and, supposing she had no objection to give her testimony even to hang him, which might happen, it must be refused; therefore, my Lords, whatever this woman says that may infer guilt against her husband must be totally thrown out of consideration; nor will I suffer one single question to be put or her to say a single word from which his guilt can be inferred; and the jury are not to give any attention whatever to it, if it should happen that anything should drop to the prejudice of her husband.

Mr. JOHN CLERK—My Lord Justice-Clerk—

The LORD JUSTICE-CLERK—What! Mr. Clerk, would you insist on being heard after the Court have delivered their opinions? It is most indecent to attempt it.

Mr. JOHN CLERK—I was heard, my Lord, on the general point of the admissibility of this witness, but not on the special objections which I have to the questions which my Lord Advocate proposes to put, and on which the Court have not delivered any opinion.

The LORD JUSTICE-CLERK—Mr. Clerk, this is really intolerable.

The DEAN OF FACULTY—My Lord, although as counsel for Mr. Brodie I am not entitled to be heard on this subject, I find myself called upon to interfere as Dean of Faculty. It is perhaps not strictly in order for Mr. Clerk to insist on being heard after your Lordships have delivered your opinions, but some indulgence ought to be shown to a young gentleman.

Lord HAILES—My Lord Justice-Clerk, though Mr. Clerk stated his objection generally, yet he did not enter into particulars, and I think he may be allowed now to state what particulars he meant to insist on.

The LORD JUSTICE-CLERK—Mr. Clerk, we will hear what you have to say.

Mr. JOHN CLERK—My Lord, I mean to offer a special objection to the interrogatory mentioned by my Lord Advocate, on which I have not yet been heard, nor do I understand that any opinion has been given respecting it by your Lordships. It is proposed to ask this woman what dress Mr. Brodie wore when in her husband's house on the 5th of March last previous to the robbery of the Excise Office. I formerly observed, my Lords, that my client and Mr. Brodie are accused of the same crime, and are nearly in the same circumstances, and this is a question from the answer to which it may appear that Mr. Brodie was guilty of the robbery laid to his charge. But at the same time, my Lords, it will appear that Mr. Brodie was at the house of my client in a suspicious dress and in suspicious circumstances, and will it not be from thence concluded that my client was engaged with him in the very design which he at that time intended to put in execution? Such a presumption would likewise be most forcibly corroborated by their known intimacy, by their being frequently concerned in the same pursuits, and, above all, by the presence of the other two persons who are supposed to have committed this crime. I say, my Lords, on the supposition that Mr. Brodie is guilty, the circumstance of his dress is one of the strongest presumptions that can be figured against my client.

But, farther, my Lords, my client has an interest in preventing the conviction of Mr. Brodie; if his guilt is not proved an inference is afforded me of the innocence of my client, for Mr. Brodie being with my client so recently before the crime was committed presumes that they were employed in the same manner; and the suspicion against Mr. Brodie being groundless is an argument that the suspicion against my client is equally groundless. Now, my Lords, if this woman be examined her evidence may, though indirectly, tend to the crimination of her husband. And if the law does not allow the evidence of a wife to be taken against her husband, I cannot see that there is a good distinction between her evidence as taken directly and indirectly; and therefore, my Lords, I hope that your Lordships will sustain the objection.

The LORD JUSTICE-CLERK—The Court will take care not to allow the witness to give any answer against her husband. But, as she is a good witness against Brodie, the Court cannot help it if, by establishing his guilt, a presumption thereby arises against Smith. I am therefore for repelling the objection.

The objection was repelled accordingly.

[The witness was then brought in.[4]]

Mr. WIGHT, for the pannel Brodie—My Lords, I must object to this witness upon another ground, and shall not take up the time of the Court any longer than simply to state the objection, which appears to me perfectly irresistible. The law of this country requires that the name and designation of every witness to be examined against the pannels should be intimated to them at least fifteen days before; but the name of the woman who now appears in Court is not to be found in the list of witnesses served upon the prisoner. There is indeed a "Mary Hubbart or Hubburt, wife of George Smith," mentioned as a witness in the indictment, but the present is no such person; her name is perfectly different, being Mary Hibbutt, as appears by an extract of the parish register where she was born, which I now produce. The objection, therefore, of a misnomer applies in full force to this witness.

The LORD ADVOCATE—This appears to me a very extraordinary and frivolous objection, for, even supposing the witness's name is Hibbutt instead of Hubbart or Hubburt, still there could not possibly be any mistake as to the person, since she is designed the wife of George Smith, and it is not pretended that she is not the wife of that person. This woman emitted several declarations before the Sheriff; in some of them she is called Mary Hubbart and in others Mary Hubburt. At first she pretended she could not write, and the only declaration subscribed by her is signed Mary Smith; so that the prosecutors, who had no other opportunity of knowing her real name than from the declaration, were left altogether in the dark as to it. As the witness allowed herself to be called Hubbart or Hubburt in the declaration without challenge it is not competent for her now to deny it.

My Lords, it is of no sort of consequence in the present case that there has been a mistake of a letter or two in the witness's name; it was perfectly unnecessary to have designed her in any other way than Mary Smith, wife to George Smith, and if that would have been sufficient, certainly an attempt

Lord Hailes.
(After Kay.)

to be more particular cannot have the effect of injuring the pannel, and therefore can be no valid objection against this witness.

The DEAN OF FACULTY—My Lords, I cannot help considering this as a question of the greatest consequence, for if this objection is not sustained, then the objection of misnomer cannot have any longer effect, for if the change of a letter or two, as insisted on by the Lord Advocate, does not afford that objection, there can be no such thing as a misnomer, since the whole difference betwixt names consists only in change of letters.

I am free to admit that if this witness had only been libelled Mary Smith, wife of George Smith, particularly as she had subscribed her name Mary Smith, then there could not have been stated any objection to her examination. But as she is particularised to be Mary Hubbart, it is a sufficient objection to me that the name of the woman now present is not Mary Hubbart, but Mary Hibbutt, a perfectly different name. There still may be a mistake of the person although she is designed wife to George Smith, for it may happen that Smith may have two wives. There is not a greater difference betwixt Erskine and Friskin, which last name is not uncommon in this country, than betwixt Hubbart and Hibbutt. It is all one under what name she is mentioned in the precognition, as that was not her doing; neither is it probable that she knew by what name she was there called. My Lords, there has not been a witness examined here this day that can know by what name he has been taken down by the Clerk.

The LORD ADVOCATE—My Lords, I beg that the witness may be desired to write her name.

The LORD JUSTICE-CLERK—Mary Hubburt, you will sign your name.

[The witness signed her name accordingly.]

The DEAN OF FACULTY—My Lord, the witness has subscribed her name "Hibbutt."

Lord HAILES—The name of Hobart is the name of the very respectable family of Buckinghamshire, in England, and I would have supposed that this woman's name, since it so nearly resembles it, was the same, and would not have taken her own word to the contrary. Hibbutt, nevertheless, is perfectly different from Hubbart, and, however obscure it might be, still, as it is proved by the parish register to be the name of the person now called, I consider myself obliged to give weight to the misnomer.

The DEAN OF FACULTY—I beg pardon for interrupting the Court, but I am just informed that this point has been decided by Lord Eskgrove and Lord Stonefield at the Glasgow Circuit, where a misnomer of "James Roberton" instead of "James Robertson" was sustained. There, there was only the want of a letter, whereas there is certainly a much greater difference betwixt the names here in question.

Lord ESKGROVE—As to the case mentioned by the Dean of Faculty, Robertson and Roberton are two perfectly distinct names. In the case before your Lordships there can be no doubt that if this woman had only been libelled as wife to George Smith, without her maiden name, there could have been no question whatever. It is the universal custom in England that the maiden name sinks into that of the husband's, but my great difficulty is, in this case, that the public prosecutor, in giving this witness a further description than was necessary, has totally mistaken her name, I do not think that there is any force in her being called Hubbart in the precognition for the same reason given by the Dean.

[Here his Lordship was interrupted by the Lord Advocate.]

The LORD ADVOCATE—My Lords, the circumstances which I meant to prove by the witness are so immaterial that I will give the Court no further trouble with the matter. I agree to pass from this witness.

Lord ESKGROVE—I am very happy I am relieved from deciding it, as I was going to deliver an opinion for sustaining the objection.

The LORD JUSTICE-CLERK—Mary Hibbutt, you are at liberty to go where you please.

Daniel Maclean

---

19. DANIEL MACLEAN, waiter to William Drysdale, innkeeper in the New Town, called in and sworn.

WITNESS—On the night of Wednesday, the 5th of March, on which the Excise Office was broken into, I was in company with John Brown and Andrew Ainslie in the house of one Fraser in the New Town from about half-past nine to eleven o'clock at night; we drank some punch together, and there was one Price and some others in company with us. I remember to have received a five-pound bank-note from the prisoner, George Smith, on the next night after the Excise Office was broken into, in order to purchase a ticket in the mail-coach for his wife to Newcastle. The note was battered on the back. I carried it to John Clerk, Mr. Drysdale's book-keeper, but he could not change it, and therefore I applied to Mr. Drysdale himself, and then carried back the change of the note, after deducting the price of the ticket, to Mr. Smith.

John Clerk

---

20. JOHN CLERK, book-keeper to the before-mentioned William Drysdale, called in and sworn.

WITNESS—I remember that Daniel Maclean, Mr. Drysdale's waiter, came to me the next night after the Excise Office was broken into for a ticket in the mail-coach to Newcastle for some person, and offered a five-pound bank-note in payment. I had not change myself, and therefore desired him to apply to Mr. Drysdale. He laid the bank-note upon the table, but I did not then look at it. Mr. Drysdale changed the note. On the Monday following I received it from Mr. Drysdale, with directions to carry it to the Sheriff-Clerk's Office, which I did.

David Robertson

---

21. DAVID ROBERTSON, merchant in Edinburgh, called in and sworn.

WITNESS—I am a hardware merchant. I remember that Mr. Brodie, the prisoner at the bar, purchased a spring saw from me about eight or nine months ago. [Here one of the saws libelled on was shown to the witness.] This saw bears my shop mark, and it was such a one that I sold to Mr. Brodie. [The counsel for the pannels here repeated the objection against adducing the two spring saws, as mentioned in the general objection and interlocutor before taken down.] I have sold the same kind of saws to different persons. Cabinetmakers sometimes make use of such saws in the way of their business, but Mr. Brodie told me that the one he purchased was for cutting off the natural spurs of game-cocks. Some time afterwards another person, whom I do not know, came to my shop and purchased another spring saw; he asked for such a one as Mr. Brodie had bought. [Here the other saw was shown to the witness.] This saw also bears my shop mark, and it was such a one that I sold to the person I have already mentioned.

William Middleton

---

22. WILLIAM MIDDLETON, indweller in Edinburgh, called in and sworn.

WITNESS—I am in the employment of the Sheriff-Clerk's Office. I have been acquainted with John Brown *alias* Humphry Moore for some time past, and I remember the robbing of the Excise Office. Brown came to me upon Friday, the 7th of March last, about eleven o'clock at night, and informed me that he wanted to make some discoveries concerning that robbery and the other late robberies which had been committed in this place. I desired him not to give me any information, but to keep his mind to himself, and I would take him to a person to whom he might communicate whatever he had to say. Accordingly I conducted him that same night to Mr. Scott, the Procurator-Fiscal, and afterwards, at his own desire, to the bottom of Salisbury Crags, where Brown pointed out a place in which we found a number of false keys under a large stone. These we brought to town with us to the Procurator-Fiscal's house. The next day I was sent into England along with Brown in search of the goods belonging to Messrs. Inglis & Horner, silk mercers, which had been stolen from their shop; and Mr. Frier, a partner of that house, accompanied us.

The DEAN OF FACULTY—My Lords, it is not proper that the witness should be allowed to speak of facts that have no relation to the present trial.

The LORD JUSTICE-CLERK—William Middleton, you are to confine yourself to such facts as relate to or are immediately connected with the breaking into the Excise Office, which is the charge brought against the prisoners.

WITNESS—Upon Sunday, the 16th of March last, the prisoner, George Smith, was carried at his own desire to the bottom of Warriston's Close,[5] and I accompanied him, along with Alexander Williamson and James Murray, sheriff-officers. Smith there pointed out a hole in a wall where a false key, a pair of curling irons, and a small iron crow were hid, which, he said, had been used in breaking open the Excise Office; whether they were covered with earth or not I cannot say, as the prisoner himself put in his hand and brought them out. [Here a false key, a pair of curling irons, and a small iron crow were shown the witness.] These are the same articles that were so found. [The counsel for the pannels here repeated the objection against adducing the iron crow, the curling irons or toupee tongs, and dark lanthorn, as mentioned in the general objection and interlocutor before taken down.] I was present at the search that was made in Smith's house; there was nothing found in it. I was likewise present on the day following at a search that was made in Brodie's house and yard, when one part of a dark lanthorn was found in a necessary house, and another part in a pen where fowls or game-cocks had been kept. [Here the dark lanthorn libelled on was shown to the witness.] These are the two parts of the dark lanthorn which were so found. The prisoner, George Smith, informed me that the small crow was used in breaking into the Excise Office.

Cross-examined by the DEAN OF FACULTY—Did Brown inform you, previous to your going to England, that the prisoner, William Brodie, had any concern in the robbery of the Excise Office?

WITNESS—He told me that there was a gentleman whom I knew, and whom I little suspected, concerned in it, but he did not mention his name.

> Alexander Williamson

23. ALEXANDER WILLIAMSON, sheriff-officer in Edinburgh, called and sworn.

WITNESS—I was present, along with George Williamson and James Murray, when there was a search made in the house of William Brodie, the prisoner, upon the 10th of March last, and in the course of the said search I saw a pair of pistols wrapped in a black stocking taken from under the earth in the fireplace of a shed in his yard. [Here the pistols libelled on were shown to the witness wrapped in a green cloth.] These are the pistols, and they were found in that green cloth. [The counsel for the pannels here repeated the objection against adducing the pistols, as mentioned in the general objection and interlocutor before taken down.]

Cross-examined by the DEAN OF FACULTY—How came you to say that they were found in a black stocking?

WITNESS—I saw a black stocking on the table, and that misled me.

The DEAN OF FACULTY—You are to speak from what you know, sir, and not from what you see on the table.

WITNESS—I am certain that it was in a green cloth they were found.

James Murray

---

24. JAMES MURRAY, sheriff-officer in Edinburgh, called in and sworn.

WITNESS—I was employed, along with Alexander Williamson and some others, to search the prisoner's (William Brodie) house upon the 10th of March last. In the course of the search we found a pair of pistols in a green cloth covered with earth in the fireplace of a shed. I think that it was myself that dug them out of the earth. [Here the pistols libelled on were shown to the witness.] These are the pistols that were so found. I afterwards saw one part of the dark lanthorn found in a necessary house, and another part of a dark lanthorn found in a pen where game-cocks had been kept. I accompanied the other prisoner, George Smith, upon the 16th of March, to the bottom of Allan's Close,[6] and he there pointed out a hole in a wall, where, he said, there were some articles hid. I put in my hand and brought out a false key, a pair of curling irons, and a small crow. [Here the articles formerly produced were shown to the witness.] These are the same that were so found.

Cross-examined by Mr. JOHN CLERK—You say that you put in your hand and brought out these articles; are you sure it was not George Smith who did so?

WITNESS—I put in my hand; George Smith could not, being handcuffed.

George Williamson

---

25. GEORGE WILLIAMSON, messenger-at-arms in Edinburgh, called in and sworn.

WITNESS—I was employed with others to search the house of the prisoner, William Brodie, on the 10th of March last, and found several keys of an uncommon construction in a room off Brodie's shop. We likewise found a pair of pistols wrapped in a green cloth under the earth in the fireplace of a shed in the woodyard. These were discovered by Smith, the prisoner, poking with an iron. [Pistols shown to witness.] These are the same that were so found. We also found several pick-locks in Mr. Brodie's house, all of which were lodged by me in the Sheriff-Clerk's Office. [Here the pick-locks were shown to witness.] These are the same pick-locks that were so found. [The counsel for the pannels here repeated the objection against adducing the pick-locks, as mentioned in the general objection and interlocutor before taken down.] I was sent in quest of Mr. Brodie, who was supposed to have gone to London, by Mr. Scott, the Procurator-Fiscal, upon the 11th of March last. I left Edinburgh about eleven o'clock at night. When I arrived at Dunbar I got some accounts of him; Mr. Brodie had left that place in a post-chaise. At Newcastle I was informed that he had taken the "Flying Mercury" post-coach to York; and I was afterwards informed that he had continued in it till he came to London. When I arrived in London I was informed by the coachman that Mr. Brodie did not go with the coach to the stage office, but that he had quitted it at the foot of Old Street, Moorfields. I waited upon Sir Sampson Wright, and at his desire I called upon Mr. Walker, solicitor-at-law in the Adelphi, and inquired for Mr. Brodie. He told me he was bad, and that I could not see him. I said I had a letter for him and wanted only to deliver it; but Mr. Walker replied that it might perhaps be dangerous to allow me to see him.[7]

The DEAN OF FACULTY—My Lords, without meaning any reflection on the witness, whom I know and believe to be a very good man and an active officer, the greatest part of what the witness says is "hearsay." He tells your Lordships that he was told one thing at Dunbar; that he received another piece of information at Newcastle; that a coachman told him so-and-so in London, and that Mr. Walker said this, that, and the other thing. My Lords, this is exceedingly improper. I have been taught to understand that in criminal trials the best evidence that can be got ought always to be brought; and surely it will not be pretended that that has been done in the present case. In a question of this kind, hearsay evidence is not admissible. The witness has said that he was informed so-and-so by coachmen; why were not these coachmen called as evidences? He has given you an account of a conversation that passed between him and Mr. Walker; why is not Mr. Walker brought here to speak for himself?

The LORD ADVOCATE—My Lords, it was thought a material circumstance to be proved that the prisoner, William Brodie, fled from this country; that he secreted himself in London; and the witness, who was sent in pursuit of him, was considered as a proper person to be examined as to the fact. In the course of informing the Court what he himself did he has necessarily mentioned what passed between himself and some other persons. This cannot be said to have been hearsay evidence, being what the witness himself knows.

My Lords, the Dean of Faculty has asked why the different post-boys and coachmen who drove the prisoner to London, why Mr. Walker and others were not all cited as witnesses? The bringing forward of such a variety of witnesses is not only unnecessary but expensive. By the forms of criminal procedure in this country a trial must be finished at one sederunt; but, my Lords, if the mode contended for by the Dean of Faculty had been pursued in the present case this trial could not have been finished in a month.

The LORD JUSTICE-CLERK—George Williamson, you will confine yourself to what you know or did yourself, and do not speak of what you were told by others.

WITNESS—I searched for the prisoner in London, but could not find him. I also went out to Deal and Dover, but could receive no intelligence of him. Accounts were afterwards brought to this place that he had been apprehended in Holland and brought to London. I went to London for him. He was delivered over to me at Tothilfields Bridewell, and I conducted him to this place and lodged him in the Tolbooth.[8]

Andrew Ainslie

The SOLICITOR-GENERAL—The next witness is Andrew Ainslie.

The DEAN OF FACULTY—Before this witness is called I rise to state to the Court an objection against his admissibility. This witness is alleged to have been guilty of the same crime of which the pannels at the bar now stand accused, and therefore the objection of his being a *socius criminis* might apply to him. But although by our former law the objection of a witness being *socius criminis* might render him inadmissible, yet I have no occasion, nor is it my intention, to insist on the present objection in that view, for I freely own that the practice of this Court has for some time past, and with great propriety, I think, over-ruled that objection.

But, my Lords, I contend that this witness is inadmissible from the particular circumstances attending his case. For, according to the information which I have received, when this witness was apprehended and committed to prison, in the month of March last, to stand trial for this crime, he never charged Mr. Brodie as having been in any measure accessory thereto. On Ainslie's first examination he positively affirmed that Mr. Brodie had no sort of accession to the crime of which he is now accused, or was concerned in any other bad action whatever to his knowledge, unless playing at cards and dice should be reckoned such; and in the different declarations which he made before the Sheriff he still persisted in denying that my client had any concern in this robbery. But after Mr. Brodie was apprehended and brought from Holland Ainslie was again brought before the Sheriff, when he was informed that either he himself must be hanged or he must accuse Mr. Brodie. Further, I am now instructed to say that when this witness was carried before the Sheriff his life was offered to him on his becoming King's evidence against Mr. Brodie, and accusing him of having been concerned in this robbery, and that, even notwithstanding this offer, he persisted in denying that Mr. Brodie was guilty of this crime, until John Brown *alias* Humphry Moore, another of the witnesses cited, and alleged also to have been a *socius criminis*, was allowed to see and converse with him in prison, when at length he came into the measures proposed. I mean to say nothing against the conduct of the Sheriff, which may have been very proper—with the motives which may have influenced a public officer to a particular line of conduct I have nothing to do—but I state it as an insuperable bar to the admissibility of this witness, that hopes were suggested to him of saving his own life by criminating my client. And I offer to prove, by the evidence of the Sheriff of Edinburgh himself, that a bargain of this nature was made with Ainslie, and that it was not till then he was prevailed upon to say that Mr. Brodie had any concern in this crime. No man could withstand such a temptation, and it is impossible that the Court can receive the testimony of a witness in such circumstances.

The LORD ADVOCATE—My Lords, I hardly expected that such an objection would have been made at this time, as it has long been the universal practice to admit *socii criminis* as evidence, and at the last trial in this Court such a witness was received without even an objection being stated. All the arguments on the other side could only affect the credibility of the witness, which properly belongs to the jury, and not the admissibility, which alone is before the Court. It is indeed true, and I am even surprised that the honourable counsel had not appealed to the authority, that Sir George Mackenzie has laid it down that *socii criminis* could not be admitted as evidence; but upon what principle of law or reason Sir George formed that opinion I could never discover. Sir George Mackenzie, indeed, is an author by whom I never was much instructed. He is often contradictory, always perplexed, and in many instances unintelligible. But even supposing the law had so stood in his time, the Court and the practice have long since deviated from it.

My Lords, the fact as stated by the Dean of Faculty is

Lord Eskgrove.
(After Kay.)

erroneous in every respect. For although Ainslie in his first declaration did not accuse Brodie or any other person, and denied all knowledge of the crime, yet in the second declaration which he emitted before the Sheriff on the 14th of March, which I now hold in my hand, and would read did the forms of the Court permit me to do so, he in the most express terms charges both Brodie and Smith as being equally concerned in the crime libelled. And, my Lords, it will not easily be believed—indeed, the thing is incredible—that so respectable an officer of the law as the Sheriff of Edinburgh would ever have entered into such stipulations with Ainslie. But even had such transaction taken place before any inferior judge or magistrate, still that cannot deprive the public prosecutor of the evidence of this witness, for it will not be said that any such transaction passed between him and the witness, and therefore the objection ought to be repelled, reserving the credibility of his evidence to the jury.

The DEAN OF FACULTY—My Lords, I offer to prove my assertion.

The LORD ADVOCATE—My Lords, I am willing, if the Dean of Faculty and the Court consent to it, to hold the second declaration, emitted long before Mr. Brodie was apprehended, as the evidence to be delivered by Ainslie on this occasion.

Lord ESKGROVE—No transaction of any kind can possibly take place where life and death are concerned; and, therefore, even although the counsel on the other side consent to such a proposal, the Court would not allow it.

The LORD JUSTICE-CLERK—Dean of Faculty, do you say that my Lord Advocate has made a corrupt bargain with the witness to accuse Mr. Brodie upon condition of receiving a pardon?

The DEAN OF FACULTY—No, my Lord; but I repeat my offer to prove a bargain to that purpose with the Sheriff.

Lord HAILES—My Lords, the objection of *socius criminis*, if it ever was sustained in our law, has long since been obsolete. Nor can I understand how Sir George Mackenzie laid it down that *socii criminis* could not be admitted in evidence, since in his time we have instances of their having been actually received as witnesses. This assertion of Sir George Mackenzie's is, like many others in the same work, founded neither on principle nor fact. But the Dean of Faculty's objection amounts to a kind of *reprobator* against this witness. But even supposing that any credit could be given to the circumstances upon which this objection is principally founded, yet it could not affect the admissibility of this witness, as it is not pretended to be said that the alleged stipulation had taken place with the consent of the prosecutor for the Crown. I am therefore, upon the whole, for repelling the objection.

Lord ESKGROVE—My Lords, there is no doubt that the objection of the witness being a *socius criminis* cannot be admitted in the present state of our law, whatever might have been done formerly. By the common practice, such witnesses are every day admitted; nor do I see how crimes of this nature could be discovered if a contrary practice were followed.

As to the special circumstances qualified by the Dean of Faculty, that a bargain was made by the Sheriff with Ainslie to procure him His Majesty's pardon on condition of his accusing the pannel, I am likewise of opinion that these do not go to his admissibility. For your Lordships will observe that Ainslie cannot possibly be under any temptation now to accuse the pannel in consequence of that bargain. If I understand the law, my Lords, the calling any person as a witness on a trial is completely departing from any right to indict that person himself as being guilty of the crime concerning which he is called as a witness. Nor does it signify whether the pannel be convicted or not; it is clear that the witness can never be questioned for that crime; and Ainslie is quite safe from the consequences of his being accessory to the robbery of the Excise Office, if he was so. But, my Lords, it will be proper, before examining Mr. Ainslie, to inform him of his situation; and it will be proper, and the counsel for the pannels are entitled, to put such questions *in initialibus* of his evidence as will tend to satisfy your Lordships and the jury whether such a bargain had been entered into with him by the Sheriff or not, and how far he considers himself bound by it.

Lord STONEFIELD—My Lords, I am for repelling this objection.

Lord SWINTON—My Lords, the objection made to the admitting of Andrew Ainslie is that he was an accomplice. I am clear to repel the objection in so far as it goes against the admissibility of the witness, but reserving it in full force, and leaving it to the conscience of the jury, in so far as it strikes against the credibility of the witness. In all my practice, ever since I knew this Court, although I have often heard the objection made, I never knew one instance in which it was sustained. If the jury were bound to believe every word a witness said, be his character what it may, there would be good reason for sustaining the objection, but where objections are reserved against the credibility of a witness, the jury are left at liberty to believe as much or as little of what he says as they see good cause for so doing.

The repelling of this objection, which is now the uniform practice, was founded upon good sense and reason, for as accomplices are best qualified to make discoveries, so, many crimes, were they excluded from being witnesses, would pass unpunished; and any hazard of their being guilty of perjury may be easily prevented by the Court's informing them that the evidence they are to give cannot affect themselves.

The LORD JUSTICE-CLERK—My Lords, were such an objection as this to be sustained, we would find very few instances, as one of your Lordships has very well observed, where a crime such as the present, of an occult and secret nature, could be brought to light. My Lords, as to the objection of the *socius criminis*, I will not say a single word upon it. I always thought, my Lords, that it contained in itself a complete answer, since the allegeance that the witness is a *socius criminis* implies that the pannel is guilty of the crime.

What is said by the Dean of Faculty about a supposed bargain betwixt the Sheriff of Edinburgh and Ainslie is by no means such an objection as affects his admissibility, although I will not say that his credibility may not be in some degree diminished by it; and the Dean of Faculty will be right in making his own use of it to the jury. Had the Dean of Faculty alleged that this bargain was corruptly made by my Lord Advocate, I could have understood him. But the Sheriff is only an inferior officer, and had no power to enter into any such transaction. Had he been ever so willing he could not have given Ainslie the smallest security that the terms and conditions of the bargain were to be fulfilled on the part of the Crown in consequence of Ainslie performing what was required of him. A higher authority was necessary, and none but the Lord Advocate himself could with any effect enter into an agreement with a witness to procure him His Majesty's pardon for becoming King's evidence. It is therefore not enough to say that offers were made him, whatever they were, by the Sheriff, and we must examine him, reserving all objections to his credibility.

The Court then pronounced the following interlocutor:—

The Lord Justice-Clerk and Lords Commissioners of Justiciary having considered the foregoing objections with the answers thereto, they repel the objections stated, and allow the witness to be examined, reserving the credibility of his evidence to the jury.

ROBT. M'QUEEN, I.P.D.

26. ANDREW AINSLIE, sometime shoemaker in Edinburgh, present prisoner in the Tolbooth of Canongate of Edinburgh, called in and sworn.

The LORD JUSTICE-CLERK—Andrew Ainslie, you are called here as a witness to give evidence as to certain matters in which it is generally understood you yourself had a concern. You are informed by the Court that whether you had any such concern or not you are in no danger in telling the truth, for, being called here as a witness, you can never afterwards be tried for the crime with which the prisoners are charged. You are to pay no regard to the declarations you formerly emitted; these are now destroyed. And you will remember that by the great oath you have sworn you are bound to tell the truth, and if you say anything to the prejudice of the prisoners which is not true, or if you conceal any part of the truth with a view to favour them, you will be guilty of the crime of perjury, and liable to be tried and punished for it, and you will likewise commit a heinous sin in the sight of God, and thereby endanger the eternal salvation of your own soul.

WITNESS—I am acquainted with both William Brodie and George Smith, the prisoners at the bar, and also with John Brown *alias* Humphry Moore. I remember that the Excise Office was broke into upon Wednesday, the 5th of March last. I knew before that that it was to be broken into, but how long I cannot tell. Brown and the prisoners and I frequently talked of it before, and Brown and I went often to the Excise Office in the evenings in order to observe at what hour the people left it, and in consequence of repeated observations we discovered that the door was usually locked about eight o'clock, and that there were two men, an old and a younger man, who came night about to watch the office about ten o'clock. Afterwards Brown and I went out one afternoon to a house at Duddingston, where we drank a bottle of porter, and saw a woman whom I took to be the landlady. We then went to a field in the neighbourhood, from which we took the coulter of a plough and two iron wedges, which we carried to the Salisbury Crags and hid there. At this time there was a black dog in company with us. We had fixed on Wednesday, the 5th of March, for committing the said robbery, and we allowed the coulter to remain in Salisbury Crags until about six o'clock of the evening of that day, when Brown and I, it being then dusk, went out and brought the coulter of the plough to the house of the prisoner, George Smith, on purpose to use it in breaking into the Excise Office. We found Smith at home, and we expected Mr. Brodie to join us and to accompany us to the

Excise Office. Brodie did not come until a good while after, when he joined us in the room above-stairs in Smith's house. Mr. Brodie was at this time dressed in a light-coloured great-coat, with black clothes below (in which I had often seen him before), and a cocked hat. When he came in he had a pistol in his hand, and was singing a verse of what I understood to be a flash song. By a flash song I mean a highwayman's song. We spoke together concerning the Excise Office; and it was settled upon that I should go before to the Excise Office and get within the rails and observe when the people went out. I went there accordingly a little before eight o'clock, carrying the coulter of the plough with me, and waited till I saw the porter come out with a light and lock the outer door. In a short while thereafter Smith came to me and asked if the people were all gone, and when I informed him that they were gone out Smith then went forward and opened the door with a key, which, I had heard him say, he had previously made for it, and went into the office. In about five minutes thereafter Brodie came down the close, and when I told him that Smith had gone in, but that Brown was not yet come, he went up the close again towards the street, and returned in a little with Brown, who said he had been dogging the old man who watched the office in order to see where he went, and that he had gone home. Brown then asked me whether or not I had "Great Samuel"—by which he meant the coulter. I told him I had, and gave it him through the rails, and he and Brodie then went down towards the door of the office and went in, as I supposed. I had no arms myself, excepting a stick, but Smith had three loaded pistols, Brown two, and Brodie one; at least, I saw Brodie, when he came into Smith's house, have one in his hand. It had been previously settled amongst us, before leaving Smith's house, that Brodie was to stand in the inside of the outer door, and that Brown and Smith were to go into the office. I was to remain without to watch, and in case of danger, to give an alarm to Brodie, which Brodie was to communicate to Brown and Smith. The signal of alarm agreed upon was to be given by me in this manner—A single whistle if one man appeared, so that they might be prepared to secure him; but if more than one man, or any appearance of danger, I was to give three whistles, in order that those within might make their escape by the door or by the back windows, as they thought best. I had an ivory whistle prepared for the purpose, which was given me by Mr. Brodie in Smith's house in the afternoon. I took my station within the rail and leaned down, so that no person either going in or coming out could see me. Some short while after Brodie and Brown went into the office, a man came running down the close and went in also. I gave no alarm, for before I had time to think what I should do another man came immediately running out at the door and went up the court. In a very little afterwards, to my great surprise, a second man came out from the office. I got up and looked at him through the rails, and perceived that he was none of my three companions. I had not seen the other man who came out first so distinctly, owing to my lying down by the side of the parapet wall on which the rail is placed, in order that I might not be observed. I was afraid that we were discovered; and, as soon as the second man had gone up the close, I gave the alarm by three whistles as the agreed-on signal of retreat and ran up the close myself. I went down St. John's Street and came round opposite to the back of the Excise Office, thinking to meet my companions coming out by the back way, having escaped from the windows. I remained there for some little time, and, not meeting with them, I then went directly to Smith's house. Finding none of them there, and Mrs. Smith telling me that they were not yet come in, I went back to the Excise Office by the street, went down the close, saw the door open, and, finding everything quiet, I returned to Smith's, where I saw him and Brown. They accused me of not having given the alarm as I promised, and said that when they came out they found that Brodie had gone from his place. I told them what I had observed, and that I had given the alarm. I remained in Smith's only a few minutes, and I did not see Brodie again that night.[9] Brown and I then went over to the house of one Fraser in the New Town, and sent for Daniel Maclean, Mr. Drysdale's waiter. We spent the evening with him there. There was one Price likewise in company with us, and we remained together till about two o'clock in the morning. It was near eight o'clock when I went first to the Excise Office, and it was about half-an-hour afterwards that I quitted my station. Brodie called next morning at our room—the room occupied by Brown and me. He came in laughing, and said that he had been with Smith, who had accused him of running away the previous evening. I told him that I also thought he had run off; but he said that he had stood true. Brodie had no great-coat on when he came to the Excise Office and spoke to me at the rails; he was dressed in black. When the whistle was given me by him in Smith's house in the afternoon Brodie had on the white-coloured clothes which he usually wore. He afterwards changed them before we went to the Excise Office. Before I left Smith's I saw Brodie have a pick-lock in his hands, and I think we all had it in our hands looking at it. Brodie was in his own hair. I did not observe him have a wig. We had prepared three crapes to disguise our faces; one of them was intended for Brown, another for Smith, and the remaining one for myself, but I did not see either Brown or Smith put a crape in their pockets that night. [Here the pistols libelled on were shown to the witness.] These pistols belonged to Mr. Brodie, and Smith had them with him at the Excise Office. They were given to him by me, and I had borrowed them from Mr. Brodie a month or two before for another purpose. That same evening Brown told me, as we went over to the New Town, that they had found sixteen pounds and some silver in the Excise Office; and on the Friday evening following, when I called at Smith's house, in the room above stairs I found Smith and Brodie, and saw the money lying on a chair. I got a fourth share of it in small notes, and at the same time I got some gold from Mr.

Brodie in payment of money he owed me. Brodie and Smith also each got a fourth share of it. There were two five-pound notes amongst the money that was on the chair, and I signified a desire to have one of them. I accordingly gave back some of the small notes I had received and some of the gold and got one of them in exchange. I afterwards gave the note to Smith, and saw him change it at Drysdale's in the New Town the same evening, when he was purchasing a ticket for his wife in the mail-coach to Newcastle for the next day.[10] Brown and one Price were then present.

The SOLICITOR-GENERAL—Have you any particular mark by which you could know the said note again?

WITNESS—It was a Glasgow note, and battered on the back with paper.

[Here the Solicitor-General proposed to show the witness the bank-note libelled on.]

The DEAN OF FACULTY—My Lords, here I must interrupt the witness. It is stated in the libel that a five-pound bank-note is to be produced in evidence against the pannels; but the witness says that the note given him to change was a Glasgow five-pound note, and the paper on your Lordship's table is a promissory note for five pounds issued by John Robertson in name of Spiers, Murdoch & Company, a private banking company in Glasgow. This cannot in propriety of language be termed a bank-note. In Lombard Street, where such notes as that on the table are daily negotiated, they never think of calling them bank-notes. This term, my Lords, is exclusively appropriated to the notes issued by a bank constituted by a Royal Charter, such as the Bank of England, and the notes of a private banker are distinguished by the name of banker's notes. Neither does such a note come under the description of money, as it is not a legal tender in payment. I hold in my hand this objection in writing, which, to save the time of the Court, I shall read, and I crave that it may be entered on the record.

The SOLICITOR-GENERAL—This objection appears to me to be so entirely frivolous as hardly to be worthy of an answer. The note in question is one issued by a very respectable banking company in Glasgow, and well known in this country by the name of the Glasgow Arms Bank. Such notes are commonly held to be bank-notes, and are so described in common language every day. Many instances might likewise be given of their being described in the same manner in criminal indictments, nor was it ever before objected that the description was insufficient. We need not go so far off as Lombard Street; there is no necessity for going further than the Parliament Close, where thousands of these notes are issued, known by no other name than that of bank-notes. The honourable counsel on the other side of the table, as well as myself, have received the greatest part of our fees in bank-notes of this kind, and both of us would have reason to complain, I believe, if what we received in that manner were not really bank-notes or considered as money.

The DEAN OF FACULTY—My Lords, the common use of language, as well as the technical and legal description of the writing on the table, join in supporting this objection. That there is a distinction in common phrase between a bank-note and a banker's note there can be no doubt. Every private company which is instituted with a view to the purposes of banking may indeed issue promissory notes, which meet with a voluntary credit from the country; but these are distinguished from the public banks instituted by the authority of Government, and where credit does not depend upon the goodwill of any individual, as every man must accept in payment their notes when tendered to him. These notes are alone properly termed bank-notes as the notes of a bank which is a public corporation, while the notes of a private company are termed banker's notes, or those of an individual. Although the one may, in common discourse, be sometimes confounded with the other by those who are ignorant of the real distinction, there is no doubt that that distinction exists and is acknowledged by any one acquainted with the subject; and where they are best acquainted with it there the distinction is most explicitly acknowledged, as in Lombard Street, where no other term is known for the note of a private banker than a banker's note. The inaccuracy of the description in the indictment is therefore evident, and can by no means be defended by the vulgar error which sometimes, I admit, is fallen into of confounding it with the note of a public bank.

My Lords, it will be allowed me that accuracy is at least as necessary for an indictment as to proceedings in the civil Courts; and your Lordships cannot have forgotten the late decision upon the application of the Bankrupt Act, when it was found that money belonging to creditors could not be lodged in the Bank of Dundee, in respect, the Act declares, that the bankrupt funds recovered should be lodged in a bank. And if the Bank of Dundee, my Lords, was held in that judgment not to be a bank under the meaning of the Act, with what propriety could your Lordships determine in a criminal case that their notes were bank-notes? No case can be figured more precisely in point; and if your Lordships approve of that decision, you will necessarily find that the note on the table is improperly described, and cannot be used in evidence.

I might safely admit, my Lords, that if this note had been described as a five-pound bank-note of a certain company, supposing it had been a bank-note of Sir William Forbes & Company, that this would have been a good description, for then it would have appeared by the indictment that the writing meant was a promissory note of that company. But from its being termed generally a bank-note, I could never suppose that it was not a note issued by one of the public banks, as that is the description that applies to no other species of document known in this country. For these reasons I hope your Lordships will not allow any questions concerning this paper to be put to the witness.

Lord HAILES—When I had the honour to serve the Crown as a depute-advocate, I learned from a most eminent judge, Lord Tinwald, Justice-Clerk, from whom I derived much instruction in the principles of law, that the note of a private banking company could not be termed in law a bank-note, nor could it be considered in any respect as money. On one occasion he obliged me to correct an indictment where I had fallen into the same error which I perceive here. The word bank-note, in legal acceptation, is applied exclusively to the notes issued by a bank instituted by Royal Charter, and I remember well the case alluded to by the Dean of Faculty, which was determined on the same principles. I am therefore clear for sustaining the objection.

Lord ESKGROVE—My Lords, I am clearly of the opinion that has been given by my honourable brother. The promissory note of a private banking company is not held in the language of our law to be a bank-note, and therefore I am for sustaining the objection.

The LORD JUSTICE-CLERK—I suppose there are none of your Lordships of a different opinion? The Lords therefore sustain the objection.

The Court then pronounced the following interlocutor:—

The Lord Justice-Clerk and Lords Commissioners of Justiciary having considered the objection, with the answers thereto, they sustain the objection to this piece of evidence libelled on, and refuse to allow the same to be produced.

ROBT. M'QUEEN, I.P.D.

[Here the witness was shown a false key, a pair of curling irons, a small iron crow, and the coulter of a plough.]

WITNESS—I know these articles; they were all used in the breaking into the Excise Office. The coulter we called "Great Samuel," and the iron crow, "Little Samuel." When I gave the coulter to Brown through the rails at the Excise Office he asked me if I had "Little Samuel," and I said that I believed that Smith had it in his pocket.

Lord HAILES—Andrew Ainslie, you gave an account of this matter formerly before the Sheriff; but you have been very properly told by the Court that what you said there is now of no avail, and that your declarations are destroyed. You have this night, in presence of the Court and the jury, given evidence against the prisoners at the bar. Before you leave the Court, I desire you to consult your own breast whether or not you have said anything to the prejudice of these men that is not true. You have it still in your power to correct any mistakes you have made, but this opportunity will never recur to you. If, therefore, you are conscious of having said anything against the prisoners contrary to truth, and if you leave this house without informing the Court and the jury of you having done so, you will commit a most heinous offence against the Almighty God, and you will be guilty of perjury and of murder.

Cross-examined by the DEAN OF FACULTY—At what hour went you first to the Excise Office on the night in which you say it was broke into?

WITNESS—I left Smith's house about a quarter before eight o'clock; I went away before the rest.

The DEAN OF FACULTY—What o'clock was it when you returned the last time to Smith's that evening?

WITNESS—I cannot say, but I think it would be about an hour from the time I went first to the Excise Office.

The DEAN OF FACULTY—How long were you at the Excise Office before Brodie came to you?

WITNESS—About a quarter of an hour; he came to the Excise Office just about eight o'clock.

The DEAN OF FACULTY—You have said that you had resolved to break into the Excise Office a considerable while before you carried that design into execution, and you have told us that it was broke into upon a Wednesday night? Now, you will inform the Court and the gentlemen of the jury what your reason was for fixing upon that night more than any other?

WITNESS—Brown and I having seen, in consequence of frequent observations, that an old man watched night about with the other porter, and knowing that it was his turn to watch on Wednesday night, we therefore fixed upon that night for carrying our design into execution. We knew that there was usually nobody in the office from eight to ten o'clock for the purpose of watching it. I do not remember who it was that first proposed robbing the Excise Office.

> John Brown

27. JOHN BROWN *alias* HUMPHRY MOORE, sometime residing in Edinburgh, present prisoner in the Tolbooth of Canongate of Edinburgh, called.

Mr. WIGHT, for the pannel, William Brodie—My Lords, before this witness, who is also a *socius criminis*, is called in, I have to object to his being received as a witness upon grounds which, I imagine, are insuperable. This man, my Lords, was convicted at the General Quarter Sessions for the county of

Middlesex, by the verdict of a jury, of stealing twenty-one guineas and fourteen doubloons, in consequence of which he was adjudged to be transported beyond the seas for the term of seven years, in April, 1784, and this is instantly instructed by a copy of the said conviction, under the hand of the proper officer, now produced; and further, the witness, under the name of John Brown, was banished by the Justices of Peace for Stirlingshire from that county in September, 1787, upon his confessing a theft committed at Falkirk, as appears from a certified copy of the said sentence under the hand of the Clerk of the Peace of the said shire. I shall not take up your Lordships' time in proving that a man thus infamous is altogether inadmissible as a witness in any cause, especially where life is concerned, and I have no doubt that your Lordships will sustain the objection.

The SOLICITOR-GENERAL—My Lords, in answer to this objection, I here produce His Majesty's most gracious pardon in behalf of this witness, under the Great Seal of England, dated 28th July last, which, by the law of England, renders the witness habile and testable.

Mr. WIGHT—The production of this pardon, my Lords, will by no means answer the objection which I have stated. The infamy attending the commission of the crimes of which Brown has been convicted is not, cannot be, done away by the King's pardon. He still remains a man unworthy of credit, in whom the gentlemen of the jury can place no confidence. His situation, in short, is just the same as it was before the granting of the pardon, unless that the pardon saves him from the punishment awarded against his crimes. This doctrine is delivered by Sir George Mackenzie in very strong terms, and it is the doctrine of common sense.

[During this time some desultory conversation took place about what was the felony for which Brown was sentenced, the Lord Advocate saying it was only swindling.[11]]

The LORD ADVOCATE—My Lords, as to the sentence against Brown, supposed to have been pronounced by the Justices of Peace for Stirlingshire, it does not appear with certainty, nor do I know whether Brown, the witness, be the same person who was the subject of that sentence or not, as the certified copy of the sentence of banishment produced is against one John Brown from Ireland. I admit, my Lords, that if he had been tried by a proper Court and convicted in consequence of the verdict of a jury that the objection would have been a very good one; but the sentence of the Justices of Peace here produced cannot afford an objection which your Lordships can sustain in bar of his evidence. Granting him to be the same person, there is here no trial or verdict of a jury. It appears that a petition was presented for him to avoid the trouble of a trial, and the Clerk of Court has most improperly taken down an acknowledgment of his guilt. There was no occasion for his accusing himself, it was sufficient for him to state that he wished to avoid the consequences of a trial; and therefore, my Lords, this sentence can in no view of the matter be held to infer his actual guilt of the crime laid to his charge before the Justices. My Lords, I admit in the fullest manner the effect of the first sentence against Brown for the felony, but I maintain that it is completely taken off by the subsequent pardon.

I do not reckon myself obliged to answer to the general objection of *socius criminis*: that is fully answered by the practice and the uniform course of your Lordships' decisions. A specialty was argued in the case of Ainslie; but this witness is in a situation very different. He never was charged with this crime, nor was he ever liable to the temptation which it was alleged, for the pannels, might have influenced the former witness.

My Lords, many daring robberies have been committed in this city, and, in spite of the utmost vigilance of the police, no discovery could be made of the perpetrators. At length, upon the Friday after the robbery of the Excise Office, Brown went to Mr. Middleton, a person employed by the Sheriff, and told him such circumstances as led to a discovery. From this, my Lords, I am bound to suppose that he had repented of what he had done, and I conceived it to be my duty not to prosecute him, but, on the contrary, to make use of his evidence as a means of discovery of the rest of his accomplices. After this, my Lords, it was found that he had been convicted at the Old Bailey. I then applied for advice to those whom I thought were best enabled to assist me concerning the law of England on this subject, and I learned, my Lords, that the proper method to be followed was to apply for a pardon. There is no occasion for making a mystery of the matter, it was the Recorder of London I did apply to. He is a gentleman necessarily more versant in these matters than any other man in the kingdom. By his advice, I applied for a pardon and accordingly obtained it.

But, my Lords, there was no occasion for a pardon in this case; the witness, in my opinion, would have been just as admissible without it. The sentence by which he was condemned is to us entirely a foreign sentence, and, therefore, upon the universally received principle of law, that *statuta non obligant extra territorium statuentis*, it can be of no force with us, unless from that politeness, termed *comitas* by the law, which civilised nations pay to the decrees of each other, and, accordingly, unless your Lordships shall, *ex comitate*, be disposed to give effect to the decree of a foreign Court, this objection is such as cannot even be listened to in the first instance, the crime said to be committed by Brown having been committed in England, and the sentence pronounced against him being the sentence of an English Court.

My Lords, your Lordships in another capacity, in the civil Court, do not as a matter of course give effect to foreign decrees. In every instance you must be satisfied that the decree is consistent with equity and justice before you interpone your authority. And this holds more particularly in such decrees as infer a penalty, in which case, indeed, some lawyers think, and my Lord Kames declares himself to be clearly of that opinion, that no weight whatever is attached to a foreign decree.

But, my Lords, even laying this out of the question, His Majesty's most gracious pardon, which I hold in my hand, puts an end to all objection at once. There is not, indeed, a clearer point than that a pardon from the King takes away the effects of any former sentence, and makes the person pardoned precisely the same person he was before the sentence was pronounced against him.

This question must be judged of according to the law of England, and English authorities are express to this purpose. Thus Blackstone, B. iv. ch. 31, in fine says, "The effect of such pardon by the King is to make the offender a new man, to acquit him of all corporeal penalties and forfeitures annexed to that offence for which he obtains his pardon, and not so much to restore his former as to give him a new credit and capacity." And another authority, my Lords, equally respectable—I mean Bacon's Abridgment, p. 809—lays down exactly the same doctrine. This witness, therefore, is and must be admissible, notwithstanding the sentence pronounced against him. He has a new credit and capacity given him by this pardon, which enables him to be adduced as a witness, whatever may have been his character previous to obtaining it.

The authority of Sir George Mackenzie has, indeed, been stated as in opposition to this argument. But things have varied so much since his days, and his opinions are frequently so loose and confused, that no weight can be given to his opinion in opposition to such direct and recent authorities as I have quoted. It is perhaps no great authority, my Lords; but I hold a newspaper in my hand, from which it would appear that a case in England exactly in point was determined in July last in consistency with the authorities I have mentioned; and another case in the year 1782 was determined in the same manner.

As to the sentence of the Justices of Peace, I confess I was surprised, my Lords, that the counsel on the other side of the bar should have urged it, when in so late a case as that of *Brown and Wilson*, in the year 1774, your Lordships found that a sentence of the Justices of Peace was no bar against the admissibility of a witness, nor any sentence which proceeded without a jury. I therefore sit down, my Lords, in the full conviction that your Lordships will over-rule the objection against this witness.

The DEAN OF FACULTY—My Lords, this case, so far as I know, has never yet been decided by your Lordships. The witness is in a new situation, and in one so extraordinary that it well deserves your Lordships' serious consideration, whether he ought, in law or in common justice to the pannels, to be allowed to give evidence. My Lord Advocate is mistaken in saying that Brown was not under the same apprehension with Ainslie when he accused the pannels; for I cannot conceive that any man could have better ground than he to be afraid of the justice of his country; and certainly no man ever spoke under more strong and immediate fears of a halter.

When he made his confession he was under sentence of death, at least he knew well that he was liable to a capital conviction for not having transported himself conformable to the sentence at the Old Bailey. He knew that a pardon was necessary to preserve his life, and that it was impossible for him to remain in safety without it in this country. The game he played, therefore, was very evident—he did not accuse Mr. Brodie at first, and gave no information whatever but against the pannel Smith. My Lords, was it unnatural for a man of his complexion in such circumstances to have recourse to fiction? Accordingly, whenever Mr. Brodie was taken, a strong accusation against him was for the first time made by Brown, and this pardon was the immediate consequence. Let your Lordships reflect upon the whole of his conduct; let the jury take it into their most serious consideration; and I will aver that no evidence was ever offered under more suspicious circumstances.

The effect of the pardon, my Lords, is another point, and it is one which involves the most important consequences.

It is admitted on the other side of the bar, and, indeed, without their admission it is in evidence, that this man John Brown or Humphry Moore was sentenced to transportation by the Courts in England for a felony. It is not denied that a sentence of this nature precludes of itself the admissibility of that person as a witness against whom it is awarded, but it is said that this sentence is a foreign decree, to which we are not bound to pay any respect.

My Lords, are not the Courts of this country in the practice every day of paying respect to foreign decrees? It is true that the decrees of foreign Courts receive effect in this country only *ex comitate*. But it is nothing to me upon what principle the Courts here give effect to such decrees, if effect be really given. And that such respect is paid to foreign decrees, unless where they are contrary to our own law, is a position which no man will contest. To what purpose, then, is it stated, that this is the sentence of a foreign Court, unless it be stated at the same time that it is a sentence which your Lordships would not have pronounced in the same circumstances? The crime of which Brown was convicted is equally punishable in both parts of this island, and the effects of the sentence following upon the crime must, therefore, upon the universal principles by which all nations are now guided, be the same in both parts of the island also. The objection, then, that the decree is foreign, cannot be listened to by your Lordships without overturning those settled maxims by which your decisions, both in this Court and in another Court where all your Lordships sit, are constantly directed.

But His Majesty's pardon, it is said—this pardon now produced to your Lordships, and obtained for the sole purpose of endeavouring to enable this man to be a witness—has now placed him in the same situation as if he had never been condemned.

My Lords, I have heard it said that the King could make a peer, but that he could not make a gentleman; I am sure that he cannot make a rogue an honest man. This pardon, therefore, at the utmost can only avert the punishment which follows from the sentence. It cannot remove the guilt of this man, though it may save his life. Can it, indeed, my Lords, be supposed that this amiable prerogative, lodged in the hands of the King for the wisest of purposes, and to be exerted by him as the father of his people, should have the effect to let loose persons upon society, as honest, respectable men, as men who may be witnesses, who may be jurymen, and may decide upon your lives or my life to-morrow, although these very persons were yesterday in the eye of the law and the eye of reason held as hardened villains from whom no man was safe, considered as wretches guilty of, and fitted to, perpetrate the most abominable crimes; and that although every man knows them to be the same as they were, and is equally afraid of, and would as little trust them as before they obtained a remission of their crimes?

My Lord Advocate has talked of their obtaining a new credit by the pardon. What is this, my Lords? Can it be a new credit to cheat and rob and plunder? Is this pardon to operate like a settlement in a banker's books, when he opens a new credit upon the next page, after old scores are cleared off? My Lords, it is impossible. To suppose a pardon to have such effects is to suppose it the most unjustifiable of all things.

My Lords, I am willing to allow that this pardon should have every consequence beneficial to Mr. Brown; that he should derive all the benefit from it which the pardon itself expressly declares to be competent to him, and that no part of the punishment to which he was liable before this extension of His Majesty's clemency can now be inflicted upon him. But this is very different from the proposition, that he is a good evidence in this or any other cause; it is no part of his punishment that he is not allowed to swear away the life of his neighbour; on the contrary, it is rather a favour to him. That he is intestable was never a punishment even before the pardon was granted; it is only a consequence of the sentence for a crime of an infamous nature which fixes an indelible character upon him, and describes him as a man whose testimony is worthy of no regard; and that character is no more removed by the pardon than the original truth and authenticity of the evidence upon which he was convicted is falsified by it; on the contrary, the pardon contains in itself the most unexceptionable evidence of the guilt and infamy of the person who is obliged to plead it.

Authorities have been quoted on the other side of the bar, but they are not the authorities of our law. The authority of Sir George Mackenzie is expressly in their teeth. This is the second time to-day, my Lords, that I have heard this respectable writer talked lightly of. I cannot but express my surprise at it. He was undoubtedly a man of the highest abilities, and he is our only criminal lawyer. I think he is the most intelligible and clear of all our writers, and I have read him with great profit. But his authority is to be held light in this matter, because his opinion is decisive in favour of this objection—an opinion which, though it were not delivered by such high authority in our law, is yet so much in unison with the common reason and common feelings of mankind that I should deem it to require no other support.

The sentence of the Justices of Peace of Stirlingshire, it has been said, forms no objection to the admissibility of this witness, because it was pronounced without a jury, as all their sentences are. My Lords, this is not the reason. Sorry I am to say that, by a decision of your Lordships, magistrates of burghs and Sheriffs of counties have been found entitled to whip and imprison British subjects without a jury. But will it be maintained that persons so punished will not be accounted infamous and their testimony rejected?

My Lords, the reason why the sentence of the Justices of Peace was held not to bar the admissibility of a witness was because they are not a Court of record, and your Lordships could not be legally certified of what was their judgment. Could this information have been legally obtained the *infamia facti* would have been sustained as sufficient without the *infamia juris*.

A man is equally infamous in either case if his punishment is merited. And why is *infamia facti* not always admitted in our law as a sufficient bar, but merely because all objections to witnesses must be instantly verified, which would produce an infinite number of trials within trials, and, besides, which is far worse, would be trying a man without a libel, without allowing him time to produce witnesses, and without a jury. But the *infamia facti*, if proved—and in this case the proof is beyond dispute—is equally strong to render a witness inadmissible as any *infamia juris*. For it is not merely the sentence of a Court which makes a man intestable, but the fact that he is a villain. And this is an additional proof that His Majesty's pardon, which undoubtedly does not justify the act, though it saves the actor, cannot take away the infamy attendant upon the crime of which he stands convicted.

But the matter does not end here. My Lords, supposing that His Majesty really had this incomprehensible prerogative of changing, by a sheet of parchment, a corrupt and dishonest heart, and cleansing it from all its impurities, I still maintain that it has not been exercised. Where is the clause in this pardon restoring Brown to his character and integrity? You have heard the pardon read, and there is no clause in it to that effect. He is screened against punishment and every effect of a prosecution; but it would have required a very express clause indeed to give the pardon the additional force of removing the infamy of his sentence, and surely the warmest advocates for prerogative cannot be offended at its being said that the King must exercise that prerogative before its power can be felt.

My Lords, I shall trouble you with nothing farther upon this subject, which appears to me very clear. The sentence of the English Court is no more foreign than those to which the Courts of Scotland give effect every day. It is such a sentence as your Lordships would have pronounced had the crime been committed in this country. His Majesty's pardon cannot, by our law, restore this man from the infamy annexed to this sentence, and common reason tells us that it is beyond the power of kings, because it is beyond the power of man, to reinstate a man in his original integrity by their fiat.

Lord HAILES—My Lords, the Dean of Faculty has done more for Sir George Mackenzie than I was ever able to do, though I studied him before the Dean of Faculty was born. Sir George Mackenzie's work on the criminal law is a medley of opinions formed from the civilians, with what occurred in his own practice, and desultory observations upon them. He is exceedingly inaccurate. He mentions, for instance, an Act of Sederunt which has no existence, and in many other instances talks equally loosely.

With regard to the present objection, my Lords, it is clear that the decree is foreign. By the articles of the Union, our own laws and forms of procedure are secured to us, and we have as little connection with those of England as with the laws of Japan, being as little bound to obey them. At the same time there is always a *comitas* to foreign decrees, where not inconsistent with our own law. Here, however, there is no necessity to enter into this question, as the sentence in this case is superseded by the pardon. The sentence of the Justices of Peace weighs nothing with me. No such sentence ought ever to render a witness inadmissible, for Justices of Peace are always ready enough to banish a man who is accused from their own territory. I am therefore for repelling the objection.

Lord ESKGROVE—My Lords, I think this a matter of very great importance. I am clearly of opinion that it is beyond the prerogative of the Crown to render a person capable of being a witness by granting him a pardon. I know no such prerogative.

But, my Lords, the decree here is a foreign decree, and in judging of it we must consider the law of the country where it was pronounced, and from the authorities, my Lords, which have been quoted, it appears that a pardon in England does take off the whole consequence of the sentence. And in my opinion it would be highly unjust that the English sentence should be allowed to militate against a person exactly as it would do in England and not at the same time to give the pardon the same effect which it would have in that country. The *comitas* due to the sentence of an English Court is also due to the pardon, or to the sentence which an English Court would pronounce in consequence of that pardon. I cannot figure a more grievous punishment than that of being held out as a person incapable of giving testimony in any cause; and if by the law of England all the consequences of a sentence are done away by His Majesty's pardon, then this goes among the rest.

Had the crime been committed, or the sentence pronounced, in Scotland I would have had another opinion. I do not sit here, my Lords, to pass judgment upon authors long since dead. But the same opinion is delivered by Dirleton, which is given by Sir George Mackenzie; and *his* authority will not, I suppose, be questioned by any lawyer. And I hold it to be the law of Scotland, that a pardon does not restore the person pardoned, so as to free him from the infamy attending his crime. But as the law of England—the law of that country where the crime was committed, and the sentence pronounced—says otherwise, I am bound to repel the objection.

Lord STONEFIELD—My Lords, I am for repelling the objection. It was repelled in the case of Lord Castlehaven in the State trials.

Lord Stonefield.
(After Kay.)

Lord SWINTON—My Lords, this is a question of so much delicacy and importance that I could have wished more time to have weighed what I have heard from the counsel than the forms of Court will admit of.

The question is—Whether His Majesty's pardon did so far restore John Brown to the character and reputation he held before his conviction as to make his evidence admissible in the present trial?

In substance, my opinion concurs with that of my brethren, for repelling, in the circumstances of the present case, the objection to the admissibility of the witness, leaving his credit to the consciences and good sense of the jury.

Had John Brown's conviction proceeded upon a jury trial in Scotland, I would have been of a different opinion. There are, in the first place, several texts in the civil law upon this topic, all clearly purporting that a remission, so far from restoring, even blemished, the reputation of him whom it relieved from punishment. Next, our municipal law is perfectly explicit to the same effect. The statutes of Robert I., among others therein debarred from giving evidence, mentions convicts redeemed from justice. This act is expressly quoted and laid down as law by Sir George Mackenzie, who is, at least, our most ancient author upon the criminal law, and there is no practice or decision to the contrary.

These observations, however, I do not apply to the present case, for here the conviction and sentence are from England. The infamy, therefore, disabling Brown to be a witness arising in the law of that country, and coming here, must bring its character and construction and effects along with it.

I observe that one of these effects was the restoring a criminal pardoned to the state and character that he held previous to the conviction. The authorities referred to by the Lord Advocate prove this, and, in addition to these, I shall only mention to your Lordships Mr. Justice Buller's Treatise on Trials, a book of great authority, which lays down that if a person found guilty, on an indictment for perjury at common law, be pardoned by the King, he will be a good witness, because the King has power to take off every part of the punishment.

As to the sentence of the Justices of Peace of the county of Stirlingshire, banishing Brown by his own consent from that county, no stress can be laid on it, as it is now a settled point that no sentence of an inferior Court, proceeding without the verdict of a jury, is sufficient to set aside any person from being a witness.

The LORD JUSTICE-CLERK—My Lords, I will not say a word about the sentence of the Justices of Peace, nor of what would have been the case had the crime been committed, or sentence pronounced, in Scotland. I would hold the decree in England *pro veritate*, and give it effect accordingly. But, my

Lords, if the pardon frees this man from the penal consequences of his sentence, although I were to hold that it does not rehabilitate him in Scotland, still it leaves only the *infamia facti*, for the *infamia juris* is, *eo ipso*, done away. And, my Lords, nothing can set aside a witness unless *infamia juris*.

The Dean of Faculty argued this objection with great ingenuity, but he founded his whole argument on the proposition that an *infamia facti*, if it was capable of proof, was a sufficient objection to the admissibility of a witness; and, indeed, unless this proposition were true, his whole argument falls to the ground. But, my Lords, this proposition is evidently fallacious, and I need use no other instance than that of Ainslie, who, like every other King's evidence, admitted in the very bosom of his deposition an *infamia facti*, in so far as he was concerned in the commission of the crime charged against the pannels, and yet it was not even pretended that this was an objection to his admissibility; and your Lordships every day allow the examination of witnesses in the same situation. I am therefore clear for repelling the objection.

The Court then pronounced the following interlocutor:—

The Lord Justice-Clerk and Lords Commissioners of Justiciary having considered the foregoing objections with the answers thereto, they repel the objections stated and allow the witness to be examined, reserving the credibility of his evidence to the jury.

ROBT. M'QUEEN, I.P.D.

[The witness was then called in and sworn.]

The LORD JUSTICE-CLERK—John Brown, you are called here to give evidence regarding a matter in which it is generally supposed that you yourself had some concern. You are now informed by the Court that although you may have had such a concern you are in no danger to speak the truth, because, being adduced as a witness against the prisoners at the bar, you cannot be tried for the crime of which they are accused; and you will take notice that whatever you may have said against these men, in the different declarations which you emitted before the Sheriff, which are now destroyed, you are now bound by the great oath which you have sworn to tell the truth; and that if you say anything to the prejudice of these men that is not true or if you conceal any part of the truth, with a view to favour them, you will thereby be guilty of the crime of perjury, for which you will be liable to be tried by this Court, and severely punished, and you will commit a heinous offence in the sight of the Almighty God, and thereby endanger your immortal soul.

WITNESS—I am acquainted intimately with both the pannels, and have been frequently in company with them, and with Andrew Ainslie, then a shoemaker in Edinburgh. I have met Brodie often at Smith's house and other places. I know that the General Excise Office in Chessels's Buildings was broken into upon Wednesday, the 5th of March last; I was myself one of them that broke into it, and Andrew Ainslie and the two prisoners were along with me. George Smith and I were within the office, Brodie was at the door, and Andrew Ainslie was without, keeping watch. We had resolved three months before to break into it; and on the 30th of November last, the night on which the Free Masons made a public procession last winter, Smith, Ainslie, and I went to the Excise Office and unlocked the outer door with a false key. We went in together, and opened the inner door to the hall with a pair of toupee irons, but none of the keys we had would open the cashier's door. Smith said a coulter would be a good thing to open it with. Thinking it too late to remain longer, we came out again; but we could not lock the outer door with the key, and therefore left it unlocked. Last spring Ainslie and I went to Duddingston, and drank a bottle of porter in a house there; afterwards we went into a field in the neighbourhood, in which there were two ploughs, and carried off the coulter of one of them, which we hid in Salisbury Crags. On the evening of the 5th of March last, which was two or three days afterwards, when it was about dusk, Ainslie and I went out to Salisbury Crags for the coulter, and brought it in with us to Smith's house. Smith was at home, but Brodie was not yet come, although we expected him. The hour at which we had agreed to meet was seven, but Mr. Brodie did not come until near eight. The purpose of our meeting was to go and rob the Excise Office that night. We were in Smith's room above-stairs when Brodie joined us, and we there drank some gin and "black cork," and ate some herrings and chicken. By "black cork" I mean Bell's beer. Mr. Brodie was then dressed in black; in the preceding part of the day I saw him in white or light-coloured clothes. I do not remember that he had a great-coat on when he came to us at Smith's in the evening. When he entered the room he took a pistol from his pocket, and repeated the verse of a song of Macheath's from a play, words like—"We'll turn our lead into gold," or such like.[12] After we were all met together, it was agreed upon that Ainslie should remain on the outside of the Excise Office, within the rails, with a whistle, to give the alarm in case of danger; that Brodie was to be stationed within the outer door for the same purpose; and that Smith and I should go into the cashier's room. Accordingly, Ainslie left Smith's first, and in some time after I followed. Brodie was not disguised, but Smith and I had crapes in our pocket, and Smith had likewise a wig, which, I believe, had once belonged to Brodie's father. When I came to the mouth of the entry to Chessels's Buildings, I met the old man who usually locked the door coming out, and went after him and saw him go home. My reason for so doing was to see that he had not gone on an errand and to return. When I came back to the court I met Brodie in the entry, who told me that Smith had gone into the office, and desired me to go in. I went down the close with him, saw Ainslie at his post, and received the coulter, or "Great Samuel," from him, and carried it in with me to the office. I found the outer door open and Smith in the hall. The outer door of the cashier's room was opened by Smith with a pair of curling irons, and I assisted him to force open the inner door of the cashier's room with the coulter and a small iron crow. After we got in, Smith, who had a dark lanthorn with him, opened every press and desk in the room where he suspected there was any money; some by violence and others with keys which we found in the room. We continued there about half-an-hour, and found about sixteen pounds of money in a desk in the cashier's room, which we carried away with us. It consisted of two five-pound notes, six guinea notes, and some silver. We heard some person come upstairs, and cocked our pistols, which were loaded with powder and ball. Smith said he supposed it was some of the clerks going into one of the rooms. We heard no whistle while we were in the office. When we came downstairs, Brodie and Ainslie were both gone. We left the outer door of the Excise Office unlocked, and carried the key away with us. We then came up to the Canongate, and went across it, and down another street a little below—Young's Street. I stopped in the middle of the last street, pulled off my great-coat and gave it to Smith. I then returned, went down to the Excise Office door, where everything seemed to be quiet; afterwards I went to Smith's house, where in a little I was joined by Smith, and soon afterwards by Ainslie. I did not remain there long, when Smith recommended it to me and Ainslie to go over to Fraser's house in the New Town, that we might avoid suspicion; and we went accordingly. I knew at the time that Smith was making a key for the outer door of the Excise Office. [Here the witness was shown a key.] That is the key he so made, and with which he opened the door. We had three pair of pistols along with us, all of which were previously loaded by Smith with powder and ball. [Here the pistols libelled on were shown the witness.] These are a pair of them, but whether that pair was carried to the Excise Office by Smith or me I cannot say. I saw Mr. Brodie have a pistol in his hand in Smith's house. When Brodie came to Smith's first that night he brought with him some small keys, and a double pick-lock, which we all looked at. [Here the pick-lock libelled on was shown to the witness.] This is the same that was used on that occasion. On Friday, the 7th of March, I was sent for to Smith's house. Brodie, Smith, and Ainslie were there, and the money which we got in the Excise Office was then equally divided between us. I got about four pounds from Brodie to my share. I saw all the money in Smith's room above-stairs before it was divided, and there were two five-pound bank-notes amongst it. On the same Friday evening, I went with Smith and Ainslie to Drysdale's, in the New Town, and saw Smith change one of the five-pound notes there, when purchasing a ticket for his wife in the mail-coach to Newcastle. I went to William Middleton on Friday night, the 7th of March last, and told him that I wished to make a discovery as to the late robberies; he carried me the same night to Mr. Scott, the Procurator-Fiscal, but I did not at that time mention anything of Brodie's concern in them. The next day I was sent to England to trace some goods taken from Inglis & Horner's shop. I returned on the 15th of March, and was the same day examined by the Sheriff. I was informed that Smith had emitted a declaration, informing of Brodie's guilt, in consequence of which he (Brodie) had absconded, and then for the first time I mentioned that Mr. Brodie had been concerned with us.[13] Ainslie informed Smith and me that he had seen two men come up the close before he quitted his post at the Excise Office and went away. Smith carried the money which was found in the Excise Office away with him, and he afterwards gave it to Brodie, who made a fair division of it on the Friday. On the Thursday I did not see him.

Lord HAILES—John Brown, you have already been told by the Court that you ought to pay no regard to what was contained in your declarations before the Sheriff, and that, whatever you may have formerly said, you cannot now hurt yourself by speaking the truth. I intreat you to reflect on the evidence you have given this night, and if you are conscious of having said anything which you ought not to have said, that you may say so to the Court and to the jury. It is not as yet too late, but if you neglect the opportunity which you now have it will never recur to you again; and I earnestly desire you to beware of this, that if you have said anything this night to the prejudice of these men at the bar that is not true, and if you do not undeceive the Court and the jury before you leave this house, you will commit a most heinous sin against the God of heaven, in whose presence you now stand, and you will be guilty of perjury and of murder.

Cross-examined by the DEAN OF FACULTY, for William Brodie—When you went first to Mr. Scott, the Procurator-Fiscal, did you say anything concerning the breaking of the Excise Office?

WITNESS—I did.

The DEAN OF FACULTY—Who did you say was concerned with you?

WITNESS—George Smith. I did not mention either Brodie or Ainslie until I returned from England.

The DEAN OF FACULTY—Are you sure that Mr. Brodie brought his pistols to Smith's in the afternoon?

WITNESS—I am certain.

The DEAN OF FACULTY—Did you not say that when he came to Smith's before eight o'clock he had his pistol in his hand?

WITNESS—I did.

The DEAN OF FACULTY—How could he have left them at Smith's, then, in the afternoon?

WITNESS—I did not say he left them there; he brought them there, but carried them away with him again. I am certain as to the small pistols that Mr. Brodie carried in his breeches pocket.

The DEAN OF FACULTY—Was Mr. Brodie present when the pistols were loaded?

WITNESS—He was.

The DEAN OF FACULTY—When did Mr. Brodie first come to Smith's that day, and how was he dressed?

WITNESS—He came in coloured clothes, between dinner and tea.

The DEAN OF FACULTY—Might that be four o'clock?

WITNESS—I could not tell what o'clock it was.

The DEAN OF FACULTY—Was it after three o'clock that afternoon?

WITNESS—I am not certain.

The DEAN OF FACULTY—Was it after two o'clock?

WITNESS—Yes, I am certain it was.

The DEAN OF FACULTY—Were these the pistols he brought with him? [The pistols produced.]

WITNESS—No, not these; I did not say these, but another pair, since the truth must be told. Do not think to trap me; you may make something of me by fair means, but not by foul. I do not understand the meaning of being thus teased by impertinent questions.

The DEAN OF FACULTY—The more violent the gentleman is, so much the better for my client. The jury will take notice of the manner in which he gives his evidence.

Lord ESKGROVE—My Lord Justice-Clerk, the witness should be told that he ought not to talk in that manner to the counsel.

The LORD JUSTICE-CLERK [to witness]—Mr. Brown, you are going too far; it is the duty of these gentlemen to put any questions to you which they think proper, relating to the crime charged.

WITNESS—My Lord, in giving my evidence, I have said nothing but the truth, and I have rather softened the matter than otherwise, with regard to Mr. Brodie.

The DEAN OF FACULTY—At what hour, sir, did you go to the Excise Office on the night you have mentioned, and when did you return to Smith's?

WITNESS—As I was going down to the Excise Office the clock struck eight, and I was back again at Smith's house about nine o'clock.

Cross-examined by Mr. JOHN CLERK, for George Smith—Pray, sir, how do you know that to be the key with which Mr. Smith opened the door of the Excise Office? You said just now that you were not present when Smith opened the door; that he was in before you arrived.

WITNESS—I know very well that that was the key, because I knew he made it for that purpose.

Mr. JOHN CLERK—But how do you know that he opened the door with that key on the 5th of March?

WITNESS—I know he made the key so far back as November last. I know the key very well; there is not a key in five hundred like it. You will not show me such a key in Edinburgh. There is no smith in this city could make such a key.

Mr. JOHN CLERK—That is no answer to my question.

The LORD JUSTICE-CLERK—It is enough to satisfy any sensible man.

Mr. JOHN CLERK—It is for the jury, my Lord, to judge of that.

[To Witness]—You mentioned your having on a great-coat when you broke into the Excise Office; pray, sir, was that great-coat your own, or to whom did it belong?

WITNESS—It belonged to Michael Henderson, stabler in the Grassmarket, and I carried it home to him the following night.

Mr. JOHN CLERK—Did you carry anything to Mr. Henderson along with it?

WITNESS—I did not.

The LORD JUSTICE-CLERK—John Brown, you appear to be a clever fellow, and I hope you will now abandon your dissipated courses, and betake yourself to some honest employment.

WITNESS—My Lord, be assured my future life shall make amends for my past conduct.

The LORD ADVOCATE—My Lord, the parole evidence on the part of the Crown being now closed, the declarations and other writings, which have been authenticated in the presence of your Lordships, fall now to be read to the jury, but as there are some parts of Smith's declarations which relate to matters not immediately connected with the subject of the present trial, I do not desire that these parts of his declarations should be read by the Clerk of Court or communicated to the jury.

[After some conversation, this proposal, which did much honour to his Lordship, was agreed to, and such parts of the declarations as were not read in Court were pasted over with paper, that they might not be looked into through mistake by the jury after they were inclosed.]

Declarations of George Smith.

No. I.

At Edinburgh, 8th March, 1788.

The which day compeared, in presence of Archibald Cockburn, Esq., His Majesty's Sheriff-depute of the shire of Edinburgh, George Smith, grocer in Edinburgh, who, being examined and interrogated by the Sheriff, declares,

That it is about a year and a half since the declarant came to Scotland; that he was never in it before; that he was born at Boxford, within four miles of Newburgh, Berkshire; that the declarant and his wife travelled the country of England as hawkers, with a horse and cart; that he brought a horse to this country but no cart; that, when he first came to Edinburgh, he put up at Michael Henderson's, having heard his house mentioned by travellers in England as a traveller's inn; that he was taken ill after his arrival in this country, and confined for about four months in Michael Henderson's, which obliged him to send for his wife to this place; that he sent for goods from England, which he sold, as also his horse, in order to support himself.

That since he came to this country, he has frequented Clark's in the Flesh Market Close, which is a gambling house, and in which house he was in use to meet with a variety of people, and among the rest Andrew Ainslie and John Brown; that the declarant first got acquainted both with Ainslie and Brown in Michael Henderson's; that Ainslie gave himself out for a shoemaker, but the declarant cannot tell of what profession Brown is; that the club, as it was called, at Clark's, as the declarant believes, has been doing little these three months past; that the declarant never played there to go very deep, and was never seen to win or lose above thirty shillings, having never taken more than that sum in his pocket alongst with him, but, upon recollection, thinks that he has won above thirty shillings; that the declarant inclines to believe that John Brown has rather been unfortunate at the club.

Declares and acknowledges that the declarant took a cellar in Stevenlaw's Close from a woman whom he now sees in the office; that the declarant afterwards took Ainslie to the said woman and told her that this was the gentleman who was to possess her cellar; but he does not remember of calling him by the name of Campbell, or any other name; that the declarant gave the rent, which was ten shillings, to Ainslie, who gave it to the woman.

Declares that the declarant went with Ainslie to Mrs. Clark's house in George's Square, where Ainslie took a stable from that lady, but the declarant and Ainslie remained in the kitchen, and neither of them saw Mrs. Clark, as he thinks; that the declarant does not now recollect for what purpose Ainslie said it was he wanted to rent the stable; that the declarant saw Ainslie pay five shillings, or some such sum, as a month's rent for the stable per advance.

And being interrogated, What was the purpose of the vice which stands in the cellar of his house?—Declares that he has had that for seven or eight years, and that he used it for putting tongues in buckles, or any thing of that sort, but he has not used it since he came to his present house; that his wife intended to have set out this day on a visit to her relations in England, and for that purpose the declarant took out for her a ticket in the mail-coach at Drysdale's, where he exchanged a five-pound bank-note and paid for it.

Declares that the black dog now in the office belongs to a neighbour of his, but, from the declarant's giving him now and then some bones to pick, he frequents the declarant's house, and follows him and his wife; that the note he exchanged at Drysdale's the declarant has had in his possession for above two months past; that he got it from a smuggler, and it was battered then as it is now. This he declares to be truth, and declares he cannot write.

ARCHIBALD COCKBURN.

No. II.

At Edinburgh, 10th March, 1788.

The which day compeared, in presence of the Sheriff of Edinburgh, George Smith, formerly examined on Saturday, the 8th current, after having sent notice to the Sheriff that he wished to speak with him. Came to the office and told the Sheriff that he wished to have an opportunity of making a clean breast, and telling the truth, upon which the Sheriff informed him that, as he, the Sheriff, knew he stood in a very ticklish situation, it was his duty to let him know that whatever he told or discovered was not to be accepted of under any condition or promise whatever, or that his doing so would operate anything in his favour, and that therefore he was at perfect freedom, either to speak or hold his tongue, as he judged best. And that the said George Smith having declared that he wished to tell the truth, and communicate all the guilty scenes in which he had been concerned for some time past, since he came to the town of Edinburgh, he was desired to proceed.

Declares that, in the end of October, or beginning of November last, the declarant, in company with Andrew Ainslie and John Brown, whose real name is Humphry Moore, went to the College of Edinburgh about one o'clock in the morning. Having got access at the under gate, they opened the under door leading to the Library with a false key, which broke in the lock, and thereafter they broke open the door of the Library with an iron crow, and carried away the College mace.

Declares that the declarant has, almost since his first arrival in Edinburgh, been acquainted with Deacon William Brodie, and he saw him first at Michael Henderson's, where he was introduced to the declarant by one Graham at the time the declarant was confined in that house; that Brodie, in the course of conversation, suggested to the declarant that several things could be done in this place, if prudently managed, to great advantage, and proposed to the declarant that they should lay their heads together for that purpose.

That, in consequence of this concert, the declarant and Brodie were in use to go about together, in order to find out the proper places where business could be done with success; that Brodie, in their walks, carried the declarant to the College Library, where, having observed the mace standing, Brodie said that they must have it; that Andrew Ainslie was afterwards sent by the declarant and Brodie to look at the Library, under pretence of calling for somebody, in order to see if the mace was always in the same place, as they suspected it might be one day in the Library and another somewhere else, which would have rendered an attempt upon the Library precarious; that Ainslie reported that the mace was in the same place that the declarant and Brodie had seen it, and, upon getting this report, the theft of the mace was committed as before mentioned.

Declares that, since the mace was stolen, as the declarant thinks, the declarant, along with Brown and Ainslie, laid a plan of breaking into John Tapp's house and taking his money; that this business was suggested, and pressed, by Brown, the declarant rather being averse to it; that Brown told the declarant that he knew the key of Tapp's shop opened the door of his house, and brought it to the declarant to look at, which, upon seeing, the declarant said there was nothing in it, meaning by that, that the lock to which it belonged could easily be opened.

Declares that, accordingly, soon after this, and, as he thinks, about Christmas or near to it, Brown kept Tapp in his shop drinking, and the declarant and Ainslie, betwixt nine and ten o'clock at night, opened the door of the house with a false key and took out of his drawers eighteen guinea notes and a twenty-shilling one, a silver watch, some rings, and a miniature picture of a gentleman belonging to Tapp's wife, which picture they broke for the sake of the gold with which it was backed.

Declares that in the month of August last, as he thinks, the declarant, in company with William Brodie and Andrew Ainslie, went to a shop in Leith, which they broke into by means of two pick-lock keys, one for the padlock and another for the stock-lock; that the declarant and Ainslie went into the shop and Brodie kept watch, to give an alarm in case of danger; that from this shop they carried off two pair of wallets full of tea, which were taken from four chests; that Ainslie was ill at this time, and Brodie being weakly, Ainslie and he could scarcely manage one of the wallets, which obliged him to put it into an old press bed (as the declarant took it to be) which they found standing in a shed in a field adjoining to the Bonnington Road to Leith; that it was proposed to lodge the tea in Brodie's, but he afterwards objected to it, which was the reason that they never inquired after it more.

That about two months ago the declarant, in company with Andrew Ainslie, broke into the shop of Inglis, Horner & Company, and took therefrom a large assortment of valuable goods, composed of silks and cambricks; that the silks were mostly black, excepting two pieces, a piece of plain white sattin, a piece of variegated ditto, and a lead-coloured silk, in quantity about ten yards, which Brown gave to a girl, an acquaintance of his, of the name of Johnston; that the silks were all sent to England, except the silk before-mentioned, a piece of black silk of about two yards and a quarter, in two odd bits, which the declarant gave to his wife to make a cloak to her child, and about twelve yards and a half of thick tweel'd black silk for gentlemen's vests and breeches, and two yards and a half of black florentine sattin, with about six yards of cambrick.

That Brodie suggested to the declarant the doing of Inglis & Horner's shop, as the goods there were very rich and valuable, and a small bulk of them carried off would amount to a large sum; that Brodie and the declarant went frequently to try the pad and stock-lock of Inglis & Horner's shop, and they did so most commonly on the Sunday forenoon, when the people were in church; that the padlock was of a difficult construction, and was opened at last by a key of the declarant's own making; that Brodie made one that did it also, and he on one occasion went by himself with his key and unlocked the padlock, but could not lock it again, upon which he came to the declarant and told him what he had done, which he did also to Ainslie and Brown; that they were all very angry with him, and said that he had more than likely spoilt the place after all the trouble they had been about, but Brodie told them he hoped not, as he had fixed the padlock with a bit stick in a way that it would not be discovered, and, upon looking at the place afterwards, which they all did, they found the lock to be just as it was.

Declares that on Wednesday evening, the 5th instant, the declarant, along with William Brodie, John Brown, and Andrew Ainslie, between the hours of eight and ten o'clock at night, broke into the Excise Office and carried off from that about sixteen pounds, consisting of two five-pound notes, four guinea notes, one twenty-shilling note, and about seventeen shillings and sixpence in silver; that this money was divided among them, and Brodie received his share.

That Brodie first planned the Excise Office, and repeatedly carried the declarant there under pretence of calling for Mr. Corbett from Stirling, and other people, in order to learn the situation of the place, and, on one of these occasions, the declarant observed the key of the outer door hung upon a nail near by it, and, without taking it down, he clapped some potty upon it, and carried away the wards; that Brodie took a drawing of the wards of that key, which the declarant thinks he has in his possession; that Brodie told the declarant how to get into the cashier's desk, and where the money lay, which was in two places, and in each of these places some money was found; that Brodie came to the knowledge of these circumstances, by being present, when Mr. Corbett, from Stirling, who is a connection of Brodie's, drew money at the cashier's office.

That, when they broke into the Excise Office, the outer door was opened by a key which the declarant had filed from the pattern before-mentioned; that the plan of accomplishing this business was as follows:—Ainslie was to keep on the outside of the office, hanging over the palisadoes in the entry with a whistle of ivory, which was purchased by Brodie the night before, with which, if the man belonging to the Excise Office came, he was to give one whistle, and if any serious alarm was perceived he was to give three whistles, and then make the best of his way to the Excise gardens in the Canongate in order to assist the declarant, Brodie, and Brown to get out at the back window of the hall, it being determined in case of surprise to bolt the outer door on the inside and make the best of their way by the window.

That Ainslie was armed only with a stick, which he left somewhere in the court, and which stick was purchased by the declarant; that Brodie had a brace of pistols, the declarant a brace and a half, and Brown a brace, which the declarant borrowed from Michael Henderson; that these arms were all loaded with double balls, as they were determined not to be taken, whatever should be the consequence.

That the declarant and Brown were told afterwards by Brodie and Ainslie that a person had come running down the court and gone in at the outer door and upstairs; that upon this Ainslie had given the alarm by a whistle, as was agreed upon, and made the best of his way, but none of them in the inside heard the whistle, at least neither Brown nor the declarant did, and Brodie said he did not; that when the door opened Brodie was standing behind it, and, upon the person's running up stairs, Brodie made off; that the declarant and Brown, when in the cashier's room, heard the outer door open, but, trusting to Brodie's being at the door and staunch, they did not mind it; that the declarant and Brown, when coming out of the cashier's office, heard a person coming hastily down stairs, which made them stop or they must have met him; that upon this the declarant said to Brown, "Here must be treachery; get out your pistols, and cock them," which they did accordingly; that upon coming to the outer door they found it shut, the declarant and Brown having seen the person that came down stairs smash the door after him when he went away.

That the declarant and Brown went down into Young's Street, where Brown gave the declarant a small crow, with some wedges, and a shirt, as also a large chissel; that the chissel and the shirt were given to Brodie afterwards, with the bank-notes, the declarant's dark lanthorn, and two bottles, which they had carried off from the Excise Office, and took for wine; that the key with which the outer door was opened, the crow, and a pair of curling irons with which the outer door of the cashier's room was opened, were all hid by the declarant in a wall between the Earthen Mound and the North Bridge.

That, in virtue of repeated observations, it was discovered that two men watched the Excise Office time about, and Ainslie and Brown found out that from eight to ten o'clock at night there was commonly no man in the Excise Office, which was the reason of the thing being done at that time.

That it was concerted by Brodie, in case of interruption, by the man coming into the office before the business was accomplished, to conceal themselves quietly until he was gone to rest, and then to secure him; and they were, if this happened, to personate smugglers who came in search of their property that had been seized, and the declarant had a wig of Brodie's father's in his pocket in order to disguise himself; that the wig and scarf and small wedges were left in the second arch from the south of the North Bridge; that the scarf was within the wig.

That Brodie, after having been in the Excise, where he had on black clothes, went home and changed them to his ordinary dress, of a marbled colour, and a round hat; and that Brodie told the declarant that his sister had remarked him changing his dress in such a hurry.

That there is in Brodie's house a horse-pistol belonging to the declarant, as also a very large, remarkable key, which Ainslie and Brodie stole from the Abbey when there was a sale there; that Brodie has a parcel of keys of different sorts, which he has been altering, and among them is the key which he had made for Inglis & Horner's padlock; that, in Brodie's bedroom, there is a chest containing a false till, in which the declarant inclines to think some of Brodie's false dice and other things leading to a detection of his guilt may be found.

That the College mace and Tapp's watch were sent to Chesterfield, under the direction of William Ward, at William Cowley's, "Bird in Hand,"

Chesterfield, Derbyshire, to which place, and at which time, the rings taken from Tapp and the gold from the miniature picture were also sent; that a private letter was wrote by Brown, as he thinks, to one Tasker, formerly of this place, and whose real name is Murray, a man of bad character, which letter had no name at it but only a G. and S., and a stroke for each of the other letters in the declarant's name; that the pocket-book taken from Tapp's, with the money, was thrown by Ainslie and the declarant into a deep piece of water to the south of the Meadows.

That the goods taken from Inglis & Horner's shop were sent to Chesterfield in trunks, one of which was purchased by the declarant and another by Ainslie; that the declarant knows the places where they were purchased, and will point them out.

That the first trunk went from this by the Berwick carriers three weeks ago on Wednesday next; that the goods were removed from a cellar, in which they were originally put, in Stevenlaw's Close, taken for the purpose, notwithstanding of what was said by the declarant in his declaration of Saturday last; that Ainslie went and brought a porter from the street, who received the goods from the declarant and Ainslie half-way or more up Burnet's Close, where Brown and Ainslie lodged, near the bottom; that the porter had no creel, but only ropes, with which he tied the trunk upon his back; and Ainslie followed him and saw him carry and deliver it to the Berwick carrier's quarters, for which he received sixpence.

That the second parcel of the above goods were sent under the direction of Elizabeth Scott or Sprott, at William Cowley's, "Bird in Hand," Chesterfield, and the reason of putting this was because the initials of her name were upon the top of the trunk; that no letter was wrote to Tasker or Murray about the last parcel of goods, as the declarant's wife was to have left this on Saturday last, and the declarant told her he had some goods for her to dispose of at Chesterfield; but she knew nothing how the goods were obtained, and is entirely innocent of any participation or knowledge of his crimes.

Declares that Brodie brought with him to the declarant's house, a day before, as he thinks, the Excise Office was robbed, a coil of ropes, new, which he either had in his possession or must have bought, as also a strong chissel with a brass virral, and two pieces of wax taper; that the brass chissel is, as the declarant believes, now in Brodie's shop or house.

That the coulter with which the inner door of the Excise Office was broke open, and two iron wedges, were taken from a plough by Brown and Ainslie near to Duddingston, as they said, the Friday before; and the declarant makes no doubt but a black dog, Rodney, might be with them, which used to follow the declarant and them; that the coulter and wedges were left in the cashier's office, and were concealed in Salisbury Crags from the time the coulter was taken away to the time the Excise Office was broke. This he declares to be truth.

And further declares that the ropes brought by Brodie, as before mentioned, are in the declarant's house, as also a vice and files and a spring-saw, with which the declarant used to make and alter keys; that the saw the declarant got from Brodie about five or six months ago; that the declarant, before this, bought a saw, with a pair of large pincers, at a hardware shop below Peter Forrester's, on the High Street, and the declarant inclines to think that Brodie bought his saw at the same place; that in the declarant's drawer, along with the said saw and files, there will also be found a keyhole saw, which was bought and given to the declarant by Brodie.

This he also declares to be truth; and declares that the declaration emitted by him on Saturday last, so far as is inconsistent with the present, is not true.

GEORGE SMITH.
ARCHD. COCKBURN.

No. III.

At Edinburgh, 19th March, 1788.

The which day compeared, in presence of Archibald Cockburn, Esq., advocate, His Majesty's Sheriff-depute of the shire of Edinburgh, George Smith, present prisoner in the Tolbooth of Edinburgh, who, being examined, declares,

That the small crow, the false key, and the curling tongs, now shown to him, are the same that were found by the declarant, William Middleton, A. Williamson, and J. Murray, in an old dyke on the 16th instant, and the label annexed to them is signed by the declarant as relative hereto, of this date.

Declares that the said crow was carried to the Excise Office for the purpose of opening the desks in the cashier's room; that the said false key is the one that opened the outer door of the Excise Office, and the curling tongs were squared at the point by the declarant and taken to the Excise Office for the purpose of opening the spring latch of the outer door of the cashier's room, which it did.

And, being shown a coulter and two wedges, declares that he believes they are the same that were used in forcing open the inner door of the cashier's room in the Excise Office and were left there.

And, being also shown a spur, with the upper leather at it, declares that it belonged to William Brodie; and the declarant tore the end of the leather in order that it might appear, when found, to have dropped from the foot by its being torn by accident by the buckle; that Brodie brought the said spur to the declarant's house, and from thence it was taken to the Excise Office, on purpose that it might be left there, to make it believed it had been done by some persons on horseback; that the spur was left in the Excise Office by John Brown, as the declarant was told by him upon the declarant's questioning him if he had done it, and the label annexed to the spur is signed by the declarant as relative hereto, of this date.

And, being shown a parcel of ropes which the declarant is now told were found in his house, declares that the declarant has no doubt but that they are the same ropes which were brought to the declarant's house by Brodie, and, after being knotted into a ladder, were carried to the Excise Office by the declarant, brought from thence by him, and unknotted again in the declarant's house, in which case he now sees they are.

And, being shown a pick-lock, which the declarant is informed was found in William Brodie's counting-room in the shop, declares that it is the same which William Brodie gave to the declarant in his own house before they went to the Excise Office, and which Brodie wanted to fasten with some nails, as the handle of it went round when the pick-lock was much pressed; declares that the declarant carried that pick-lock to the Excise Office, and, after they had left it, it was returned by the declarant to Brodie when under the arch of the North Bridge, where Brodie's father's wig, the scarf, and wedges were left, as mentioned in his declaration of the 10th instant; and the label annexed to the said pick-lock is signed by the declarant as relative hereto, of this date.

And being shown a black case, with a lid to it, the case full of potty, declares that it was found, as the declarant thinks, in Mr. Brodie's drawers by the declarant and George Williamson on Monday, the 10th instant; that the declarant had often seen the said case, with potty in it, before in Brodie's possession when in the declarant's house, and the declarant approved of Brodie's keeping the potty in a case, as the lid prevented an impression of a key when taken from being defaced; and the said case and potty having now a label annexed to it, the same is signed by the declarant as relative hereto, of this date.

And, being shown a five-pound note, declares it is the same five-pound note which the declarant carried to Drysdale's and changed there, to purchase his wife a ticket in the Newcastle stage; that the declarant believes it to be one of the five-pound notes taken from the Excise Office, they being both of the Glasgow Bank, but the other five-pound note was not ornamented with the same colour with the one now shown to him; that the notes were pasted on the back by Brodie, and the one now produced is signed by the declarant on the back as relative hereto, of this date.

And being shown a parcel of keys, declares that they are the same which were pointed out by the declarant concealed in Salisbury Crags, on the 7th instant, to William Middleton, Alexander Williamson, and James Murray, and the label annexed to them is signed by the declarant as relative hereto, of this date. Declares that among this parcel there is the false key which opened the outer door of Inglis & Horner's shop, to which the declarant now sees a label annexed, and which is signed by him as relative hereto, of this date.

And being shown a parcel of keys which were found by the declarant and George Williamson upon the 10th current, declares that the double clank among the said parcel was brought by the declarant from Sheffield, and given to Brodie, the reason of which was for fear it should be found in the declarant's possession and thereby create suspicion, but it was not likely to be discovered in Brodie's. Declares that the heads and stalks of two keys in the said parcel were cut from old keys by Brodie, and were intended to be finished for the purpose of opening the spring latch of the outer door of the cashier's room in the Excise Office; that a false key in the said parcel, finished, was made by Brodie for the purpose of opening the door of the Chamberlain's cash room of the city of Edinburgh; and to the said double clank, the heads and stalks of two keys for the Chamberlain's room, the declarant sees labels annexed, of this date, and are signed by the declarant as relative hereto. The declarant and Brodie had frequently been at the door of the Chamberlain's office, in order to take the impression of the keyhole; that Brodie showed the declarant the said key after it was made, and Brodie told the declarant that it did not answer.

And being shown two parcels of keys, with labels annexed to them, and two pieces of black stockings, declares that they are the property of the declarant, and were concealed by him in Salisbury Crags, and the labels annexed to them are signed by the declarant and Sheriff as relative hereto, of this date.

And being shown two trunks, declares that they are the same two trunks that were purchased by the declarant and Andrew Ainslie; that the round one was purchased by the declarant from a man opposite to Todrick's Wynd, whom he saw this day in the office, for which the declarant paid three shillings, and the other was purchased by Ainslie from a man nearly opposite to Richardson's, the smith, in the Cowgate; that the declarant first bargained for it himself, but the declarant afterwards sent Ainslie, who bought it for five shillings and sixpence, or six shillings.

That the goods taken from Inglis & Horner's shop were put into the said two trunks, sent to the said Berwick carrier's quarters, and to the Newcastle waggoner's, as mentioned in his former declaration; that the direction on the round trunk is, as he believes, of the handwriting of Ainslie, and the direction upon the other of the handwriting of Brown, of which he is certain. All which is truth, &c.

GEORGE SMITH.
AR. COCKBURN.

No. IV.

At Edinburgh, 17th July, 1788.

The which day compeared, in presence of the Sheriff-Substitute of the shire of Edinburgh, George Smith, late grocer, Cowgate, now prisoner in the Tolbooth of Edinburgh, who being examined and interrogated, declares—

That on the 10th of March last the declarant was carried to Mr. Brodie's yard and workshop by Alexander and George Williamson, in order to point out a place where it was supposed some false keys, which Mr. Brodie had, were hid.

That in the under workshop, and in the bottom of a vent which was used as a fireplace for melting the glue, the declarant, when digging for the false keys, found a little under ground a pair of pistols wrapped in a piece of green cloth, which the said Alexander and George Williamson took into custody, and lodged in the Sheriff-clerk's office.

That the declarant saw the said pistols and piece of green cloth yesterday in the Sheriff-clerk's office, and knew them to be the same that were found as above, and the reason of the declarant's knowing them was, that he had these pistols in loan from Mr. Brodie for a considerable time; and the declarant had the said pistols with him when the Excise Office was broke into on the evening of the 5th of March last.

Declares that the same evening, after breaking into the Excise Office, the declarant delivered the pistols to Mr. Brodie, being afraid of taking them to the declarant's house in case of a search. This he declares to be truth.

GEORGE SMITH.
JOHN STEWART, Sh. Subst.

Declaration of William Brodie.

At Edinburgh, this 17th July, 1788.

The which day compeared, in presence of Archibald Cockburn, Esq., advocate, His Majesty's Sheriff-depute of the sheriffdom of Edinburgh, William Brodie, wright and cabinetmaker in Edinburgh, who being examined and interrogated by the Sheriff, declares—

That he does not at present recollect the name of the vessel in which the declarant went from the river Thames to Holland in the month of April last; that is, in which he arrived at Holland in April last.

That, before he left the vessel, he gave some letters, at present he does not recollect the number, written by himself, to one Geddes, a passenger on board the vessel.

And being shown a letter directed to Michael Henderson, signed W. B., dated Thursday, the 10th of April last, declares that he cannot say that the letter was not wrote by him and given to Geddes.

And, being interrogated, if one of the letters given to Geddes was not directed to Mr. Matthew Sheriff, upholsterer in Edinburgh, and signed John Dixon, dated Flushing, Tuesday, the 8th of April, 1788?—Declares that the declarant cannot give any positive answer to that question, and he does not suppose he would have signed any letter at that time by the name of John Dixon, especially as he had wrote some letters at the same time, and given them to Geddes, signed by his initials W. B.

Declares that the declarant, when taken into custody at Amsterdam, on the 26th of June last, went by the name of John Dixon.

Declares that the declarant first became acquainted with George Smith in Michael Henderson's a long while ago, when Smith was indisposed and bedfast there; that the declarant has been in George Smith's house in the Cowgate. And being interrogated, declares that he cannot say positively whether he was in Smith's house any day of the week before the declarant left Edinburgh, which, to the best of the declarant's recollection, he did upon the 9th of March last, and upon a Sunday, as he thinks.

Declares that, having received a message that some person in the jail of Edinburgh wanted to see him, he went there and found it was either Smith or Ainslie who had been inquiring for him; but the declarant, when going there, was told by the keeper that neither Smith nor Ainslie could be seen; and that this was the night preceding his departure from Edinburgh.

Being interrogated, If reports had not been going of the Excise Office having been broke into the week before the declarant left Edinburgh, if he, the declarant, would have taken that step?—declares that it was not in consequence of that report that he left Edinburgh, but that the declarant, being acquainted with Smith and Ainslie, then in custody, did not know what they might be induced to say to his prejudice, was the cause of his going away.

Declares that the declarant has frequently been in company with John Brown, *alias* Humphry Moore (as is reported to be his real name), Andrew Ainslie, and George Smith, and drank with them.

And, being shown three letters, one dated Thursday, 10th April, 1788, directed to Mr. Michael Henderson, Grassmarket, signed W. B.; another dated Flushing, Tuesday, 8th April, 1788, directed to Mr. Matthew Sheriff, upholsterer in Edinburgh, and signed John Dixon; another, dated Thursday, 10th April, 1788, directed to Mrs. Anne Grant, Cant's Close, Edinburgh, signed, W. B., and, desired to say whether or not the said three letters are holograph of the declarant?—declares that he does not incline to give any positive answer, the appearance of writing varies so much. This he declares to be truth.

WILL. BRODIE.
ARCH. COCKBURN.

COPY of a LETTER from William Brodie, under the name of John Dixon, to Mr. Matthew Sheriff, upholsterer in Edinburgh.

Flushing, Tuesday, 8th April, 1788,
12 o'clock forenoon.

My dear Friend,

Sunday, the 23rd ult., I went on board a ship cleared out for Leith, but by a private bargain with the captain was to be landed at Ostend. I have been on board ever since the 23rd. Most of the time we lay aground a little below Gravesend. Owing to thick weather and cross wind, we are obliged to land here; but this afternoon I will set off, by water, for Bruges, and then for Ostend (so I begin my travels where most gentlemen leave them off), where I shall remain, for some time at least, until I hear from Mr. Walker; and, indeed, I will require three weeks to recruit, for I have suffered more from my sore throat than sufficient to depress the spirits of most men. There was for twenty days I did not eat ten ounces of solid meat; but, thank God, I am now in a fair way. My stock is seven guineas, but by I reach to Ostend will be reduced to less than six. My wardrobe is all on my back, excepting two check shirts and two white ones, one of them an old rag I had from my cousin Milton, with an old hat (which I left behind), my coat, an old blue one, out at the arms and elbows, I also had from him, with an old striped waistcoat, and a pair of good boots. Perhaps my cousin judged right, that old things were best for my purpose. However, no reflections; he is my cousin, and a good prudent lad, and showed great anxiety for my safety; rather too anxious, for he would not let me take my black coat with me, nor Mr. Nairn's great-coat, which makes me the worse off at present; but I could not extract one guinea from him, although he owes me twenty-four pounds for three years past. He turned me over to Mr. Walker, who supplied me with twelve guineas. He is a gentleman I owe much to. I wish I may ever have it in my power to show my gratitude to him and Mr. Nairn. Had Milton been in my place, and me in his, my purse, my credit, and my wardrobe, my all, should have been at his disposal. However, let not this go farther, lest it should have an appearance of reflection upon a worthy man. He cannot help his natural temper.

I would have wrote to Mr. Nairn, but for certain reasons I believe it is not proper at present. Please to communicate this to him. And I beg that everything may be sent to me that you, Mr. Nairn, and my sisters may think useful to me, either in wearing apparel, tools, or even a small assortment of brass and iron work. Please send my quadrant and spirit level; they lie in a triangular box in my old bedroom. My brass-cased measuring line, and three-foot rule, my silver stock buckle, it is in the locker of my chest, and my stocks, they will save my neckcloths. If my sister pleases to send me some hand towels, they will be serviceable to me, whether I keep a house or a room.

I most earnestly beg of Mr. Nairn that my remittances be as liberal as possible; for without money I can make but a poor shift; for, you must think, my days for hard labour is near expiring, although, with my constitution, I may be able to carry on business for many years, and perhaps with success.

I have not yet received the trunk with my shirts and stockings, but will write Mr. Walker to forward it to Ostend, where I will be under the necessity of buying some things. And I hope by the time I come to New York I will have some things waiting me there. Whether it is best to send them by the Clyde or Thames, you and Mr. Nairn will judge best. And I hope to have a long letter from each of you, and one from my sister Jeany; and your's will include your wife's. They may be put in with my things, and any other letters my friends are pleased to send. Direct for Mr. John Dixon, to the care of the Revd. Mr. Mason, at New York. I am not sure of settling there, but will make for it as soon as I can.

I have no more time, the boat just going off for Bruges or Ostend.

I am,
Dear Sir,
Yours for ever,
JOHN DIXON.

Wrote on the back thus—

Let my name and destination be a profound secret, for fear of bad consequences.

(Addressed) Mr. Matthew Sheriff, Upholsterer, Edinburgh.

COPIES of two LETTERS, upon one sheet of paper, from William. Brodie to Mr. Michael Henderson.

Thursday, 10th April, 1788.

Dear Michael,

I embrace this opportunity of writing you, and I make no doubt but it will give you, Mrs. Henderson, and a few others satisfaction to hear that I am well.

Were I to write you all that has happened to me, and the hairbreadth escapes I made from a well-scented pack of bloodhounds, it would make a small volume.

I left Edinburgh Sunday, the 9th, and arrived in London Wednesday, the 12th, where I remained snug and safe in the house of an old female friend until Sunday, 23rd March (whose care for me I shall never forget, and only wish I may ever have it in my power to reward her sufficiently), within 500 yards of Bow Street. I did not keep the house all this time, but so altered, excepting the scar under my eye, I think you could not have rapt[14] to me. I saw Mr. Williamson twice; but, although countrymen commonly shake hands when they meet from home, yet I did not choose to make so free with him, notwithstanding he brought a letter to me; he is a clever man, and I give him credit for his conduct.

My female gave me great uneasiness by introducing a flash man to me, but she assured me he was a true man, and he proved himself so, notwithstanding the great reward, and was useful to me. I saw my picture[15] six hours before exhibited to public view, and my intelligence of what was doing at Bow Street Office was as good as ever I had in Edinburgh. I left London on Sunday, 23rd March, and from that day to this present moment, that I am now writing, have lived on board a ship, which life agrees vastly well with me. It is impossible for me at present to give you my address, but I beg you will write me, or dictate a letter to Thom, and let it be a very long one, giving me an account of what is likely to become of poor Ainslie, Smith, and his wife; I hope that neither you, nor any of your connections, has been innocently involved by those unfortunate men, or by that designing villain Brown; I make no doubt but he is now in high favour with Mr. Cockburn, for I can see some strokes of his pencil in my portrait. May God forgive him for all his crimes and falsehoods. I hope in a short time to be in Edinburgh, and confute personally many false aspersions made against me by him and others. Write me how the main went; how you came on in it; if my black cock fought and gained, &c., &c. As I can give you no directions how to write me, you'll please seal your letter, give it to Robert Smith, and he will deliver it to my sister, who will take care that it be conveyed safe to me wherever I may happen to be at the time, for I will give such directions that everything that is sent to me shall be forwarded from place to place until it come to my hand. I have lived now eighteen days on board of ship, and in good health and spirits, although very bad when I came on board, having my tongue and throat in one ulcer, not a bit of skin upon either, and the medicines I took in my friend's and by her direction (for she is one of experience), just beginning to operate; but I found it necessary, at all events, to remove, so I underwent a complete salivation on board ship. During all my trials since I left Edinburgh, my spirits nor my presence of mind never once forsook me, for which I have reason to be thankful. My best compliments to Mrs. Henderson, and I will order payment of the two guineas as soon as I have accounts from the gentleman I have intrusted with my affairs; let her not be anxious about it, for, if I live, it shall be paid.

Dear Michael,

I am very uneasy on account of Mrs. Grant and my three children by her; they will miss me more than any other in Scotland; may God, in His infinite goodness, stir up some friendly aid for their support, for it is not in my power at present to give them the smallest assistance; yet I think they will not absolutely starve in a Christian land where their father once had friends, and who was always liberal to the distressed.

I beg you will order the inclosed to be delivered into her own hand; and I will take it kind if Mrs. Henderson will send for her and give her good advice. I wish she may be enabled to keep what little furniture she has together.

I think she should endeavour to get her youngest daughter Jean sent to Aberdeen to her friends, where she will be well brought up, and I will order an yearly board to be paid for her, perhaps six pounds per annum; it will be an ease to Mrs. Grant, and better for the child. My eldest daughter Cecill should be put apprentice to the milliner or mantua-making business; but I wish she could learn a little writing and arithmetic first. I wish to God some of my friends would take some charge of Cecill; she is a fine, sensible girl, considering the little opportunity she has had for improvement. I have been now eighteen days on board, and I expect to land somewhere to-morrow. The ship rolls a good deal, and it is with some difficulty I get this wrote, and my paper being exhausted I shall conclude this epistle. Please make my compliments to Mr. Clark, and a few other friends, and in particular, to Mr. Balmano, and acquaint him I glimed the scrive[16] I had of him. He is a gentleman I have a great regard for. Pray do not forget writing me a long letter. I am,

Dear Michael,
For ever your's.
W. B.

Pray do not show this scroll to any but your wife.

(Addressed) Mr. Michael Henderson, Grass-market, Stabler, Edinburgh.

COPY of a LETTER or UNSIGNED SCROLL, in the handwriting of William Brodie, and founded on in the Indictment, marked No. 1.

My dear Sir,

By short instructions sent me when I left London, which I think were drawn up in my cousin Milton's hand, I was forbid writing to any one in Britain, Mr. Walker excepted, for a year or two; but this order, if necessary, I find it not easy for me to comply with, for I must correspond with my friends in whatever part of the globe I am, and I hope they will do so with me, and write them when an opportunity offers. I have gone through much, in every sense of the word.—J. D. and M.

I wrote Mr. Walker from this the 12th current. I received an answer the 18th, and wrote again the 23rd current, and upon receiving his next I hope to be enabled to embark in the first ship for America, to whatever port she is bound, which will probably be Charlestown, South Carolina, as there is a ship lying-to for that port; and notwithstanding the climate is very hot, and not so salutary to British constitutions, especially at the time I will arrive, which will be about the dog days. I will settle there if I think I can do better than at Philadelphia or New York. Longevity to me is now no object; but, at any rate, I will be at New York, and I hope to find there letters, and, if possible, some clothes and tools, otherwise I will be badly off indeed.

It grieves me to hear my creditors were so rigorous hasty, but well pleased on hearing the deed and conveyance had the proper effect. I hope all my creditors will be paid, and a reversion, which can be no object to the Crown. Were an application made to the Solicitor, and, if needful, a supplication in my name to his mother, and uncle the Treasurer, perhaps it might be a means either of quieting or getting easier through the threatened suit with the Crown; but this is only my idea.

At any rate, if my clothes and tools must go to sale, a proper assortment of tools, put into my best chest, might be put up in one lot, and my wearing apparel and linens in another lot. They are worth more to me than any one, and I think few in Edinburgh will bid for them if known they are designed for me; but if any one bids their value, in God's name let them have them, otherwise I hope they will be bought for me. I wish it were possible for me to know, before I left this, if I might expect them at New York; if otherwise, I will be under an absolute necessity of laying out what little money may remain, after paying my passage and clearing my board and lodging here, to my last shilling, and buying a few necessaries, otherwise I will land almost naked; and, if possible, to reach a few tools, both of which, I am informed, are 50 per cent. dearer in America than here.

I received from Mr. Walker, in all, £12 16s., and he would pay something for three days I slept in Mr. Rose's, though I am at present three guineas in debt to my landlord, and not a stiver in my pocket for four days past. This is the dearest place I was ever in.

I beg I may hear from you when at New York, and, if directed to Mr. John Dixon, to the care of the Reverend Dr. Mason, I will certainly receive it (as I know no other name there to desire you to direct it to), for I will certainly call there, whatever part I land or settle in, in expectation of letters, &c., and, in particular, a long letter from you, in which please answer the following questions without reserve. I am prepared to hear the worst:—How does my dear sisters keep their health? I hope the shock of my departure, and what followed, has not injured either of them in health. How did they stand it? Where does my sister Jeany live? I hope there is no alteration in Mr. Sheriff's friends to my dear Jamie. If money is an object, it is all in his favour. How is Mr. and Mrs. Grant, and Mr. William, to whom I am for ever much obliged for settling my passage. It was a deep cut, but the more I am obliged to him and shall never forget it. He is a feeling and a generous gentleman.

I am sorry I cannot say so much of my cousin Milton, although he, too, was anxious for my off-going. How does my uncle and Mrs. Rintoull keep their health? From his conduct and repeated expressions, I never had much reason to expect anything from him, but now far less, although I be more needful. I believe few at my age ever went out more so. At present I am destitute of everything. I can put every article I have upon my back, and in my pocket. How does Mrs. Campbell and her son's family?

Who were the most forward of my creditors to attach? How does my affairs turn out in the whole? If Robert Smith is employed, has he been active and attentive? He would need to be looked after, although he may be useful; and any news or alterations relating to my friends that may have happened.

What has been done, or likely to be done, with the two unfortunate men, Smith and Ainslie, and the greater villain, John Brown *alias* Humphry Moore? Was John Murray *alias* Jack Tasker brought from England?

Whatever these men may say, I had no hand in any of their depredations, *excepting the last*, which I shall ever repent, and the keeping such company, although I doubt not but all will be laid to me. But let me drop this dreadful subject.

[Signed with the following initials]:—

S. W., T. L., R. S., J. M., J. S.

COPY of a LETTER or UNSIGNED SCROLL, in the handwriting of William Brodie, founded on in the Indictment, marked No. 2.

Pray write me what is become of Anne Grant, and how is her children disposed of. Cecill is a sensible, clever girl, considering the little opportunity she has had of improving. My dear little Willie will be, if I can judge, a brave and hardy boy.

Jean is her mother's picture, and too young to form any opinion of.

What has become of Jean Watt? She is a devil and a ———. I can form no opinion of Frank or his young brother; but pray write me how they are disposed of.

If you please, write me what is become of the two unhappy men, Smith, and his wife, and Ainslie. Are they yet? Is their trial come on? and the greater villain John Brown *alias* Humphry Moore? I shall ever repent keeping such company, and whatever they may alledge, I had no direct concern in any of their depredations, excepting the *last fatal one*, by which I lost ten pounds in cash; but I doubt not but all will be laid to my charge, and some that I never heard of.

[The following is written at the foot of the page:—]

I often went in a retregard. I have been all my life in a reteregard motion.

[What follows is written on the other side.]

Does Mr. Martin stand his bargain? Is any of my late property sold? Who is making out my accounts? Has Robert Smith been useful and active in my affairs? He is double and would need looking after.

Perhaps, in the course of making out and settling my accounts, some questions may occur that I may solve. If there is any such, please write them down, and I will answer them in course. Has any settlement taken place with Mr. Little? I am afraid my affairs will be a laborious task to you; but I hope all my creditors will be paid, and a reversion.

If all my moveables are not yet sold, I beg my clothes and linen, and a set of useful tools may be preserved for me; they are worth more to me than another.

I wrote more fully some time ago to Mr. Walker on this head, and also Mr. Sheriff, the 8th April; but I know not if he received it. Pray let me know if he did, and how he stands affected towards me. Whatever be his sentiments, I shall always esteem him and regard him as my brother, but I shall never write another friend until I hear from you, and have your opinion how they will take it.

Pray, did Captain Dent ever make any discovery who I was when he arrived at Leith.

J. L., J. M., R. S., J. S.

COPY OF AN ACCOUNT OR STATE, IN THE HANDWRITING OF WILLIAM BRODIE, FOUNDED ON IN THE INDICTMENT.
(Hitherto Unpublished.)

A State of my Affairs as near as I can make out at present from Memory, having no other Assistance.

COPY of a LETTER from Messrs. Lee, Strachan & Co., merchants in London, to Messrs. Emanuel Walker & Co., merchants in Philadelphia.

London, 1st May, 1788.

Messrs. Emanuel Walker & Co.

Sirs,

You will please to supply the bearer, Mr. John Dixon, with cash to the amount of fifty pounds sterling, taking his bill on Mr. William Walker, attorney in the Adelphi, London, for the same, which will be duly honoured, and oblige,

Sirs,
Your most obedient
Humble Servants,
LEE, STRACHAN & CO.

Messrs. Emanuel Walker & Co., Philadelphia.

Evidence for Defence.

[The counsel for Mr. Brodie here observed that the object of the exculpatory proof was to show that, on Wednesday, the 5th of March last, the night on which the robbery of the Excise Office was committed, Mr. Brodie was otherwise employed the whole of that afternoon and evening, which, if established, excluded the possibility of his being concerned in that robbery.]

Matthew Sheriff

1. MATTHEW SHERIFF, upholsterer in Edinburgh, called.

The LORD ADVOCATE—My Lords, this gentleman is the brother-in-law of the prisoner, and therefore is certainly a very improper witness. I am at all times very averse to object to a witness adduced for a pannel, but I thought it my duty to mention the fact to your Lordships, and to leave it with you to determine whether or not this gentleman's evidence ought to be received.

Mr. WIGHT, for William Brodie—My Lords, this is the first time I have ever heard that a brother-in-law is not a competent witness in a criminal trial. This gentleman being brother-in-law to the pannel, is a circumstance which may, and which perhaps ought, to be attended to, as affecting his credibility, if his testimony stands contradicted by other proofs; but it is surely no objection to his admissibility.

The LORD JUSTICE-CLERK—What do you mean to prove by this witness?

Mr. WIGHT—My Lord, I mean to prove that he was in company with the prisoner until about eight o'clock of that night on which the robbery is said to have been committed.

The LORD JUSTICE-CLERK—You may call him in. The circumstance of his being brother-in-law to the pannel will no doubt go a great length to discredit his testimony, in so far as it may be contradictory of other evidence; but this will fall to be considered by the jury when they come to judge of the proof brought by both parties.

[The witness was then called in and sworn.]

WITNESS—I know that the prisoner left Edinburgh in March last, and I think it was on the 9th of March, the Sunday after the Excise Office was broke into. I dined with him in his own house on the Wednesday preceding—the 5th of March. I think I went there to dinner about a quarter before three

**Charles Hay (afterwards Lord Newton).
(After Kay.)**

o'clock.[17] Mr. Brodie was then at home. I was in his house from dinner until within a few minutes of eight o'clock at night. There was present at dinner in company a stranger gentleman whose name I do not know, the prisoner's two sisters, and an old lady, his aunt. We drank together from dinner to tea, which I think was brought in about six o'clock, and then the stranger gentleman went away. We sat in the same room all the while I was there. Mr. Brodie was dressed in lightish-coloured or grey clothes. Before I came away, Mr. Brodie pressed me to stay supper with him, but I declined his invitation, saying I was engaged. When I came away, I left Mr. Brodie in his own house. I went directly from his house to my own house in Bunker's Hill.[18] Mr. Brodie dined with me next day (Thursday), and remained with me in my house from three o'clock until eleven o'clock at night.[19]

Cross-examined by the LORD ADVOCATE—What was the gentleman's name who was in company with you?

WITNESS—I do not know; I do not remember his name.

The LORD ADVOCATE—Did you hear his name mentioned?

WITNESS—I may perhaps have heard him named while at table with him, but as he went away early in the evening, and as I had no reason at the time to pay any particular attention to his name, it has escaped me.

The *Lord Advocate*—When did you sit down to dinner?

WITNESS—We sat down to dinner about three o'clock.

The LORD ADVOCATE—Are you sure Mr. Brodie did not leave the room from dinner until you parted with him?

WITNESS—I am certain Mr. Brodie did not leave the room.

The LORD ADVOCATE—Did you, on your way home, hear any clock strike or bell ring? or how do you know that it was precisely a few minutes from eight o'clock when you left Mr. Brodie?

WITNESS—I do not remember to have heard any clock strike or bell ring on my way home, but I had a clock in my house and a watch in my pocket. I am sure that I reached my own house within a few minutes of eight, either before or after it, and I had occasion to remark the hour from Mr. Brodie being so immediately afterwards accused of having that night broke into the Excise Office, a thing which I did not then, and which I do not yet, believe.

Jean Watt

---

2. JEAN WATT, residenter in Libberton's Wynd, called in and sworn.

The LORD ADVOCATE—I wish to know from this woman whether or not she is married. (To witness)—Are you married?[20]

WITNESS—No; I am not married.

[The examination was then allowed to proceed.]

I am well acquainted with the prisoner, William Brodie. I remember that on Wednesday, the 5th of March last, Mr. Brodie came to my house just at the time the eight o'clock bell was ringing, and he remained in it all night, and was not out from the time he came in until a little before nine o'clock next morning. We went early to bed, about ten o'clock, as Mr. Brodie complained that night of being much indisposed with a sore throat.

Cross-examined by the LORD ADVOCATE—How do you recollect that it was Wednesday night more than any other night of that week?

WITNESS—On the following Monday I heard that Mr. Brodie was suspected of being concerned in the breaking into the Excise Office; that his house had been searched for him; and that he had gone away on the Sunday. This made me particularly recollect, and also because it was the last night Mr. Brodie slept in my house. He slept with me that night. I have a family of children to him. I saw him again on the Saturday night afterwards, but not till then; and he was in my house in the forenoon of the Tuesday preceding.

3. PEGGY GILES, servant to Mr. Graham, publican at Mutton-hole, near Edinburgh, called in and sworn.

WITNESS—I was servant to Mrs. Watt, the preceding witness, last winter, and I remember that the prisoner, Mr. Brodie, came to my mistress's house about eight o'clock at night of Wednesday, the 5th of March last, and that he slept there all night, and remained until about nine o'clock next morning. My mistress and Mr. Brodie supped together early, about half-an-hour after eight o'clock, on bread and beer and a piece of cheese, for which I was sent out soon after Mr. Brodie came in. I was out about ten minutes, and when I returned Mr. Brodie was still in the house. I remember when he came in to have heard the eight o'clock bell ringing.

GENTLEMAN OF THE JURY—Was it the Magdalen Chapel bell you heard ringing? or what bell was it?

WITNESS—It was the Tron Church bell.

Cross-examined by the LORD ADVOCATE—Are you sure of that?

WITNESS—I am very sure.

Mr. WIGHT—Pray, where does the Tron Church stand?

WITNESS--In the Parliament Close.[21]

The LORD ADVOCATE—How do you know that Mr. Brodie slept all night in your mistress's house?

WITNESS—He was in bed when I arose in the morning, and I gave him water to wash his hands before he went out.

The LORD ADVOCATE—Did you see Brodie in your mistress's house at any other time during that week?

WITNESS—He came back in the forenoon and again in the afternoon of the same day, that is of Thursday,[22] and likewise on the Saturday night following. Mr. Brodie was in use to sleep frequently at my mistress's house.

4. HELEN ALISON or WALLACE, spouse to William Wallace, mason, in Libberton's Wynd, called in and sworn.

WITNESS—I reside in Libberton's Wynd, and I know the prisoner, Mr. Brodie. I heard of his leaving Edinburgh in March last, and I remember to have seen him come down Jean Watt's stair a little before nine o'clock on the morning of the Thursday before he went off—the 6th of March. I was then standing at my own door at the foot of the stair; and I had Francis Brodie, the prisoner's son, a boy of about seven years of age, by the hand. As his father, Mr. Brodie, passed he put a halfpenny into the child's hand, and clapped him on the head. I said to the boy, "Poor thing, thou hast been too soon out, or you would have seen your daddie at home"; he said, "No, I have not been too soon out, for my daddie has been in the house all night." After my husband got his breakfast, I went upstairs to Mrs. Watt, and I said to her in a joking way, "You will be in good humour to-day, as the good man has been with you all night." She answered, "He has; but, poor man, he has not been well of a sore throat." On the Monday following, I heard that there were messengers upstairs in Mrs. Watt's, searching her house for Mr. Brodie; and when I went up and was told what was the matter, I said to one Murray, a sheriff-officer, then present, "Dear sirs, who would have thought this would have happened, when I saw Mr. Brodie come downstairs and give a bawbee to his own son on Thursday last?" To which the man answered, "Indeed, few would have thought it."

Cross-examined by the LORD ADVOCATE—How do you recollect that it was upon the Thursday you saw Mr. Brodie come down stairs? Can you give any reason for doing so?

WITNESS—Indeed, I can give a reason, but to be sure it is a very mean one to mention to your Lordships.

Lord ESKGROVE—Tell us the reason, good woman.

WITNESS—I had purchased three pair of shoes on the Wednesday in the market; that is, a pair for each of my sons, and one for my husband. On Thursday morning I missed my husband's shoes, and, thinking they were stolen, I was waiting for my husband at the door at the time he usually returned to breakfast, which was about nine o'clock, to see if he knew anything of them; and had it not been for this I would not have been at the door nor seen Mr. Brodie come downstairs.

James Murray

5. JAMES MURRAY, sheriff-officer in Edinburgh, called in and sworn.

Examined by Mr. WIGHT—Do you remember having searched the house of Jean Watt, at the foot of Libberton's Wynd, in the course of your pursuit after Mr. Brodie?

WITNESS—I do.

MR. WIGHT—What day was that upon?

WITNESS—It was upon the Tuesday after he left Edinburgh I searched the house—the 11th of March; but finding nothing in it, I ordered Mrs. Watt to come up to the Sheriff, and I waited until she got ready.

MR. WIGHT—Did you see any person in the house, except Mrs. Watt and her servant? and had you any conversation with her?

WITNESS—I saw Mrs. Wallace, who lives at the foot of the wynd, whom I saw among the witnesses just now, and she said, "Oh, Jean! who would have thought on Thursday morning, when Mr. Brodie came down this stair and clapped his son's head, and put a halfpenny in his hand, that such a thing as this would be soon after here?" To which I answered, "Indeed, Mrs. Wallace, I dare say none would have thought it."

James Laing

6. JAMES LAING, writer in the Council Chamber, Edinburgh, called in and sworn.

Examined by Mr. HAY—Do you remember of any process being brought before the magistrates against Mr. Brodie some time before he left this place, for using false or loaded dice?

WITNESS—I do.

Mr. HAY—At whose instance was the process?

WITNESS—At the instance of one Hamilton, a chimney-sweep in Portsburgh.

Mr. HAY—When was this process?

WITNESS—I do not exactly remember; but steps have been taken in it within these six months.

Lord ESKGROVE—I suppose this Mr. Hamilton is not a common sweep, but a master who keeps men and boys for the purpose?

WITNESS—He is a master, as your Lordship observes.

Cross-examined by the LORD ADVOCATE—Do you know Mr. Brodie to be a gambler?

WITNESS—I never gambled with him.

Robert Smith

7. ROBERT SMITH, wright in Edinburgh, sometime foreman to Mr. Brodie, called in and sworn.

The Lord Advocate (Ilay Campbell).
(Showing the old Parliament House.)
(After Kay.)

Examined by Mr. HAY—Do you know that a spring-saw is a proper instrument for cutting off the natural spurs of game-cocks, in order to adopt artificial ones?

WITNESS—I do.

Mr. HAY—Did you ever see Mr. Brodie using a small spring-saw for that purpose?

WITNESS—Frequently.

Mr. HAY—Is a spring-saw a usual and necessary implement for all wrights and joiners, as well as smiths?

WITNESS—I have one myself, which I use for cutting off brass knobs and several other purposes.

Mr. HAY—Are old keys and pick-locks usual and necessary implements for wrights and smiths?

WITNESS—They are.

Mr. HAY—Do you know that a box of old keys was always lying open in the corner of Mr. Brodie's workshop, to which you and the other men had access?

WITNESS—There was; and when a key of any of our customers was either broke or spoiled, we could often fit the lock from some of these keys.

[Here the witness was shown the keys libelled on.]

WITNESS—I never remember to have seen any keys of that kind before.

[Here it was proposed to show the witness a pick-lock, and to ask him whether or not joiners or cabinetmakers kept such an instrument, when the Lord Advocate admitted that it was not uncommon for a cabinetmaker to keep such articles as the above. There were several witnesses cited by Mr. Brodie to prove this fact.]

The exculpatory proof being closed a few minutes after one o'clock of the morning of the 28th day of August, the Lord Advocate then proceeded to address the jury.

The Lord Advocate's Address to the Jury.

Lord Advocate

The LORD ADVOCATE—Gentlemen of the jury, it is now my duty to offer some observations on the import of the evidence which has been led before you, and as you have already had a very long and fatiguing sederunt, I shall endeavour to state what occurs to me in as few words as possible. It is with the greatest concern that I address you in this case—a case that is attended with circumstances which must occasion to all of us the most painful sensations; but public justice requires that these feelings should be repressed.

Gentlemen, the crime with which these prisoners stand charged is of a most dangerous and heinous nature. It is a crime which, until of late, was but little known in this country, though now it seems to be every day growing more frequent, and the practice of it is almost reduced into a system. It is no longer than fourteen days ago that two men received their sentence at that bar for a crime of the same nature with this—the robbery of the Bank of Dundee— which appeared to have been conducted and perpetrated by an association in that town, similar to the association which took place, in the heart of this populous city, between the prisoners at the bar and the other two men whom you saw this day give evidence against them; and which, had it not been discovered, threatened the inhabitants of this city with the most dangerous consequences. That now charged against these prisoners, though of the most flagrant nature, is but one of many in which there is good ground to believe that this association has been concerned. And it is your province, gentlemen, if upon careful examination of the evidence you think these men guilty, to do that justice to your country which the public safety requires, by returning a verdict against them.

It is perhaps of no consequence to inquire into what was the former situation of the prisoners, because that is a circumstance which can have no weight with you in determining what verdict you are this night to return.

As for George Smith, he is a stranger in this country, of whom we know nothing more than what he has been pleased to inform us in his different declarations, of which a part has not been read for the reasons you heard mentioned; but from thence you will be led to conjecture that the parts which were not read contained very little to his advantage. This man, gentlemen, had the appearance of following a lawful employment and carrying on trade in a shop in this city; but I am afraid there is too good reason to conclude that the character of a grocer, which he assumed, was only meant as a cover to him that he might escape the observation of the public while he was pursuing objects of a very different nature. His counsel have attempted no defence, such as the *alibi* endeavoured to be proved by the other prisoner; no witnesses have been examined in his exculpation; and his different declarations, which though not legal evidence by themselves, yet when corroborated by the great variety of other evidence led this day, are so full and complete proofs of his guilt that I do not consider it necessary to add one word more as to him.

The other prisoner, Mr. Brodie, is in a different situation. He is known to us all; educated as a gentleman; bred to a respectable business; and removed from suspicion, as well from his supposed circumstances as from the rank he held amongst his fellow-citizens. He was far above the reach of want, and, consequently, of temptation; he had a lawful employment, which might have enabled him to hold his station in society with respectability and credit; he has been more than once officially at the head of his profession, and was a member of the City Council. If, therefore, he, too, is guilty, his situation, in place of alleviating his guilt, is a high aggravation of it. If he indeed prevailed upon himself to descend to the commission of the most detestable crimes, what excuse can be made for him? That he frequented bad company; that he had abandoned himself to gambling, and every species of dissipation; that he has by these means run himself into difficulties, is surely no apology for him.

But, gentlemen, I am not entitled to proceed without substantiating the crime libelled against him. I will go on to state the evidence; and if after a cool and dispassionate consideration, which you are bound to give, and which from the very great attention you have already bestowed, I can have no doubt you will give it; if you are not most thoroughly convinced in your minds that the prisoner is guilty, I do not desire that you should return a verdict against him. I can have no wish that is contrary to material justice.

It is totally unnecessary to go over the evidence tending to show that the Excise Office was actually robbed in the manner mentioned in the indictment, as I suppose that is a fact which will not be disputed, I will therefore recapitulate the heads of the evidence, so far as it appears to me to verify the charge.

Gentlemen, you have heard various objections stated by the prisoners' counsel against the admissibility of the evidence of Brown and Ainslie, and therefore I will in the first place call your attention to the other evidence, against which no objection has or can be made, and which is, in my opinion, sufficient in itself to establish the guilt of the pannels; and I shall afterwards speak to the evidence of these two men.

The first circumstance which you have in evidence, and to which I call your attention, is the intimate connection between the prisoner Brodie and the other three, Smith, Ainslie, and Brown, who have all confessed themselves guilty of the crime charged; it is admitted by himself in his letters and declaration, and is confirmed by the evidence of Smith's maid, who said that she had seen them often together in her master's house; his being often in company with them, gambling with them in different houses, and particularly in Clark's, a house which, from what we have heard of it this day, ought for the good of society to be razed to the ground or built up, as houses infected by the plague are in times of pestilence.

In the second place, gentlemen, the prisoner was in company with these men on the very night in which the robbery was committed. This is proved by the testimony of Smith's maid, Grahame Campbell, a witness who it is not pretended had any temptation to perjure herself. She tells you that Brodie came to her master's house that day in the dusk of the evening; that they were in the upper room all together, and had some cold fowl and herrings; that Brodie was then dressed in an old-fashioned black coat; that she mentioned this circumstance to her mistress; that he went out with Smith, Brown, and Ainslie; and that when he came back later in the evening, he had then changed his dress and had on light-coloured clothes. These are all circumstances highly suspicious, and they would have been likewise sworn to by Smith's wife, if she had been allowed to be examined; but that is unnecessary, as the facts the witness has deponed to are all probable in themselves, and they are corroborated, to the extent I have mentioned, by the other evidence, and also by Smith's declarations, which last I do not mean to found upon as evidence against Mr. Brodie, but it is a curious fact.

In the third place, gentlemen, you will observe that the Excise Office was robbed upon Wednesday, the 5th of March. On the Friday night following, information was given to the Procurator-Fiscal by Brown; on the Saturday, Smith and Ainslie were apprehended and committed to prison. And what happens? Brodie goes to the prison to visit them, but is denied access. Is it possible to suppose that a gentleman in Mr. Brodie's situation would have done this had he been innocent? No, gentlemen, it is not to be supposed.

But attend to what follows. Early the next morning, Brodie sends for Robert Smith, his foreman, and asks him if he had heard any news concerning them; he tells Brodie that Smith, the pannel, and Ainslie were in prison, and so forth, and adds that he hoped his master was not concerned with them. Gentlemen, he knew that Smith and Ainslie were Mr. Brodie's companions; and you cannot conceive that he would have presumed to put such a question to his master if he had not been convinced in his own mind of his master's guilt. Mr. Brodie makes no answer to this question. Will it be said that a man conscious of his own innocence would have remained silent upon such an occasion? Gentlemen, I appeal to yourselves; how would any one of you have felt, or what answer would you have returned to a servant who dared put such a question to you?

Brodie at this time tells Smith that he is going out of town for a few days; but you have it in evidence that he left this country, and fled to Flushing. In order to account for this flight you are told a story of a prosecution against him, at the instance of a chimney-sweep, for using false or loaded dice. This is a very strange circumstance to bring in exculpation. I have no hesitation to say that it is the most ignominious defence I ever remember to have heard maintained by a prisoner at that bar; but you cannot believe that that prosecution was the occasion of his flight. He was in no greater danger from it then than he had been in for months before; no step had been taken in that process which could alarm him at this critical time; and it is mere mockery, it is altogether a joke, to pretend that from such a circumstance the prisoner at the bar could have taken up the resolution of banishing himself from his country for ever.

Besides, Mr. Brodie, in his declaration before the Sheriff, did not assign this as the cause of his flight. He said that, as he was intimate with Smith and Ainslie, he was afraid they would accuse him of being concerned with them in robbing the Excise Office. He did not so much as mention the defence now set up for him; but his counsel saw that it would be necessary to account for his conduct in some shape or other, and no other appearance of defence occurred but this process. It is impossible to believe this story; and indeed it is impossible to assign any cause for Mr. Brodie's conduct consistent with his innocence of the crime charged against him.

I would, in the next place, gentlemen, have you to attend to the prisoner's behaviour when he flies from this place to London. He secretes himself in London for several weeks; search is made for him, but he cannot be found;

he admits in one of his letters that he knew that Mr. Williamson was in search of him, but he did not choose an interview; a vessel is freighted for him by some persons, contrary to the duty they owed to their country; she is cleared out for Leith; he goes on board of her in the middle of the night, with a wig on, in disguise, and under a borrowed name; he is carried to Flushing; he changes his name to John Dixon, and writes letters to people in Edinburgh under that false signature, explaining his whole future operations, in consequence of which letters he is traced and apprehended, just when he is on the point of going on board of a ship for New York. If he had been innocent; if he had had nothing else to fear than the story of the loaded dice, it is not possible that he could have conducted himself in this manner.

The letters he writes to Geddes are likewise very strong circumstances; but the other letters, or scrolls, found in his trunk are still stronger. You have had it clearly proven that all these letters are of his own handwriting, and in both of the scrolls he expressly acknowledges the crime for which he now stands at the bar. In one of them he says that he had no "direct" concern in any of the late depredations of Smith, Brown, and Ainslie, excepting "the last fatal one"; in the other the word "direct" is scored out, but in both of them he acknowledges his accession to the last act; by which he can mean no other than the robbery of the Excise Office; for it happened on the Wednesday evening, and Brown gave information of it on the Friday evening immediately after. It was, therefore, in all probability the last of the depredations of this dangerous combination; and Mr. Brodie's having applied the expression "fatal" to it identifies it beyond all doubt.

Gentlemen, I beg leave now to bring under your consideration what happened in this city after Mr. Brodie absconded. You have it in evidence that his house was searched, and various articles of a very suspicious nature found. A pair of pistols, identified to have been used on the occasion of the robbery, is found under the earth, and the place where they were hid pointed out by the other prisoner Smith; also a dark lanthorn, the one half of it in one place and the other half of it in another. Gentlemen, if Mr. Brodie is really innocent, it appears to me passing strange that these articles should have been so concealed.

All these circumstances, gentlemen, are established by the most unexceptionable evidence; they are connected with and corroborated by each other; and they all point to this conclusion, independent altogether of the direct evidence of Brown and Ainslie, that Mr. Brodie is guilty of the crime charged. They cannot be accounted for upon any other supposition.

In the opposite scale, gentlemen, you have the proof of *alibi* attempted by the prisoner, which is exceedingly defective and inconclusive. *Alibi* is a defence seldom resorted to but in the most desperate circumstances, and little regard is in general paid to it, for this good reason that it resolves into an immediate falsification of the whole evidence brought in support of the charge. It is suspicious at all times, but it is peculiarly so when the *alibi* is confined to the same town in which the crime was committed, within a few minutes' walk of the place, and is deponed to by witnesses at a great distance of time.

The first witness, gentlemen, brought by the prisoner to establish this defence is Matthew Sheriff, his own brother-in-law, by no means an unexceptionable witness. This gentleman depones that he dined with Mr. Brodie on Wednesday, the 5th of March, and that he was in company with him until eight o'clock that night. He is brought forward singly to prove a fact, which, if true, Mr. Brodie could be at no loss to establish by other unexceptionable evidence. There was another gentleman, he tells you, who dined in company with the pannel that day; and what appears to me to be a very odd circumstance, this gentleman is not called as a witness; nay, more, although Mr. Sheriff recollects a great variety of other circumstances, he does not remember this gentleman's name. Why is this gentleman not brought forward on this occasion? Why are not some of the servants of the house, or any other person, called to support Mr. Sheriff's testimony? Mr. Sheriff, then, is only a single witness, and from his near connection with the pannel, he gives his evidence under circumstances that are suspicious, and therefore no weight can be allowed to it.

But even supposing Mr, Sheriff's testimony to be true, it is by no means inconsistent with the guilt of the prisoner, nor affects the credibility of the prosecutor's evidence. Grahame Campbell depones that Brodie did not come to Smith's house until about eight o'clock; and allowing him to have remained with Mr. Sheriff until near eight, the expedition against the Excise Office was not then begun; and you will recollect that Brodie was the last who made his appearance at Smith's, and that he was expected by his associates a considerable time before he arrived.

Jean Watt is the next witness adduced by the prisoner, who, by her own evidence, appears to be a woman of an abandoned character. She has a family to Mr. Brodie, and was denominated by him, in one of his letters, by the appellation of "a devil." This witness and her maid no doubt concur most minutely in a very extraordinary fact, which, if it can be believed, amounts to a falsification of the whole other evidence, viz., that Mr. Brodie came to Watt's house just at eight o'clock, as the bell was ringing, and did not leave her house again till nine o'clock next morning. No doubt she swears pointedly to the night, and so does her servant; but although these two witnesses agree in the day, the hour, and even the minute of Mr. Brodie's coming to Watt's house on the 5th of March, yet, when they came to be cross-examined, they did not even agree in days; for Jean Watt said that she did not see Brodie from the Thursday morning, at nine o'clock, till the Saturday afternoon following, yet her maid said that he was twice in the house on the Thursday, both in the forenoon and afternoon; though Sheriff said that Brodie was in his house on the Thursday from three o'clock in the afternoon till eleven o'clock at night. They can give no reason for fixing the night of his visit at Watt's house to be Wednesday night, except the subsequent flight of the prisoner; and therefore it may have been any other night in that week as well as the one condescended upon.

But, gentlemen, I have no occasion to dispute, and indeed, from the evidence of Helen Alison, I am inclined to believe that the prisoner went on the Wednesday night to Mrs. Watt's house, and slept there that night; but I have heard nothing, allowing all the witnesses to have spoken what they believed to be true, that goes to prove that he went there until after the crime was committed. Gentlemen, the circumstance which fixes the hour in the memory of both Mrs. Watt and her servant is the ringing of a bell, and we all know that there is a bell that rings at ten o'clock as well as at eight. And it is very far from being improbable that they might both mistake the one bell for the other, either at the time, or afterwards, upon endeavouring to recollect the hour at which Brodie came to them.

Allowing, therefore, gentlemen, that all the witnesses adduced by the prisoner are to be believed, there appears to be nothing in their testimony contradictory to the evidence of the prisoner's accession to the crime charged; and therefore I can have no doubt that, although the matter rested upon the evidence I have already stated, you could have no hesitation in pronouncing both the prisoners guilty.

But, gentlemen, when, in addition to that evidence, you take into your consideration the testimony of Ainslie and Brown, the two associates of the pannels, if any doubt did remain, it would necessarily be removed. The counsel for the prisoners, aware of this, have objected to the admissibility of both of them.

I admit that the credibility of these witnesses is liable to suspicion, and that if the proof rested upon their evidence alone, I would not call upon you to find the prisoners guilty upon it, but in so far as their evidence is corroborated by the general tenor of the other unexceptionable parts of the proof they are entitled to credit.

To Ainslie it has been objected that a corrupt bargain was made with him by the Sheriff, which, in other words, amounts to this, that he must be a false witness. If the prisoners' counsel were serious in stating this objection, they ought certainly to have proved it; but, gentlemen, it proceeded entirely upon a mistake in point of fact—upon a supposition that Ainslie had not spoke out until Brodie was apprehended. Gentlemen, I hold Ainslie's declaration in my hand, and which I offered to read, and which I would now read, if the forms of the Court would allow me, emitted a short while after the robbery was committed, and containing a full and complete disclosure of the whole transaction. But, gentlemen, you will not, you cannot, suspect that there was any such bargain; that there was anything in the present case out of the common course.

A similar objection was made by the counsel for the prisoner to the evidence of Brown, with this addition, that he had been convicted of felony at the Old Bailey. The last part of this objection, gentlemen, is completely answered by the pardon which, by the law of England, where that sentence was pronounced, completely rehabilitated him. Brown is then in even a more favourable situation than Ainslie, for, as he never was charged with the crime for which the prisoners are tried, nor any intention taken up to prosecute him for it, he had even less temptation than Ainslie to swear falsely.

There is therefore nothing in the objections stated to these witnesses, and accordingly the Court have found so. These men, gentlemen, have told you that Brodie was with them when the breaking into the Excise Office was originally planned that he met them at Smith's house on the night when the robbery was committed, in which particular their evidence is corroborated by the testimony of Grahame Campbell; that he was with them at the commission of the crime, which is the time when he endeavours to prove an *alibi*; that some of the pistols carried to the Excise Office belonged to him, which pistols were afterwards found in his possession. They have likewise informed you that it was agreed upon that Brodie should be stationed within the door and Ainslie without, and this exactly corresponds with the testimony of James Bonar.

Brown and Ainslie are so consistent with each other and with the whole other evidence adduced, both real and circumstantial, that I am unable to discover a single discrepancy in the whole, excepting where Brown and Ainslie say that, after the robbery, they did not either of them see Brodie again that evening, but Smith's maid said that they all met again in Smith's house and supped there, and that Brodie supped along with them. This, however, does not appear to be a fact of any importance or that tends to discredit either of the witnesses, as it is evident that Smith's maid has confounded the first and second meetings together.

But it is unnecessary for me to enlarge upon particulars which cannot have escaped your own observation, and I shall therefore conclude with remarking that you have in this case more direct evidence of the pannels' guilt, corroborated by a greater variety of circumstances all coinciding in a most remarkable manner, than I remember to have met with in any other which has occurred to me in the course of my practice.

Gentlemen, I shall only further add that if the prisoner William Brodie, a person who from the nature of his employment had frequent opportunities of being introduced into the houses of others, has been guilty of the crime laid to his charge, and is allowed to escape punishment, the consequences to the inhabitants of this populous city may be of the most serious nature. But, gentlemen, the evidence is before you, and if, upon a fair and deliberate consideration of it, you are convinced of the pannels' guilt, I can have no doubt that you will do justice to your country by returning a verdict accordingly.

Mr. John Clerk then rose to address the jury on behalf of George Smith.

Mr. John Clerk's Address to the Jury.

John Clerk

Mr. CLERK—Gentlemen of the jury, it is now my duty to state the evidence to you for the pannel, Mr. Smith, and I shall trouble you with a very few observations only.

My unfortunate client is a very poor man; and although he was in a situation, before he was apprehended on suspicion of this crime, to support himself and his family upon the produce of his industry in his trade as a grocer, he has, in consequence of this unlucky affair, been reduced to absolute beggary, so that he has not been able to make those extraordinary exertions either in procuring evidence or counsel, which the more opulent prisoner has done. He is an Englishman, a stranger in this country, and in great straits for his life, and whatever is favourable in his character or conduct is unknown; while, on the other hand, everything that tended to blacken his character and fix guilt upon him has been brought forward. He has no one to say a good word for him, as that great villain, John Brown *alias* Humphry Moore, has, who, you will remember, was so highly complimented by their Lordships when he left that box. But, I, as his most inexperienced and imperfect counsel, will try and do the best I can for the poor man.

The LORD JUSTICE-CLERK—Be short and concise, sir, at this time of the morning.

Mr. CLERK—Pray, your Lordship, let me proceed.

The LORD JUSTICE-CLERK—Well then, proceed, young man.

Mr. CLERK—It is easy to account from this cause, gentlemen, for what my Lord Advocate observed concerning the obscurity of my client's history before the robbery of the Excise Office; and I imagine that no argument against him can be drawn from it. I know that I speak to a jury who will lay nothing into the scale against him that does not arise from the evidence which has been adduced.

My Lord Advocate has told you, gentlemen, that the guilt of my unfortunate client is so clear as to admit of no doubt, and it is in consequence of that opinion, I suppose, that his Lordship has made so few observations upon it. I cannot, however, yield my assent to this proposition; and I shall endeavour to show you, on the contrary, gentlemen, from a statement of such parts of the proof as affect my client, that the fair and legal evidence against him is incomplete and will not warrant a verdict for the Crown.

The evidence may be reduced to three distinct branches—his own declarations, which have been read; the direct evidence of the witnesses adduced for the prosecutor to the commission of the crime; and the real evidence of circumstances.

With regard to the declarations, the Lord Advocate has told

John Clerk (afterwards Lord Eldin).
(After Kay.)

you, gentlemen, that they contain a variety of particulars which have not been read, and have been omitted by the consent of the pannel; and from this, his Lordship observed, an inference might be drawn that the declarations contain many more particulars little to the credit of the pannel. Gentlemen, an inference more candid, or at least more charitable, might, in my opinion, be deduced from the circumstance. It is easy to conceive the state of mind in which the pannel must have been when apprehended. Connected with those infamous men who were supposed to have committed the crime, a partner in their most dissolute scenes, no wonder, gentlemen, that he was struck with terror when seized upon an accusation of being joined in their guilt.

After having resisted for some time the impressions arising from his confinement, his panic most naturally increased almost to a delirium; a fit of temporary frenzy, an insanity, seized him, and he accused himself of an atrocious crime as the only means of safety. But this accusation is rejected by his cooler judgment, and accordingly he pleaded not guilty at this bar. In accusing himself in such a manner, the greater variety of crimes he laid to his own charge, the greater is the improbability of their being true, for it was folly to balance the merit of confessing a crime eagerly inquired after by the guilt of other crimes which were out of head. And it was folly of such a sort as to prove that the pannel was incapable of rational conduct; and thus the credit of his declaration, in so far as it injured himself, is in charitable reasoning considerably diminished.

But, at all events, gentlemen, it is sufficiently known and acknowledged, and it was even admitted—at least, it was not denied by the Lord Advocate himself—that the extrajudicial declaration of a pannel is not legal evidence against him. It is undoubtedly a circumstance in evidence, but not of weight to convict unless it be adminicled by other proof. This will be admitted, on all hands, to be the law of Scotland, and I shall make no comment on it.

If, therefore, it is shown to your satisfaction that the parole and circumstantiate evidence is either contradictory, inconsistent, or incredible, you will lay very little stress on the extrajudicial confessions of the prisoner.

And this leads me to the second branch of the evidence, or the attempt at a direct proof of the accession of the pannel, Smith, to the crime charged.

The first witness after those to the declarations, whose deposition affects the pannel Smith, is M'Lean, Mr. Drysdale's waiter. He is the nineteenth witness. I need not enter into the particulars of his evidence, since all of you must recollect that he could say nothing more than that Smith bought a ticket in the mail-coach for his wife; gave him in payment a five-pound bank-note, battered on the back, and received the change. It does not appear from whence the pannel had the note which he gave to M'Lean, nor whether it was among the money which was stolen from the Excise Office or not.

John Clerk, Mr. Drysdale's cashier, the twentieth witness, could not even say so much as M'Lean. It does not appear from either of these depositions whether the paper on the table was that which was presented to them or not, as the Court determined that it is not properly described in the indictment, and on that account it cannot be used in evidence against the pannel.

I may therefore leave these witnesses, gentlemen; and I am persuaded that none of you will think that they said anything which militates against my client in the smallest degree.

Grahame Campbell, the seventeenth witness, was examined as to a variety of particulars, but her whole deposition, in so far as it regards the pannel Smith, amounts to no more than that he was in company with Brodie, Ainslie, and Brown that evening on which the Excise Office was broken into; that they supped together, ate herrings or a fowl, whilst she was in a back cellar; and upon her coming out of this back cellar the company had left the house, and Smith, her master, had likewise gone out; but there is no evidence of their having gone out together, and although they had, it does not follow that they went to the Excise Office together.

It would be very hard if a man should be suspected of a robbery merely because he leaves his house about the time that the robbery is committed, and in this case—there is little more; for it was by no means extraordinary that Brown and Ainslie should be with Mr. Brodie in Mr. Smith's house that night, as they were there every night, always playing at cards and dice, and amusing themselves in company together.

And further, gentlemen, although they had not been drawn together by constant habits and the love of similar amusements, a good reason was given why Brown and Ainslie were constantly at the house of Smith. You were informed that these two men dined and supped there every day, that is, were day boarders in his house.

Putting all this together, I may dismiss this witness with the same observation which I applied to the former ones. As far as I understand her evidence, she said nothing which has a tendency to criminate my client.

I come next to the testimony of Ainslie and Brown. Gentlemen, you have heard a variety of objections stated to the admissibility of their evidence—all of which has been over-ruled by the Court. But notwithstanding the judgment of their Lordships, I must adhere to these objections and maintain that they ought not to have been admitted as witnesses. Gentlemen, I think a great deal of most improper evidence has been received in this case for the Crown.

The LORD JUSTICE-CLERK—Do you say that, sir, after the judgment which the Court has pronounced? That, sir, is a most improper observation to address at the outset to the jury.

Lord STONEFIELD—It is a positive reflection on the Court.

Lord HAILES—It is a flat accusation that we have admitted improper evidence.

Lord ESKGROVE—I never heard the like of this from any young counsel at the beginning of his career at this bar.

The LORD JUSTICE-CLERK—With these admonitions, go on, sir; proceed, sir.

Mr. CLERK—Aweel, my Lords, if I go on, I beg to assail at the outset the evidence of these two corbies or infernal scoundrels, Ainslie and Brown.

The LORD JUSTICE-CLERK—Take care, sir, what you say.

Mr. CLERK—Yes, my Lords, I say that they are both most infamous characters. Gentlemen, you should discard such vagabonds, and not rely on their evidence in any way; and if you knock out the vile brains of their evidence in this case, there is nothing else remaining on which you can convict my poor client, except his own very candid declarations which I have already explained to you. Gentlemen, these nefarious witnesses Ainslie and Brown, should have stood at this bar this night in place of my client, who was happy in his domestic privacy with his poor, honest, inoffending wife, whom you this day saw—and my heart bleeds for her. [Here there was some applause from the audience which was at once suppressed.] Gentlemen, Ainslie contradicts himself, and Brown is not to be believed. With respect to this said Mr. John Brown *alias* Humphry Moore, you had it out of his own mouth that he was a convicted felon in England, and I say to you that no convicted felon ought, by the good and glorious law of Scotland, to be received as a witness in this or any other case in the British dominions.

[Great applause from the audience.]

MACERS—Silence in Court.

The LORD JUSTICE-CLERK—Mr. Clerk, please restrict your reflections. The Court have admitted the witness.

Mr. CLERK—Yes, my Lords, I know that very well, but your Lordships should *not* have admitted him, and of that the jury will now judge.

The LORD JUSTICE-CLERK—This is most indecent behaviour. You cannot be allowed to speak to the admissibility; to the credibility you may.

Lord STONEFIELD—This young man is again attacking the Court.

Mr. CLERK—No, my Lords, I am not attacking the Court; I am attacking that villain of a witness, who, I tell your Lordships, is not worth his value in hemp.

The LORD JUSTICE-CLERK—The Court, sir, have already solemnly decided, as you know, on the objections raised by the Dean of Faculty, that in law the objections to these witnesses should be repelled, and they were repelled accordingly; therefore you should have nothing more to say to us on that point.

The DEAN OF FACULTY—If it will satisfy Mr. Clerk, I can assure him that I will plead on this point to the jury, waiving all objections to the admissibility, which it may be rather irregular to plead after the decision of the Court.

The LORD JUSTICE-CLERK—Dean of Faculty, I know you will attempt nothing that is improper.

Mr. CLERK—But, my Lords, the jury are to judge of the law as well as the facts.[23]

The LORD JUSTICE-CLERK—Sir, I tell you that the jury have nothing to do with, the law, but to take it *simpliciter* from me.

Mr. CLERK—That I deny.

[Consternation in Court.]

Lord HAILES—Sir, will you deny the authority of this High Court?

Mr. CLERK—Gentlemen of the jury, notwithstanding of this interruption, I beg to tell you, with all confidence and all respect, that you are the judges of the law as well as the facts. You are the judges of the whole case.

The LORD JUSTICE-CLERK—You are talking nonsense, sir.

Mr. CLERK—My Lord, you had better not snub me in this way. I never mean to speak nonsense.

The LORD JUSTICE-CLERK—Proceed—gang on, sir.

Mr. CLERK—Gentlemen, I was telling you that this infernal witness was convicted of felony in England, and how dare he come here to be received as a witness in this case?

The LORD ADVOCATE—He has, as I have shown you, received His Majesty's free pardon.

Mr. CLERK—Yes, I see; but, gentlemen of the jury, I ask you, on your oaths, can His Majesty make a tainted scoundrel an honest man?

[Great applause in Court.]

The LORD JUSTICE-CLERK—Macers, clear the Court if there is any more unruly din.

The LORD ADVOCATE [interposing and addressing Mr. Clerk]—Sir, permit me to say, after this interruption, that the prerogative of mercy is the brightest jewel in His Majesty's Crown.

Mr. CLERK—I hope His Majesty's Crown will never be contaminated by any villains around it.

[Sensation in Court.]

The LORD JUSTICE-CLERK [to the Lord Advocate]—Do you want his words noted down?

The LORD ADVOCATE—Oh no, my Lord, not exactly yet. My young friend will soon cool in his effervescence for his client.

The LORD JUSTICE-CLERK [to Mr. Clerk]—Go on, young man.

Mr. CLERK—Gentlemen of the jury, I was just saying to you, when this outbreak on the bench occurred, that you were the judges of the law and of the facts in this case.

The LORD JUSTICE-CLERK—We cannot tolerate this, sir. It is an indignity to this High Court—a very gross indignity, deserving of the severest reprobation.

Mr. CLERK—My Lords, I know that your Lordships have determined this question; but the jury have not. They are judges both of fact and of the law, and are not bound by your Lordships' determination, unless it agrees with their own opinion. Unless I am allowed to speak to the jury in this manner, I am determined not to speak a word more. I am willing to sit down if your Lordships command me. [Here Mr. Clerk sat down.]

The LORD JUSTICE-CLERK—Go on, sir; go on to the length of your tether.

[Mr. Clerk then rose and resumed his address.]

Mr. CLERK—Yes, gentlemen, I stand up here as an independent Scottish advocate, and I tell you, a jury of my countrymen, that you are the judges of the law as well as of the facts.

The LORD JUSTICE-CLERK—Beware of what you are about, sir.

[Here Mr. Clerk again sat down.]

The LORD JUSTICE-CLERK—Are you done, sir, with your speech?

Mr. CLERK—No, my Lord, I am not.

The LORD JUSTICE-CLERK—Then go on, sir, at your peril.

Lord HAILES—You had better go on, Mr. Clerk. Do go on.

Mr. CLERK—This has been too often repeated. I have met with no politeness from the Court. You have interrupted me, you have snubbed me rather too often, my Lord, in the line of my defence. I maintain that the jury are judges of the law as well as of the facts; and I am positively resolved that I will proceed no further unless I am allowed to speak in my own way.

The LORD JUSTICE-CLERK—Then we must now call upon the Dean of Faculty to proceed with his address for the prisoner Brodie, which the Court will hear with the greatest attention. [Here the learned Dean shook his head, as if declining to do so.] Very well. The Court will proceed now and discharge its duty.

[His Lordship was then about to address the jury in his final charge.]

Mr. CLERK [starting to his feet and shaking his fist at the bench]—Hang my client if you daur, my Lord, without hearing me in his defence!

[These remarkable words produced the greatest sensation in Court; the judges retired to the robing-room to hold a consultation; but on their returning to Court, the Lord Justice-Clerk merely requested Mr. Clerk to proceed with his speech. Mr. Clerk then continued his address without further interruption.]

Mr. CLERK—I say, gentlemen, I adhere to all the objections stated on the proof, both to the admissibility and to the credibility of these witnesses.

On the other hand, it is obvious, that if they are to be listened to as good and unexceptionable witnesses, their evidence goes to prove the guilt of my client in the clearest and most unequivocal manner; so that the questions come to be, how far are they admissible at all? and how far are they credible? Is their evidence to be laid aside altogether? and if not, to what extent is it worthy of belief?

Gentlemen, before I was interrupted, I was going to observe, that in this branch of the evidence my cause is the same with that which is to be supported with so much greater abilities by the Dean of Faculty; and of consequence it would be unnecessary and even impertinent in me to take up your time in arguing at large upon the subject. I have followed the same conduct in the other particulars of the proof, where the pannels are in similar circumstances; and I have only to desire you to apply the same principles to both cases.

Gentlemen, I come now to the real evidence. Some of the witnesses deponed that Mr. Smith was taken up to Brodie's buildings, and there some of the articles on the table were found, but nothing in this part of the evidence is inconsistent with the innocence of Smith, who might be better acquainted with Mr. Brodie's shop and yard than the officers, without being a partner in the crimes of which he (Brodie) might be guilty.

The most material circumstance in the proof relates to the finding of the iron crow, the curling irons, and key, in the hole of a wall, and for that reason I reserve it for the last.

There are two capital defects in the evidence of this fact. First, a glaring contradiction concerning the place where the things were found; and, secondly, as glaring a contradiction in the account of what passed at finding them. Middleton says that they were found in Warriston's Close; Murray, on the contrary, that they were found in Allan's Close. Middleton told you expressly that the pannel put his hand into the hole in the wall and drew them out; but Murray said that this was impossible, because he had his hands tied behind him: and this witness farther added that he himself drew them out.

The Dean of Faculty (Hon. Henry Erskine).
(After Kay.)

These are no common mistakes; and I ask, what reliance can be had on evidence where two such falsehoods appear within the narrow compass of a few questions? I am willing to grant that there are slight inaccuracies which rather tend to confirm the truth of a deposition than to render it suspected; but you cannot suppose errors like these concerning such marked and important circumstances, as make an impression on the memory equally indelible with any part of the story, and which in this instance constitute its leading features.

I say there must be a radical error here, either in the candour of the witnesses, or in the events which they have related. They are either perjured, or have been deceived, about the articles on your table; and in either case their testimony is good for nothing. It is plain that the iron crow was not found both in Warriston's Close and in Allan's Close; the prisoner was not both fettered and unfettered at the same time; and it matters not to me which of the witnesses has been deceived. Whoever it is, it cannot be determined on this trial that any of them spoke the truth; and of consequence the evidence of both must be laid out of consideration.

At all events, gentlemen, what have you more than two solitary witnesses to two contradictory facts, instead of two witnesses to one consistent event? This can never be reckoned good and legal evidence on a trial for life, where equity as well as expediency require the most scrupulous accuracy.

Gentlemen, I have now stated what appear to me to be the most material circumstances in the proof. I have commented on the depositions of the witnesses in so far as they may be thought to criminate my client; and without farther detaining you, I beg leave to conclude by repeating the proposition which I have endeavoured to maintain, that there has not been adduced on this trial sufficient legal evidence to warrant a verdict against Mr. Smith.

At three o'clock in the morning the Dean of Faculty rose to address the jury on behalf of William Brodie.

—

The Dean of Faculty's Address to the Jury.

Dean of Faculty

The DEAN OF FACULTY—Gentlemen of the jury, the present trial exhibits in the person of William Brodie, in whose behalf I now address you, a singular phenomenon in the moral world: a man descended of an ancient and honourable family, left by a respectable father in opulent circumstances, and very far from indigence and temptation; educated in the manners and habits of a gentleman; bred to a reputable occupation, at the head of which he has frequently stood; and in virtue of that situation been a member of the Town Council of this great city; who, for a long series of years, has maintained an irreproachable character in society, and has often filled offices of honour and trust among his fellow-citizens, the duties of which he has discharged with attention and fidelity, standing at the bar of this High Court, accused of having leagued himself with the meanest and most abandoned of mankind, in the commission of a crime not less marked with moral depravity on the part of the perpetrators, than fraught with injury and danger to the public.

God forbid, gentlemen, that I were capable of wishing to press on your minds these circumstances in my client's once honourable and happy situation, with a view of creating in your minds an undue bias in his favour. Though your discernment were not, as I know it is, sufficient to secure you against the effect of such considerations, my feelings as a man, and a sense of my professional duty, would not allow me to resort to such arguments in opposition to justice, which is no respecter of persons.

Yet, gentlemen, there is a view in which I am entitled to call your attention to the former situation and circumstances of this unfortunate gentleman; for unfortunate I must call him, be the result of the present trial life or death. In deciding on evidence in support of a criminal charge, the former character of the prisoner, his probable temptations to commit the offence with which he is charged, must ever be a material consideration. A poor, forlorn wretch, without fortune, without friends, without education, without occupation, is he who is naturalised to support himself by private or open depredation on the public; and when such a person is accused, the minds of a jury, though they must presume his innocence, do not revolt at the charge as improbable. The situation of such men is charmingly described by an eloquent poet of this country—

The needy man who has known better days;
One whom distress has spited at the world;
Is he whom tempting fiends would pitch upon
To do such deeds, as make the prosperous men
Lift up their hands and wonder who could do them.[24]

My client was no such man. No circumstance in his situation has afforded a temptation to be guilty of such wrongs to risk his name, his life, for the acquisition of what his fortune, his profession, were fully adequate, honestly and fairly, to procure him.

In these circumstances you are called upon to examine the evidence in this case with the nicest accuracy. You are bound by more than common ties to require the fullest and most explicit proofs of such enormous guilt, so improbable, so unprecedented, before you find a verdict against a man who was once upon the same respectable footing with yourselves, and supposed to be governed by the same honourable principles.

But, gentlemen, while I mentioned the situation which Mr. Brodie once held in life, his family, his fortune, his friends, I must admit, however degrading to him the acknowledgment may be, that this unhappy man, instead of pursuing with industry the useful and reputable occupation by which his own fortune was acquired, and by which it might have been preserved, and with it his own peace, honour, and happiness, has for years past so far yielded himself to idleness and dissipation, and to what in the present age is too often the sad concomitant of such habits, an unhappy itch for gambling, as to lead him into the company of persons with whom, for any other purpose, he would have disdained to associate.

The unfortunate prisoner, Mr. Brodie, is by no means singular in his attachment to this vice; nor is it at all confined to the lower stations of life. People of the highest rank scruple not, in the course of their gambling, to mix with highwaymen and pickpockets, and to descend to practices of chicane and cunning which, in any other situation, they would themselves abhor. It was but the other day that a gentleman of Brighthelmstone, reputed worth three thousand pounds per annum, was detected in the very act of using loaded dice, and was obliged to fly the country for it; which is exactly Mr. Brodie's situation.[25]

But the gaming table levels all distinctions. There the high and the low, the rich and the poor, meet together. There, I admit—indeed, I have thought it necessary to prove the fact, in order to account for so strange a connection, from the bare existence of which strong arguments of his guilt have this night been drawn—there, I say, I admit that this unhappy, this misguided man, learned to endure, and at last to court, the society of those abandoned, those profligate wretches, who have this day come forward, in the most suspicious circumstances, to swear him their accomplice in the felony charged in the indictment.

But though the prisoner at the bar acknowledges with contrition these habits of folly and dissipation, and the disgraceful connection in which, to that extent, it unhappily involved him, yet he trusts it will appear, from a full consideration of the evidence, that

The very head and front of his offending
Has this extent; no more.

And he trusts to the candour and justice of you, gentlemen of the jury, that you will not allow this unfortunate connection to go further in your mind, as an ingredient of proof, than it justly ought; and far less to let suspicions supply the want of that legal evidence which the law of this free and happy country requires, in order to affect the life of any of its citizens, however dangerous to society the crimes charged may be, and however interested the public may be that they should be convicted.

Gentlemen, with these general observations in view, I intreat you to attend to the proof on which a verdict is asked from you against the life of this unfortunate man.

The whole evidence before you consists of three parts. In the first place, the evidence of Brown and Ainslie, who have acknowledged themselves guilty of the crime in question, and are the sole witnesses brought forward directly to fix the guilt on the prisoner; in the second place, in opposition to this there stands the direct proof of *alibi*, established by a number of unexceptionable witnesses; and lastly, the evidence arising from the various circumstances which are said to support and confirm the direct testimony of Brown and Ainslie, which, independent of such confirmation, is admitted to be deserving of little credit. Upon each of these parts I shall submit to you some remarks, trusting that you, gentlemen, and the honourable counsel on the other side of the bar, will correct me should I happen in any instance to mistake the import or nature of that proof which has been led in your hearing.

Upon the first part I have already, in the course of the trial, anticipated almost everything which relates to the evidence of Brown and Ainslie; I should therefore be ashamed to trouble you with more on that subject. I do not say that their being themselves accused of the crime in question should be a ground for totally rejecting their testimony, which the Court, proceeding on the present law and practice of Scotland, has allowed to be received. But this I will with confidence maintain, that the evidence of persons who, in the very outset of their testimony, confess the most enormous crimes, and thereby cover themselves with infamy as completely in the eye of reason as if they were convicted by sentence of a jury, can in no case be entitled to much credit, and when standing by itself is deserving of none at all.

But it is not on this alone that I impeach the testimony of these bad men; they stand in a situation different, very different, indeed, from other witnesses of that description—a situation to which I again entreat your best attention.

When Ainslie was first examined before the Sheriff, and for a long time afterwards, he persisted in maintaining the innocence of Mr. Brodie; nor was it till he learned that Brodie was apprehended, and till he was informed that to criminate him was the only means of saving his own life, that he uttered a syllable tending to infer the guilt of my client. This we offered to prove in the course of the trial, but a proof was refused by the Court.

The first testimony, therefore, which he gives in the matter is deliberately false. Is his after-information, or the evidence he has given this night, the better to be believed that it was wrung from him by the fear of death, or brought out of him by the hopes of life? It is vain to say that there is no proof that such means were used with him. There is real evidence that under these impressions he must have been when he delated Mr. Brodie. Well did he know that Mr. Brodie, from his unhappy connection with him and his associates, was suspected of being accessory to their guilt. He was not so blind as not to see that to the public prosecutor, whose duty it ever is to choose from various associates those whose situations make them the most striking examples of public justice, to accuse and convict such a person as Mr. Brodie was effectually to secure his own life.

It was a situation too powerful to be overcome even by much more virtue than the witness could boast of, and, unhappily for Mr. Brodie, his connection with the witness in scenes of another kind, while it suggested the accusation, procured it credit. I cannot ask you to believe without evidence that such a plot was laid, nor am I entitled to charge it. But surely witnesses in such circumstances should not lightly be believed. And doing so may lead to consequences of the most dreadful nature, as every man, unfortunate enough to have been innocently, perhaps, the companion of villains, may thus by falsehood and treachery be made their substitutes to the offended laws of their country. Ainslie's evidence, therefore, in such a situation, is not only suspicious, but altogether incredible.

The evidence of Brown is, if possible, still more unworthy of credit than that of Ainslie. A more hardened and determined villain can hardly be figured. You saw, gentlemen, the manner in which he gave his evidence. He appeared more like a man rehearsing and expatiating upon the patriotic acts he had performed for the good of his country than a criminal unfolding the black history of his own iniquities. You have it in proof that he was not only accused but convicted of a former felony, and sentenced to be transported; that a presentment by the grand jury stands yet against him for another felony; and that he was banished for theft by a sentence of the Justices of Peace of Stirlingshire, proceeding on his own confession.

He has no doubt received His Majesty's pardon. It has been obtained for him, at a very great expense, for the sole purpose of enabling him to be a witness in this cause. But though the Court has determined that this pardon, the crimes being committed in England, rehabilitates this man, and that his evidence is admissible; yet no pardon can restore his credibility, or render him an honest man. The pardon cannot alter the nature of the criminal; "can the Ethiopian change his skin, or the leopard his spots?" Is it possible that a King's pardon can restore purity of heart, rectitude, and integrity? Can "a piece of parchment with a seal dangling at it," a phrase employed on another occasion, perhaps with less force of application, turn wickedness into honesty, and transmute infamy into honour? The King has no such prerogative; this is the prerogative of the King of Kings alone, exerted only towards repenting offenders; and even with Him such change may well be accounted a miracle.

In the eye of reason, therefore, Brown is still a notorious convicted felon, an infamous, unrepenting villain, who, till the 28th July last, the date of the pardon, would not have been received as a witness even in a twopenny-halfpenny cause between man and man. And yet upon this evidence is now to depend the reputation and life of a once respected citizen! These things need only to be mentioned, gentlemen, in order to be fully felt, nor will I insult the understanding of so intelligent a jury by dwelling upon them for a moment longer.

But this, gentlemen, is not all. Mark the game which this man had to play, and in what manner he has played it. He had not, like Ainslie, only his accession to this offence to shake himself loose of; a sentence of transportation hung over his head. This sentence he has not obeyed; and the penal certification is in England, I suppose, as it is with us, capital. By accusing a person of such consequence as to make it worth the while of the servants of the Crown to make him King's evidence, he not only freed himself from trial for the offences committed here, but secured a pardon for the offence of which he stood convicted, as it was necessary, to qualify him to be a witness, that his former conviction be done away, and all his former crimes washed off in the fountain of Royal favour. A bribe of such magnitude flesh and blood could not resist. Thus, gentlemen, in addition to the profligacy of character, to the load of infamy under which this man laboured, you see the most powerful engines which can set in motion the human soul employed to drag him forward to an accusation which he had not originally made, and which, but for this, his conscience, hardened as it is, might have prevented him from ever making.

The Lord Advocate was pleased to commend this witness, as having spoken out from a desire of doing justice and being of service to his country. Did his appearance this day indicate any such feelings? Do not the circumstances in which he brought forward this accusation show the baseness of his views? He has sworn that at first he did not accuse Mr. Brodie. No; it was not till his return from England that he took this course, when, finding that the sacrifice of mean victims was not leading to any steps being taken to procure him a pardon, and that the other unhappy prisoner at the bar had confessed his own guilt, but without accusing Mr. Brodie, he (Brown) gave the lie to his first declaration by criminating that gentleman; and the pardon, which has this day procured admission to his testimony, was obtained for him. The measures of the public prosecutor in this respect were highly proper, believing, as he no doubt did, the testimony of this man. But I leave it to you, gentlemen, to consider whether it is possible for any witness to stand in more suspicious circumstances; and whether, as several of the judges have told you, that had his conviction been in Scotland instead of England, they would have rejected his testimony, notwithstanding the pardon, you should not so lay aside his evidence altogether in justice to the prisoner, who ought not to suffer for a distinction which, however founded in law, is contrary to common sense or reason when applied to the credibility of the witness, of which you alone are the judges.

I come now, gentlemen, to the direct proof of *alibi*. And here I readily confess that a proof of *alibi* is generally resorted to only upon the most desperate occasions; and that such proof, when it is in contradiction to facts clearly substantiated by real evidence or parole testimony beyond all suspicion, must yield thereto. But, gentlemen, this is by no means the case here. The *alibi* is established by the most direct and complete proof, in opposition to which nothing direct appears in evidence, unless the testimony of two witnesses, entitled to no credit from their characters, and swearing in circumstances the most suspicious. There are, indeed, other circumstances proved; with regard to which I am to address you afterwards. But these, if the depositions of Brown and Ainslie be laid aside, must appear to you so light when weighed against this evidence of *alibi* that they must kick the beam. The *alibi*, gentlemen, is thus proved.

You have, in the first place, the evidence of Mr. Sheriff. This gentleman, no doubt, is brother-in-law to Mr. Brodie; and it may be said that this circumstance renders his evidence suspicious. But Mr. Sheriff, gentlemen, is well known to many of you as a man of character and reputation, as a person of unblemished conduct, in a rank of life equal to many of yourselves. And I appeal to you, gentlemen of honour as you are, whether any of you, judging of this witness, as you would wish to be judged of yourselves, would for a moment indulge the thought that even to save the life of his wife's brother he would deliberately come forward to cast away his own soul? This gentleman deposes most expressly that he dined at Mr. Brodie's house on Wednesday, the 5th of March, the day on which the Excise Office was broke into, in company with two ladies and another gentleman; that he staid there till about eight o'clock; that Mr. Brodie during all that time was never absent from his company; and that he even asked the witness to stay supper.

Here is a direct contradiction to the evidence of Brown, who swore that Brodie called at Smith's in the afternoon of that Wednesday. Which of the two, gentlemen, are you to believe? But it is needless for me to ask the question. Were even the former circumstances urged against the credibility of this man's evidence not sufficient, you have him here convicted of the grossest perjury, if Mr. Sheriff is to be believed; for that gentleman has expressly sworn that they dined at a quarter past three o'clock, and that Mr. Brodie never left the company while the witness staid, which was till near eight o'clock.

It was asked on the other side of the bar how Mr. Sheriff, at this distance of time, came to recollect so precisely that it was upon Wednesday, the 5th of March, he dined with Mr. Brodie? The answer is obvious. It was publicly known upon the Monday following, and the witness has sworn he knew it, that Mr. Brodie was accused of being concerned in the robbery of the Excise Office. Was it not then natural—nay, would not the contrary have been altogether incredible—that Mr. Sheriff, having only four days to look back, should be able to recollect in a matter that touched so deeply the character, and might affect the life, of so near a relation, that he dined with him that very day on which that felony was perpetrated? Which of you, gentlemen, could not at this time recollect where you dined last Saturday or Sunday, and the precise time at which you left the company?

If, therefore, Mr. Sheriff is to be believed, and why he should not no reason can be suggested, the prisoner could not be present, as Brown and Ainslie have deponed he was, prior to the time Ainslie left Smith's to go to the Excise Office; which Ainslie has fixed at a quarter before eight; nor could he be with them at Smith's at all, as Brown swears they all left it a quarter of an hour after Ainslie, and immediately joined him at the Excise Office.

But Jean Watt depones that Mr. Brodie came to her house at eight o'clock on the Wednesday evening, when the eight o'clock bell was ringing; her reason for recollecting these circumstances, too, is a very good one, it being the last time that ever Mr. Brodie slept in her house. Her evidence is corroborated by the servant-maid, who depones exactly to the same purpose. And there is a circumstance, gentlemen, in the deposition of this witness which well merits your attention. Upon being asked what bell was ringing, she said it was the bell of the Tron Church. Here the counsel on the other side of the bar appeared to hug themselves upon the mistake into which they supposed she had fallen, by mentioning a bell which, from the distance, she could not possibly hear. But the matter was cleared up in a moment, when, on being asked where the Tron Church was, she replied, in the Parliament Close. This, gentlemen, is the natural simplicity of truth; this proves her to be no tutored witness, brought forward to rehearse a tale made up beforehand, or to assign fictitious causes of knowledge.

Both these witnesses concur in deposing that Mr. Brodie staid the whole night until next morning at nine o'clock in Mrs. Watt's house; and their evidence is corroborated by that of Helen Alison, who saw him coming down stairs at nine on the Thursday morning. The evidence of this good woman, Helen Alison, is accompanied with circumstances the most natural and striking, and is confirmed by James Murray, one of the sheriff-officers employed in the search on the Thursday morning, who swears to her having at that time mentioned Mr. Brodie's having been at Jean Watt's all the night of the Wednesday and morning of the Thursday preceding.

The whole of this evidence, taken together, affords a proof the most conclusive that Mr. Brodie could not be present at the robbery of the Excise

Office. You find him in his own house till the hour of eight; from that hour till nine on the Thursday morning you find him in the house of Mrs. Watt. It is impossible then that he could have been at Smith's a considerable time before the hour of eight, or that he could have been present at a robbery which took up an hour in the perpetration.

It was said, on the other side of the bar, that it was of no avail to prove an *alibi* which was merely confined to the city. This is strange doctrine, gentlemen, and perfectly new. That an *alibi* may be proved with greater certainty when the distance is greater than when it is small, I do not dispute; but does it follow that it may not be proved though the distance be ever so short? Suppose a felony to have been committed this day under that window, and that I should be accused of having been an actor in it. Could not I, gentlemen, bring sufficient evidence of an *alibi*, although within a few yards of the place where it was perpetrated? Could I not substantiate, by this numerous and respectable assembly, that I was here from nine in the morning till the present hour, employed in such a manner as to exclude the possibility of my being any way concerned in such felony? And could it be objected to such evidence that I had not proved myself absent from town, and that my *alibi* was confined to within a few feet of the place where the fact was committed?

It is to no purpose to say that the witnesses may not be accurate as to time, and that, making a small allowance for mistakes, the facts they swear to may be true, consistently with the evidence of Brown and Ainslie. For supposing Mr. Sheriff to have been mistaken as to the precise time he left the prisoner that night, he could not be mistaken as to his being constantly with him from the time of dinner till the time he left him, whatever it was; and this alone must defeat the testimony of Brown and Ainslie, who swear to the prisoner's having been there in the afternoon long before the meeting, previous to their setting out for the Excise Office, which cannot possibly be true, if Mr. Sheriff's evidence is to be believed.

Here, then, is the most unequivocal and positive proof that the prisoner, Mr. Brodie, could have no accession whatever to this robbery of the Excise Office, unless you, gentlemen, shall conclude that the whole of these witnesses, consistent as they are and corroborated by circumstances the most simple and natural, have perjured themselves wilfully and deliberately; while Brown and Ainslie, witnesses, from their character, unworthy of all belief and swearing in circumstances the most suspicious, are deponing in the utmost purity of truth and fairness.

Thus, then, gentlemen, the case would stand were it to be decided on the direct testimony of the witnesses on both sides weighed against each other. The circumstantiate proof, however, still remains to be considered, and I am free to confess that if it shall appear to you that these circumstances afford a chain of real evidence, either sufficiently independent of the direct depositions of Brown and Ainslie to prove the prisoner's guilt, or so fully to confirm their testimony as to remove the cloud of suspicion that hangs upon it, as to convince you that they must be speaking the truth and the witnesses to the *alibi* the reverse, your verdict ought to be against the prisoner.

But I humbly maintain that not any of those circumstances nor all of them put together are sufficient to entitle the evidence of such witnesses to credit, when the life of a man is at stake, even if the proof of *alibi* were out of the question, and far less in the face of that proof of *alibi*, which, if the witnesses have not deliberately perjured themselves, excludes even the possibility of the prisoner's guilt. For I hope to show that there is not one of those circumstances, suspicious as they may appear, that cannot rationally be accounted for without supposing the guilt of the prisoner, Mr. Brodie; nay, that some of them are totally inconsistent with the supposition of his having been guilty of this offence, whatever other errors his fatal connection with these miscreants may have led him into.

In considering the circumstantiate evidence, gentlemen, you are never to lose sight of the direct proof I had the honour just now of stating to you as to the *alibi*; and as each circumstance passes under your review, I entreat you to ask yourselves this question, whether it is so clear, so decisive, so totally irreconcilable with the possibility of the prisoner's innocence as to make the suspicious testimony of those infamous witnesses outweigh the proof of *alibi*, founded on the depositions of persons liable to objections on no reasonable suspicion?

The first circumstance founded on is the prisoner's connection with the perpetrators of this crime. I readily grant that it is clear from the evidence that Mr. Brodie was in habits of too great intimacy with these men. I acknowledge that he appears to have been too deeply engaged in courses of gambling and dissipation in their company and society. That his association with such characters was dishonourable to the reputation of my client, I do not deny.

But, gentlemen, this gambling connection is far from being any proof of his share of the guilt of the crime now charged against him and the other prisoner at the bar, though this circumstance, no doubt, gives possibility to a tale that, without it, would have been rejected at once as totally incredible. Had Mr. Brodie been in no way connected with Brown, Ainslie, and Smith, what could they have accused him in? When the hopes of life were held out to Brown and Ainslie, in order to procure a discovery of their confederates, however willing they might be to deceive the public prosecutor, they would have themselves seen that it was in vain to accuse a man as their associate who had never at any time been connected with them.

But though his having connected himself with them afforded a plausible colour to their charge, it does not follow that this connection affords either a proof or a presumption of Mr. Brodie's guilt; it is to be considered rather as the cause of his being accused. Many other persons, otherwise very respectable, are known to have gamed in company with these very men, but would this have been sufficient to criminate them had Brown and Ainslie thought proper to give them also up as their confederates in this dark business? The folly of haunting, for any purpose whatever, the company of such men is great indeed, but to subject the party guilty to the consequence of every enormity of which such associates may accuse him, on their bare testimony alone, would be a punishment far beyond the offence, as such men would never fail to find some unhappy associate of better rank than themselves to substitute as a sacrifice to the public for crimes to which he had no accession.

The next circumstance founded on in corroboration of the evidence of Brown and Ainslie, is the alleged proof by the oath of Grahame Campbell that Mr. Brodie was present with the gang at the house of Smith on the night the Excise Office was broken into, and left it in their company. The veracity of this witness I mean not to dispute, but I maintain it to be impossible that, if she be speaking the truth, the facts she swears to could happen upon that night, or if she did, it must be fatal to the whole evidence given by Brown and Ainslie, as it contradicts them in the most essential particulars.

This witness indeed swears that one night—for she fixes no precise time— soon before Mr. Brodie left this place, he, Brown, and Ainslie met at Smith's house before six o'clock; that they all left it about six; that between nine and ten they all returned; that they supped there, and remained about two hours. And she remembers particularly that Brown and Ainslie sat down to supper, but that Mr. Brodie stood all the time they ate their meal. But Brown and Ainslie expressly swore that, after coming out of the Excise Office, they did not see Mr. Brodie again that night, and that Brown did not meet with him till the Friday, when he for the first time got an opportunity of abusing him for having left his post. She differs from them also as to Mr. Brodie's dress, which she says was, when he came, an old-fashioned black coat, whereas Brown says it was his ordinary black coat, and that he wore a white surtout above it. Both these opposite stories cannot be true, and consequently the young woman has deponed to what happened on a different night, and her evidence does not corroborate that of Brown and Ainslie; or, if she swears to that night, she swears to facts totally inconsistent with the truth of part of their evidence at least, and thereby destroys the credibility of the rest of it.

The Lord Advocate has told you that this witness must be mistaken with regard to their supping, because she has also said that they had ate some fresh herrings or cold fowl before setting out. I cannot, for my part, see how their having taken this collation early in the evening can be any reason for their not supping betwixt nine and ten. And, at any rate, though she could have mistaken the smaller circumstance of their eating or not eating after their return, it is utterly incredible that she should have recollected their all being at Smith's together between nine and ten, and continuing together for two hours if, as Brown and Ainslie depone, they and Mr. Brodie never met that night after the time the two former went into the Excise Office.

The next circumstance founded on by the prosecutor is the departure of Mr. Brodie from this country, which is not only held out as a flight from justice, but as a flight applicable to this particular offence.

That the flight of a person accused of a crime may in some cases be a strong ingredient in a proof of his guilt, I readily acknowledge, but it is not necessarily so. If he has not been previously accused of that particular crime, and other reasons occur sufficient to account for his leaving his native country, the circumstance is at best equivocal.

In this case it cannot be denied that Mr. Brodie had strong reasons for taking this step separated from any consideration of guilt connected with this offence. His gambling connection with these men was too well known, and though nothing further could be proved against him, it must be a painful feeling for a man of any spirit to remain in that place where persons with whom he had been so intimate were taken up by public justice on charges of so heinous a nature. Joined to this, you find in evidence that a prosecution was depending before the magistrates of Edinburgh against my client for using loaded dice. I do not say, nor do I suppose that this prosecution was well founded, but the very report of such a charge, when added to the connection he had with these men, must have rendered his situation so disagreeable as to induce him to leave Edinburgh, at least for a time, or even to have resolved on settling in some foreign country, where his former folly and dissipation were unknown and where his professional skill might enable him to repair his shattered fortune. What were the real motives of Mr. Brodie it is not for man to judge, but, if his actions were equivocal, you are bound in charity, in justice, in humanity, to put the most favourable construction upon them.

Yet even when he abandoned this country, he does not appear to have conducted himself as one who never intended to return, or who was afraid of any consequences to himself, beyond the pain of enduring in his own country the loss of honest fame. He corresponds, as you find, with his friends in Edinburgh, and the whole tenor of his conduct seems to be such as might have been pursued by a person who intended only to retire out of view for a short time, till the clamour of a prejudiced public against him should cease. A flight under such circumstances and conducted in this manner can never be held as proof of guilt, or even as a circumstance sufficient to stamp credibility on the testimony of a witness base and profligate beyond all example, deponing under the strongest temptations to falsehood, unsupported by the direct testimony of any other witnesses, and directly contradicted by a proof of *alibi*, proved by a cloud of witnesses altogether free from suspicion.

With regard to the circumstance attending Mr. Brodie's departure, his conduct in London, on shipboard, and on the Continent, the evidence adduced by the prosecutor is in the highest degree lame and inconclusive. Indeed it ought totally to be rejected as not the best the prosecutor had it in his power to bring; and as to his being brought back to this country, the evidence is very defective. The evidence of Mr. Longlands consists chiefly of hearsay. Those persons who apprehended Mr. Brodie, who conducted him back to this country, are not produced as witnesses. Mr. Walker, who is said to have protected him in London; the owners of the ship, who are said to have altered the destination of the vessel to aid his flight; none of them are brought forward. And as hearsay evidence is only competent where the principal witness is dead or cannot be had, neither of which is here the case, I submit to you, gentlemen, whether any part of this evidence ought to have been received or ought now to be regarded by a jury.

I come now to the evidence arising from the letters said to be written by my client. Gentlemen, urgent as his case may be, I do not wish to strain anything or to evade any part of the proof. I do not mean to contest that these letters are of the handwriting of Mr. Brodie, although this point has been but slenderly proved. My client has not himself denied them; I shall admit them to be his. Now these letters contain nothing which can bring home to him the present charge. They prove that he was avoiding his native land; that he was anxious for the fate of these abandoned men; that he was afraid they might accuse him; but he expressly supposes a false accusation—an accusation that might equally involve the innocent persons he was writing to. In one passage he expressly asserts his own innocence. Yet the letters are written in full confidence, and without any seeming intention to hide anything.

It is true, indeed, that in one of these letters he says that he had no accession to any of their depredations except the last, which is laid hold of as a direct acknowledgment of the crime. But, gentlemen, supposing the word depredation could not be otherwise explained, where is the evidence that the crime in question was the last of which these abandoned ruffians were guilty? and if there were such, it would not be conclusive. The word depredation is generic, and may as well apply to the depredations of the gaming-table as to acts of theft or house-breaking; and as there is but too much reason from the evidence, particularly the process at the instance of Hamilton for defrauding him by false dice, to believe that this unhappy man was not altogether free from accession to depredations that may at the gaming table have been committed by those persons against such as were unfortunate enough to fall into their hands, why should you, gentlemen, to reach the life of a fellow-citizen, construe so equivocal an acknowledgment, couched in so general terms, as applicable to a particular act of guilt; for the proof of which, against this prisoner, you have nothing but the most exceptionable of all human testimony, contradicted by the most direct proof of *alibi*.

But this is not all. The terms of this acknowledgment, as repeated in the last of these two scrolls, exclude even the possibility that the prisoner could refer, or mean to refer, to the breaking of the Excise Office as the depredation to which he had an accession; for he expressly says that he lost ten pounds by it; but how, in the nature of things, is it possible that if he had been concerned in that affair he could have thereby lost ten pounds, or any sum whatever, seeing Brown and Ainslie have both sworn that the money was fairly divided, and that each of the parties concerned received four pounds and some old shillings for his share? To what other act of depredation, and whether to any committed at the gaming table, these words refer, it is not for me to suggest nor are you, gentlemen, bound to inquire; though it would seem that depredations at the gaming table are the only attacks upon the property of our neighbour that can be attended with patrimonial loss.

It is enough to exclude these scrolls, and also the letters, from operating as evidence of the prisoner's accession to the crime with which he is charged, that the only accession they acknowledge is inconsistent with the possibility of his guilt; and if he has been so far misguided as to have been concerned with those infamous persons in anything beyond that gambling connection, which he has all along admitted, it must have been some other offence not yet discovered, or not hitherto made the subject of prosecution; which, not being charged in the present indictment, could not have affected the prisoner, though a proof of it had come out in the course of his trial.

The only remaining circumstance brought in aid of the direct parole testimony is the different articles which have been found in the house of the prisoner or elsewhere, and which the prosecutor has attempted to connect with the commission of the act which is the subject of the libel. On this head I shall detain you but a moment, there not being the shadow of evidence to connect any one of them with the prisoner so as to afford a presumption, and far less evidence, of his guilt.

A dark lanthorn was found in his house, but there is not the appearance of evidence that it was used at the perpetration of the crime in question, or was ever out of Mr. Brodie's own house. The utensil itself is perfectly innocent. The useful part of it was found in the cock-pen, and it is well known that cocks are chiefly fed by candle-light. There were keys and pick-locks found in his house, but it was proved that these are the ordinary implements of his trade, and not one of those have been sworn to as having been used by the villains, who best knew and described the whole mystery of the iniquity. Nay, the only instruments that were used on that occasion in opening the locks or forcing the doors were found at the bottom of Allan's Close or Warriston's Close by the officers of justice, led by the other prisoner Smith to the hole in which they were concealed; and not one of those articles, being two crows, a key, a pair of curling irons, a coulter of a plough, and two wedges, is proved to have been in any way connected with Mr. Brodie, the three first of which Brown and Ainslie admit were carried to the scene of action by Brown and Smith, while the two last were stolen by themselves from a field near Duddingston.

True, indeed, it is, that a pair of pistols, which these witnesses say were the property of the prisoner, Mr. Brodie, were found in a fireplace in his house; but it is proved by the same witness that these pistols had not been in the prisoner's hands for a month before, when he had lent them to Smith; that they were in Smith's possession on the night libelled; and the sheriff-officers have proven that it was Smith himself who dug out these pistols in Mr. Brodie's house, which demonstrates that it was he who hid them there—a circumstance not very reconcilable with his considering Mr. Brodie as an accessory, as in that case he could not have chosen a more improper place to conceal them. In case of discovery, it would become the object of the earliest and most anxious search.

Gentlemen, these observations upon the proof on both sides I submit to your most careful and deliberate consideration. You have on the one side a direct and positive proof of *alibi*; which, if the witnesses are not foresworn, must preclude the possibility of the prisoner's guilt; and that these witnesses have departed from the truth there is not the shadow of reason to suspect. On the other hand, the whole direct evidence against the prisoner is the testimony of two witnesses, who, besides being destitute of all right to be believed as witnesses in any case, have been brought to give evidence in the present in circumstances of the very strongest temptation to convict my unhappy client whether innocent or guilty, as, but for their having accused him, one or both of them must have stood at this bar in his place. It is for you, gentlemen, to consider, under all the circumstances of the case, to which of those contradictory proofs you will adhibit your belief.

In the hands of an upright and intelligent jury I leave this unfortunate gentleman, confident that whatever verdict you shall pronounce will be the result of your ripest judgment, tempered, in case of doubt, with that tenderness with which it becomes you to decide when the fame and life of a fellow-citizen are at stake.

At half-past four o'clock in the morning the Lord Justice-Clerk proceeded to charge the jury.

The Lord Justice-Clerk (Lord Braxfield).
(From an Engraving by Beugo after the Portrait by Sir Henry Raeburn.)

The Lord Justice-Clerk's Charge to the Jury.

Lord Justice-Clerk

The LORD JUSTICE-CLERK—Gentlemen of the jury, the crime which is charged against the prisoners at the bar is of a kind the most hurtful to society. The situation of the pannels, and particularly one of them, is also exceedingly distressful. Mr. Brodie's father, whom I knew, was a very respectable man, and that the son of such a man—himself, too, educated to a respectable profession and who had long lived with reputation in it— should be arraigned at this bar for a crime so detestable, is what must affect us all, gentlemen, with sensations of horror. This unhappy situation seems to have arisen from a habitude of indulging vices which are too prevalent and fashionable, but it affords a striking example of the ruin which follows in their train.

That the Excise Office was broke into is not disputed. The question therefore is, who broke into it? Was it the pannels?

Now, to ascertain this point you have, in the first place, gentlemen, the evidence of Brown and Ainslie, and if they have sworn truth the prisoners must be guilty. To the admissibility of these witnesses there can be no objection. Were not evidence of this sort admissible, there would not be a possibility of detecting any crime of an occult nature. Had a corrupt bargain, indeed, been proved, by which they were induced to give their evidence, there might have been room for an objection to their admissibility. But no such bargain has even been alleged against the public prosecutor in the present case. And as to their being accomplices, this, gentlemen, is no objection at all. A proof by accomplices may display, it is true, a corruption of manners, which alone can render such proof necessary. But it is impossible to go into the idea that their testimony is therefore inadmissible.

Nor is there, in the present case, any reason to suppose that they were under improper temptations to give their evidence. Each of them was separately called upon by the Court, and it was explained to each of them that they ran no hazard unless from not speaking the truth, and that their being produced as witnesses secured them from all punishment, except what would follow upon their giving false evidence. Under such circumstances, you cannot suppose, gentlemen, that they would be guilty of perjury without any prospect of advantage to themselves, and merely to swear away the lives of these prisoners at the bar.

Their credibility, to be sure, rests with you, gentlemen; and if you find anything unnatural or contradictory in their evidence you will reject it. But there is nothing in it unnatural or contradictory. The principal objection was made against Brown, but his evidence is corroborated by that of Ainslie, and the evidence of Ainslie is again corroborated by that of Brown, and they are both corroborated by all the other circumstances deposed to. With regard to Smith, you have the best of all evidence against him, his own declarations, for it surely is not to be imagined that any man would criminate himself contrary to the truth. These declarations have been substantiated in your hearing, and where a *corpus delicti* is established, as in the present case, to which these declarations refer, there cannot be a doubt of their being the very best evidence, and therefore you can be under no difficulty of returning a verdict against him.

Gentlemen, to be sure these declarations are not legal evidence against Brodie. But they corroborate the evidence of Brown and Ainslie, who swear positively against him.

The evidence of Grahame Campbell likewise corroborates that of these witnesses. With regard to Mr. Brodie, she swears positively to his being present with them, dressed in an old-fashioned suit of black clothes. She seems, indeed, to be in a mistake about the prisoner's having supped at Smith's house that night, but the rest of her evidence is clear and explicit, and concurs precisely with what you have heard from the other witnesses.

The evidence of Brown and Ainslie likewise corresponds exactly with the deposition of James Bonar. Ainslie tells you that a man came running down the close, and it appears that when he opened the door Brodie set off with himself—and, indeed, to tell you the truth, I could not much blame him; and Mr. Bonar tells you that he went down the close at the very time when the robbery was going on, and that when he opened the door a man stepped out, of a description that exactly corresponds with the prisoner and the dress he had on that night.

It appears clear also, gentlemen, from the depositions of the sheriff-officers, that several articles were found upon the search in Brodie's house, which Brown and Ainslie depose to have been used in the robbery of the Excise Office; a pair of pistols, a dark lanthorn, keys, pick-locks, &c., and many of these last such as never were employed by Mr. Brodie in the course of his business. So that no doubt can remain in your mind of the truth of the facts sworn to by these two men, which are all consistent with, and corroborated by the other evidence.

The crime with which these prisoners are charged, gentlemen, was committed on Wednesday, the 5th of March. Two persons were taken up for it, and Brodie absconded. It is established by the evidence that he went to London, was afterwards put on board a sloop at night, and carried to Flushing; and that, upon search being made for him, he was apprehended at Amsterdam and brought back to this country. Gentlemen, when a person who is accused of a crime flies from justice, it affords a strong presumption of guilt. An innocent man would not fly without just cause. The prosecution against him for using false dice could not be the reason of his flight. Nay, he tells you himself in his declaration that he absconded because Smith and Ainslie were taken up.

The papers found in the trunk, gentlemen, and the two scrolls, all which have been proved to be of Mr. Brodie's handwriting, afford strong evidence against him. In one of the scrolls there is a fair and full confession of his direct accession to the robbery of the Excise Office. He says, "He never was directly concerned in any of their depredations, except the last fatal one." This is even a confession of more than is charged against him, for it must mean that he was concerned, though not directly, in their other depredations. It is impossible, gentlemen, to mistake the meaning of this expression, or that it can apply to anything else than the breaking into the Excise Office.

With regard to the *alibi*, gentlemen, it is no doubt proved by the oath of Mr. Sheriff that he was in Brodie's company from three o'clock of Wednesday, 5th March, till near eight at night, he having dined in Mr. Brodie's house that day along with three ladies, and a gentleman whose name he does not recollect. But then this rests entirely upon his evidence, and though I do not mean to say that he has sworn falsely, yet he is not a witness *omni exceptione major*, above all exception, being the brother-in-law of Mr. Brodie. Besides that, gentlemen, allowing the evidence of Mr. Sheriff, he is still only a single witness, and even in civil cases a fact cannot be established by the evidence only of one witness, especially where it is not supported by any other circumstances. At any rate, the evidence is not inconsistent with the guilt of the pannel, for the Excise Office was broke into after eight o'clock, and Mr. Sheriff was in his own house in St. James's Square about eight o'clock.

As to the evidence of Jean Watt, who swears that Brodie came to her house that night at eight o'clock, you are to consider, gentlemen, that although, to be sure, she is not his wife, yet she is his mistress; and love is often as deeply rooted between persons of that kidney as between lawful man and wife. And, as you see, gentlemen, that either she must be mistaken as to the hour or that the witnesses on the other side must be wrong, you are to determine with yourselves whether the witnesses for the prosecution brought forward by the Lord Advocate, who has no interest but to get at the truth, or this woman, and her servant-maid who concurs with her, are most entitled to belief. And you can have no doubt but that the presumption is greatly in favour of the witnesses for the Crown, who can be influenced by no motives but those of public justice.

This woman and her servant, Peggy Giles, have no doubt deposed that it was eight o'clock when Mr. Brodie came to their house; but, gentlemen, even supposing them to be swearing to what they think true, yet they still may be mistaken with regard to the precise time; and the mistake of an hour, or half-an-hour, would reconcile their evidences with the other proof you have heard. There is a bell rings at ten o'clock as well as at eight, and these witnesses may very probably have confounded the one with the other; for I have no doubt that Brodie did come to that house that night, and staid there till the next morning. Gentlemen, the law itself makes allowance for mistakes of this kind. Thus in the civil Court, in a competition between two arrestments, of which one, for instance, is at eight and another at nine o'clock, they are preferred *parri passu*, because the law supposes that the memories of witnesses may be so frail as not to distinguish short intervals of time with proper accuracy. So that you see, gentlemen, that even supposing these witnesses were willing to speak the truth, yet their evidence is completely reconcilable with the other depositions.

Upon the whole, gentlemen, taking all the circumstances of this case together, I can have no doubt in my own mind that Mr. Brodie was present at the breaking into the Excise Office; and as to the other man, Smith, as I have already said, there can be still less doubt as to him. If you are of the same opinion, gentlemen, you will return a verdict against both the prisoners; but if you are of a different opinion, and do not consider the evidence against Brodie sufficiently strong, you will separate the one from the other, and bring in a verdict accordingly.

At about six o'clock on Thursday morning, the Lord Justice-Clerk, having finished his charge to the jury, said that he hoped it would not be inconvenient for them to return their verdict at twelve o'clock that day; but, upon the suggestion of one of the jurymen, it was fixed to be returned at one o'clock.

The Court then pronounced the following interlocutor:—

The Lord Justice-Clerk and Lords Commissioners of Justiciary ordain the assize instantly to inclose in this place, and to return their verdict in the same place at one o'clock this afternoon, continue the diet against the pannels till that time, ordain the haill fifteen assizers and all concerned then to attend each under the pains of law, and the pannels in the meantime to be carried back to prison.

The Court then adjourned.

The Trial.

Second Day—Thursday, 28th August, 1788.

The Court met at one o'clock.

CURIA JUSTICIARIA S. D. N. REGIS, Tenta in Nova Sessionis domo de Edinburgh, Vicesimo Octavo die Augusti millesimo septingentesimo Octogesimo octavo, Per Honorabiles Viros; ROBERTUM M'QUEEN de Braxfield, Dominum Justiciarium Clericum; Dominum DAVIDEM DALRYMPLE de Hailes, Baronetum; DAVIDEM RAE de Eskgrove; JOANNEM CAMPBELL de Stonefield; et JOANNEM SWINTON de Swinton, Dominos Commissionarios Justiciarae dict. S. D. N. Regis.

Curia Legitime Affirmata.

INTRAN. William Brodie, sometime Wright and Cabinetmaker in Edinburgh, and George Smith, sometime Grocer there, both prisoners in the Tolbooth of Edinburgh.

PANNELS.

INDICTED and ACCUSED as in the preceding Sederunt.

The Court being again met, and the prisoners brought to the bar, the Clerk of Court called over the list of the jury, and all being present, the Lord Justice-Clerk asked them who was their Chancellor, upon which the Chancellor rose, and delivered their verdict to his Lordship, sealed with black wax.

The verdict being opened and read by the judges severally, they appointed it to be recorded. During this pause a deep silence prevailed.

The verdict being recorded, the Lord Justice-Clerk called upon the prisoners to attend to it, and it was then read aloud by the Clerk of Court as follows:—

> At Edinburgh the twenty-eighth day of August one thousand seven hundred and eighty-eight years.

The above assize having inclosed, did make choice of the said John Hutton to be their Chancellor, and of the said John Hay to be their Clerk: and having considered the Criminal Indictment raised and pursued at the instance of Ilay Campbell, Esq., His Majesty's Advocate, for His Majesty's interest, against William Brodie, late wright and cabinetmaker in Edinburgh, and George Smith, late grocer there, pannels,[26] with the interlocutor pronounced by the Lord Justice-Clerk and Lords Commissioners of Justiciary on the relevancy thereof together with the depositions of the witnesses adduced by the prosecutor for proving the same, and the several declarations libelled on, as also the depositions of the witnesses adduced for the pannel William

Brodie, in exculpation; they all, in one voice, find the pannels William Brodie and George Smith GUILTY of the crime charged against them in the said Indictment. In witness whereof their said Chancellor and Clerk have subscribed these presents upon this and the preceding page, place and date foresaid, in their name and by their appointment.

JOHN HUTTON, Chanr.
JOHN HAY, Clerk.

The LORD ADVOCATE—It is now incumbent upon me, my Lords, to move your Lordships to pronounce the sentence of the law against the prisoners at the bar.

Mr. WIGHT—My Lords, before your Lordships proceed to pronounce judgment, I have an objection to state on behalf of the prisoners at the bar, which, in my opinion, ought to prevent any judgment from passing upon this verdict.

My Lords, from the evidence taken in the course of this trial, it appears that the libel is insufficient, in so far as it charges "that the pannels did wickedly and feloniously break into *the* house in which the General Excise Office for Scotland was then kept," whereas it ought to have stated that they so broke into *one* of the houses so kept, describing such house particularly. For it appears from the proof that there were two separate and distinct houses in which the General Excise Office for Scotland was then kept, on the opposite sides of the court, and at a considerable distance from each other.

Besides, my Lords, supposing this uncertainty in the libel as to the *locus delicti* were insufficient to operate an arrest in judgment, yet no judgment can pass upon the verdict of the jury, on account of the uncertainty thereof, inasmuch as it finds in general terms the pannels guilty of the crime libelled; by which it is found that they have been guilty of breaking into the house in which the General Excise Office for Scotland was then kept, without distinguishing to which of the two before-mentioned houses the verdict applies. And the present plea in arrest of judgment deserves the greater consideration on this account, that the jury were called upon, by the manner in which the proof was conducted on the part of the pannels, to attend particularly to the circumstance of the Excise Office being kept in two separate and distinct houses.

The LORD ADVOCATE—My Lords, I am not a little surprised that an objection of this nature should be brought forward at this time. This plea resolves into an objection to the relevancy or form of the indictment, which ought to have been stated *in limine*. If the gentlemen on the other side of the bar meant to have stated any such objection as the present, they ought to have done it yesterday. But after they have allowed the indictment to pass without any such objection; after your Lordships have sustained it as relevant, and remitted it to the knowledge of an assize in common form; and when the jury have returned a verdict finding the prisoners guilty of the crime charged—there can be no room for any further proceeding, except to pronounce the sentence of the law upon the verdict so returned.

I do therefore, my Lords, altogether deny that it is competent, in this stage of the trial, to bring forward an objection such as the present, which ought to have been stated at first, and which your Lordships cannot now enter upon.

But, my Lords, even if the matter were open, the objection itself is altogether frivolous, for the house that was broke into, as stated in the indictment, was really and truly the house known by the name of the General Excise Office for Scotland at the time. It is indeed true that one or two of the clerks and inferior officers were accommodated in a small house within a few feet or yards of the large one, and which was joined to it by a wall like a wing. But this did not make them in any sense of the word two separate houses. The principal house which was broke into, was hired at £300 per annum of rent, and the small house at £8 per annum. This last was just as much a part of the General Excise Office as a kitchen separate from any house is a part of that house. And surely your Lordships would not cast an indictment which charged that a man's house was broke into, upon the ground that his kitchen was not joined to his house, which very often happens.

I therefore, my Lords, consider this as a very frivolous objection, and I know that the honourable counsel on the other side of the bar, who is, to speak in reply to me, knows too well the dignity of his character and the honour of his profession to insist seriously upon an objection so futile. Had this been the case of a poor man, my Lord, we would not have heard of this objection, and I do not see what title the rank and situation of this man can plead for troubling the Court with frivolous objections to the verdict of a jury after so long and so fair a trial.

The DEAN OF FACULTY—My Lords, I know what belongs to the dignity of my profession and the honour of my character as well as my Lord Advocate. [Here the Lord Advocate, laying his hand upon his heart, expressed, by the strongest gestures, that he meant to say nothing disrespectful to the Dean of Faculty, and was going to speak, when the Lord Justice-Clerk said that what my Lord Advocate had mentioned, so far from being derogatory to the Dean of Faculty, was a high compliment to him. The Dean of Faculty then resumed.] My Lords, I say that I know how I ought to conduct myself, both as a lawyer and a gentleman, and it is in the full conviction of performing my duty that I rise to enforce the present objection, which I think is such a one as ought to overturn this verdict.

It has been asked why this objection was not brought forward in an earlier stage of the trial—why it was not pleaded at the very outset, as sufficient to cast the indictment? It has been called a frivolous objection by my Lord Advocate. But many objections were styled frivolous by the gentlemen on that side of the table during the course of this trial, which your Lordships decided to be well founded. My Lords, it was impossible to plead it in this early stage, because the fact came out to be as stated in the objection only during the time that the proof in this trial was led. Though the circumstances might be known to us privately before, yet it was not substantiated by proof, and this surely is the proper time for stating an objection, the grounds of which only appeared in the course of the evidence, and could not possibly appear sooner.

With regard to the matter of fact in this case, I shall not detain your Lordships a moment. Nothing is clearer from the evidence than that there were two separate and distinct houses in which the Excise Office was kept at the time when the robbery was committed. Several of the witnesses have sworn to this, and it was admitted on the other side of the table. I therefore say, my Lords, that this verdict, which has found the prisoners guilty of breaking into the house in which the General Excise Office was kept, finds nothing.

It is in vain to say that these two houses belonged to one and the same office. If they are not under the same roof—which it is confessed these two houses are not—then it is of no importance how near they may be to each other, for neither of them is the house in which the Excise Office was kept, but only one of the houses employed for that purpose. His Grace the Duke of Buccleugh has two houses lying near each other, the house of Dalkeith and the house of Smeiton, both in the parish of Dalkeith. Would the verdict of a jury be good, which, upon the statement of an indictment that the house of the Duke of Buccleugh, lying within the parish of Dalkeith, was broke into, should simply find the pannel guilty? Surely not. It would be necessary to specify which of the houses was broke into, because an innocent man, who could prove an *alibi* with regard to the one, might not be able to prove it with regard to both, or, in short, because the libel is uncertain.

The Excise Office is now removed to the house lately possessed by Sir Laurence Dundas in the New Town of Edinburgh.[27] Suppose that part of the offices still remained in the former place, would it be sufficient to say that the house in which the General Excise Office is kept was broke into, when there were evidently two houses in which it was kept, one in the Old and one in the New Town? And the only difference betwixt that case and the present is that the distance is greater, for in both cases the houses are equally separate and distinct.

In the same way, for the sake of illustration, it was not till lately that I myself could find a house sufficiently convenient both for the purposes of business and accommodation of a numerous family. I had accordingly two houses, one in George Street and one in Princes Street, and I have done business in both of them. Now, would an indictment charging a person with having broken into the house of the Honourable Henry Erskine, Dean of the Faculty of Advocates, be sufficient, while I possessed two houses, to support a verdict which found the pannel in general terms guilty? It would not be enough to say that I employed both houses frequently for the same purposes, and that I could pass from the one into the other, though not without some little inconvenience of getting wet when it rained. This undoubtedly would not be sufficient, unless I could prove that both houses were one and the same; a verdict finding the pannel guilty of breaking into the house, could, from its uncertainty, apply neither to the one nor to the other.

My Lords, I will not detain your Lordships. The case is very short and simple, and without stating any further illustrations or arguments, I think that the prisoner cannot be more safe than in the opinions which your Lordships shall deliver upon so plain a point so fairly stated to you.

Lord HAILES—My Lords, I have great doubts concerning the competency of this objection, but it is a subject upon which I do not like to enter. I am indeed sorry that this objection has been stated, as it may flatter the prisoners with hopes which I am afraid are ill founded.

The merits of the objection itself appear to me very easy of discussion. The Dean of Faculty is mistaken with regard to the houses possessed by the Duke of Buccleugh, for they are not both in the parish of Dalkeith, as the house of Smeiton lies in the parish of Inveresk. But supposing they did both lie in the same parish, there is a great difference betwixt houses situated at some distance from each other and those which lie immediately contiguous, as is the present case. The small house adjoining to that principal one in which the Excise Office was kept is to be considered as a part of the same building, employed always for the same purpose, and used only for better accommodation.

I repeat it again, my Lords, that I have doubts whether or not this objection be now competent, but laying this out of the question, I am clear for repelling the objection, as the expression used in the indictment appears to me sufficiently descriptive of the place in which the General Excise Office was kept.

Lord ESKGROVE—My Lords, I am sorry that this objection has been stated, and I think it my duty to declare, for the sake of the prisoners at the bar, that I do not think it such as ought to induce them to hope that it will operate any change as to the verdict which has been returned this day.

It is my opinion, my Lords, that the objection itself, without entering into the question whether it be now competent to state it, cannot be listened to by the Court. The indictment states that the prisoners at the bar broke into the house in which the Excise Office was kept at the time when the robbery happened, and although a few offices may have been kept in the small house adjoining to the principal building, yet it cannot be denied that this separate tenement was considered as a part of the General Excise Office; and the witnesses themselves, who were examined upon this point have told us that had this small tenement been broke into instead of the principal house, they would have said that the Excise Office was broke into.

Upon this ground, I am clear for repelling this objection as not well founded, the whole building, which was called the Excise Office, being situated in the same place, and inclosed by the Commissioners so as to render its parts distinct from any other building.

Lord STONEFIELD—My Lords, I do not understand the bringing forward this objection at this time; it seems as if they wished to introduce the forms of the law of England. I think that the Lord Advocate has described in the indictment the place where the crime was perpetrated with sufficient accuracy, and therefore I am for repelling the objection.

Lord SWINTON—My Lords, among all the proceedings in this painful trial, the present motion gives me the greatest pain. It sets forth, first, that the libel charged the prisoners with wickedly and feloniously breaking into the house in which the General Excise Office for Scotland was then kept. The motion next sets forth that the verdict finds the prisoners guilty of the crime charged; and it concludes for an arrest of judgment, because the General Excise Office consists of more houses than one, as your Lordships will recollect from the proof taken before you yesterday.

One of the counsel yesterday stated himself as appearing not only in defence of the prisoners, but in defence of the law itself.

The motion, however, now made, if properly considered, tends to overturn the most valuable part of the law, namely, that part which gives this kingdom the security of jury trial. By the mode of trials long ago established, the libel is first of all to be read; the party accused is then at liberty to state his defences to the form of the indictment, and to the competency or relevancy of the charge; and it is the province of the judges to determine the law, that is, to decide upon the defences; which, together with the judgment upon them, must enter the record. The indictment and judgments upon it are then remitted to the knowledge of an assize. It then goes out of the hands of the judges, and the province of the jury commences, which is to try the truth of the facts, and to apply the law, that is, the judgment of the Court, to the facts, by returning such verdict as they think fit. That is their province. After they return their verdict, the cause comes back into the hands of the judges to pronounce the sentence of the law. But in doing so the only materials subject to their judgment are those which appear on the face of the record, that is, the indictment, the minutes of proceedings, and the verdict. They can take nothing else under their consideration; particularly, they have no power to look back into any part of the proof, or to take it under consideration in any manner.

In the present case, looking into the record, we see the indictment charges the prisoners with breaking into the house in which the General Excise Office was kept. We observe not in the proceedings any objections made to the form or the competency of the charge. The verdict finds the prisoners guilty. This is all that appears upon the face of the record. But what is now proposed to us by this motion? It is to look into our notes, or to recollect from our memory, that it was proved the whole offices of Excise were not precisely under one roof, and that there is a small adjoining house also made use of; and we are moved to arrest judgment, for that the libel is improperly laid, as it does not mention that there are more houses than one, and specify which of these were broke open.

Now, what does this amount to? Is it not a suggestion to the judges to look back into the proof, which is the whole province and privilege of the jury? If the judges, after a verdict, might look back into and consider the proof or any part of it in favour of the party accused, they might surely do the same thing to his prejudice, and in favour of the prosecutor. Is not this a mode of proceeding altogether incompetent? Is it not paving a way to make verdicts of no use, but our usurping a right to judge of the proof, independent of the verdict?—a proceeding which, I should think, is not only incompetent, but even criminal. Why did our ancestors establish the rules of proceeding which we have always observed? It was for the security of the lives and liberties of the subjects of this kingdom. The security handed down to us from our ancestors, we are bound to deliver unimpaired to our posterity.

My Lords, if I have expressed myself warmly upon this occasion, I hope your Lordships will forgive me. I am so clear upon the incompetency of this motion, that, however clear also upon the merits, yet, for the reasons given, I am not at liberty to say one word upon them.

The LORD JUSTICE-CLERK—I am clearly of opinion that it is not now competent to receive this objection, although the objection itself, were it received, is such as would have no weight with me. But I will not enter into its merits; it ought to have been stated in the pleading as a bar to the present trial; and the counsel for the pannels ought then to have brought forward whatever proof they had in order to prove the matter of fact. It is now impossible for the Court to review the evidence which has been led, and the objection must therefore be repelled.

The Dean of Faculty then moved the Court to allow the plea upon the arrest of judgment to be entered upon the record, which was allowed accordingly, and an interlocutor pronounced in the following terms:—

The Lord Justice-Clerk and Lords Commissioners of Justiciary having considered the foregoing debate, they repel the plea offered in arrest of judgment.

ROBT. M'QUEEN, I.P.D.

The LORD JUSTICE-CLERK—My Lords, you will now deliver your opinions as to the sentence to be pronounced against the pannels at the bar.

Lord HAILES—My Lords, after the verdict of the jury, nothing remains for us but the melancholy task of pronouncing the sentence of the law. It is not left in our option what punishment to inflict, for the law has declared the crime of which these unhappy men have been convicted, capital. It is my opinion, my Lords, that the prisoners at the bar be carried back to the Tolbooth of Edinburgh, and that they be there detained, and that they be executed on Wednesday, the first day of October next.

Lord ESKGROVE—My Lords, nothing is left for me but to agree with the opinion delivered by my honourable brother. I sincerely commiserate the fate of these unhappy men; one of them especially I pity much. Now that I see him at the bar, I recollect having known him in his better days and I remember his father, who was a most worthy man. Their situation is a miserable one, and I hope that it will have the effect to deter others from being betrayed into the same vices which have led these poor men to this ignominious condition.

Lords STONEFIELD and SWINTON delivered sentiments to the same purpose.

—

Address to the Prisoners and Sentence.

The LORD JUSTICE-CLERK then addressed the prisoners as follows:— William Brodie and George Smith, it belongs to my office to pronounce the sentence of the law against you. You have had a long and fair trial, conducted on the part of the public prosecutor with the utmost candour and humanity, and you have been assisted with able counsel, who have exerted the greatest ability and fidelity in your defence.

I wish I could be of any use to you in your melancholy situation. To one of you it is altogether needless for me to offer any advice. You, William Brodie, from your education and habits of life, cannot but know everything suited to your present situation which I could suggest to you. It is much to be lamented that those vices, which are called gentlemanly vices, are so favourably looked upon in the present age. They have been the source of your ruin; and, whatever may be thought of them, they are such as assuredly lead to ruin. I hope you will improve the short time which you have now to live by reflecting upon your past conduct, and endeavouring to procure, by a sincere repentance, forgiveness for your many crimes. God always listens to those who seek Him with sincerity.

His Lordship then pronounced sentence of death in the usual form, and the sentence having been recorded and signed by the judges, it was read aloud as follows:—

The Lord Justice-Clerk and Lords Commissioners of Justiciary, having considered the verdict of assize, dated and returned this twenty-eighth day of August, against the said William Brodie and George Smith, Pannels, whereby the assize all in one voice find them guilty of the crime libelled; the said Lords in respect of the said verdict decern and adjudge the said William Brodie and George Smith to be carried from the bar back to the Tolbooth of Edinburgh, therein to be detained till Wednesday, the first day of October next, and upon that day to be taken furth of the said Tolbooth to the place fixed upon by the magistrates of Edinburgh as a common place of execution, and then and there, betwixt the hours of two and four o'clock afternoon to be hanged by the necks, by the hands of the Common Executioner, upon a Gibbet, until they be dead; and ordain all their moveable goods and gear to be escheat and inbrought to His Majesty's use: which is pronounced for doom.

ROBT.	M'QUEEN.
DAV.	DALRYMPLE.
DAV.	RAE.
JO.	CAMPBELL.
JOHN SWINTON.	

The sentence having been read, Mr. Brodie discovered some inclination to address himself to the Court, but was restrained by his counsel. He thereupon respectfully bowed to the bench, and the pannels were removed to prison.[28]

The Court then rose.

APPENDIX I.

NOTE 1

This unhappy man was tried for sheep stealing in the year 1782, and condemned to be hanged. He afterwards received His Majesty's pardon conditionally that he should be transported for life. Government having adopted no plan for the transporting of felons from Scotland since the loss of America, he has, owing to that circumstance, been detained so long in prison; and I am sorry to add that he is not the only sufferer from the same cause.—*Morrison.*

NOTE 2

It is said that Mr. Learmonth very properly wrote immediately to the Sheriff-Clerk's office, and the intelligence was from thence sent to the Procurator-Fiscal, who at the time was in the playhouse. He immediately went out and set off with Mr. Williamson, the messenger, to Geddes's house in Mid-Calder, twelve miles from Edinburgh, and brought him in on Sunday morning with the letters.—*Creech.*

NOTE 3

On taking the precognition at the Sheriff-Clerk's chamber; a curious circumstance occurred respecting this black dog. Smith, the prisoner, was under examination, and the above witness, Kinnear, was also present. Kinnear had said to the Sheriff that he was at such a distance that he would not know the men, but he would know the dog, having been at one time near him. Soon after, a dog was making a noise and scraping at the door, which being opened, the above witness said, "There is the dog," and it ran and fawned upon Smith.—*Creech.*

NOTE 4

This witness was much affected on coming into Court. On passing her husband, the prisoner at the bar, she looked at him with much seeming agitation. He stretched out his hands, and, in a loud whisper, entreated her not to answer a word to any question that should be put to her.—*Creech.*

NOTE 5

A discrepancy here appears betwixt the above witness and a following witness, James Murray, who, with Middleton, accompanied the prisoner Smith to the place. Murray said at the foot of Allan's Close, below the Royal Exchange; and Warriston's Close is above the Exchange, or west, the other east. Since the trial, we were at pains to have an explanation of this inconsistency, and went with Middleton to the spot. He conducted us down Warriston's Close; and at the bottom of the steps at the foot of it, in the wall, immediately on the right hand, or to the east, and not three feet from the steps, he pointed out the hole where the iron crow and other instruments were found. He was asked how he and Murray came to disagree. He said it was true they went by Allan's Close, turned into Mary King's Close, and then went to the hole then, pointed out. In short, the one witness, Murray, describes it by the road they took, the other, Middleton, by the real situation of the place. Middleton acknowledged that he was wrong in saying Smith put in his hand and drew out the instruments. He was handcuffed, and could not stretch his arm. He only put his fingers to the mouth of the hole, to point it out, and Murray put in his arm as he immediately recollected after he left the Court. Both Middleton and Murray agree that the hole is the same where they found the iron crow, &c., and it is directly at the foot of Warriston's Close.— *Creech.*

NOTE 6

The further particulars of Mr. Williamson's search for Mr. Brodie are curious, and, having been favoured with them from Mr. Williamson himself, we here subjoin them:—

On Monday, the 10th of March, Mr. Williamson began his search at Mr. Brodie's dwelling-house, out-houses, &c. He searched several of Brodie's haunts in Edinburgh and Leith. He searched all the inclosed tombs in the Greyfriars Churchyard. The reason for this was that, some years ago, Brodie assisted one Hay, accused of a capital crime in making his escape from the Tolbooth of Edinburgh, and concealed him eight or ten days in one of these tombs till the hue and cry was over. Hay by this means got off, and has never since been heard of. When it was known, on Wednesday, that Brodie had gone off to London on the morning of Sunday, the 9th, Mr. Williamson was despatched after him. At Dunbar he learned that Brodie had passed there about four o'clock in the afternoon of Sunday, and traced him to Newcastle, where he took the "Flying Mercury" light coach for York and London. From the coachman he learned that a man answering Brodie's description had been set down at the end of Old Street, Moorfields, and did not proceed to the Bull and Mouth Inn, where the coach stops. Some persons of Brodie's acquaintance were examined, and from the declarations of some of them there was reason to believe that Brodie had gone to the Continent. Mr. Williamson went to Margate, Deal, and Dover, but got no intelligence of him.

On Mr. Williamson's return to London, he learned from Sir Sampson Wright's people that Brodie had been seen about Bedfordbury. Mr. Williamson repaired to the billiard tables, hazard tables, cock-pits, tennis courts, &c., &c. As no house could be searched without making oath to his being there, Mr. Williamson left the management to Sir Sampson's people, and returned, after eighteen days' search in London, to Edinburgh.—*Creech.*]

NOTE 7

On the journey from London to Edinburgh, Mr. Brodie was in good spirits, and told many things that had happened to him in Holland. He met with a Scots woman at Amsterdam, who asked him if he had been long from Scotland. She said that there was one Brodie, a citizen of Edinburgh, accused of robbing the Excise Office, and a great reward was offered for apprehending him. She little knew who she was speaking to, said Mr. Brodie. At Amsterdam, he fell in with the man who had committed a forgery on the Bank of Scotland. He (Brodie) said he was a very ingenious fellow. If he had not been apprehended he would have been master of the process in a week.

Mr. Brodie further told Mr. Williamson that the guide who had accompanied him and Mr. Groves from Amsterdam to Helvoetsluys had a fine repeating gold watch, which he (Mr. Brodie) said he could easily have possessed himself of at the time the man was taking leave of him, as he was then in liquor, and said he had often since regretted that he had allowed the fellow to go back with it.—*Creech.*]

NOTE 8

Grahame Campbell said they all came back to Smith's.—*Creech.*]

NOTE 9

This evening, Friday, Brown gave information, and Smith Ainslie, Mrs. Smith, and Grahame Campbell were taken into custody. The reason of Brown's giving the information is said to have been that he had seen the advertisement from the Secretary of State's Office that evening promising a reward and a pardon to the person who should discover the robbery of Inglis

& Horner's shop. Brown was under sentence of transportation in England, and in daily fear of apprehension. The reward and pardon were too powerful to be resisted, and he foresaw that it would be necessary for the prosecutor to obtain his pardon for his offence in England before he could be admitted as a witness. No wonder that the Lord Justice-Clerk said to him, after his examination, that he was a clever fellow.—*Creech*.]

NOTE 10

The witness seemed to be well acquainted with Macheath, but not with the "Beggar's Opera." The song is by Mat o' the Mint:—

"Let us take the road.
Hark! I hear the sound of coaches!
The hour of attack approaches;
To your arms, brave boys, and load!

"See the ball I hold!
Let the chemists toil like asses;
Our fire their fire surpasses,
And turns our lead to gold."

—*Creech*.

NOTE 11

It was clearly proved in the course of this trial, and I had otherwise occasion to know, that there was no information given against Mr. Brodie until Monday, the 10th, when the unfortunate Smith was examined. A warrant was immediately issued for apprehending him, and a search made, but it was too late; he had gone for London the preceding day.—*Morrison*.

Brown did not mention Brodie on the first information he gave, nor, indeed, till he had returned from England, where he had gone in pursuit of the goods robbed from Inglis & Horner's shop. It is supposed, by concealing Brodie, that he meant to have exacted money from him on his return to keep his secret. But Brodie was gone, and he then spoke out.—*Creech*.

NOTE 12

This is what is called flash language, and means swore to me.—*Creech.*

NOTE 13

This means the description of him which was inserted in all the Edinburgh and London newspapers, and was very minute and particular.—Creech.

NOTE 14

This is another specimen of the flash language, or slang. "And glimed the scrive" means "burned the letter."—*Creech.*

NOTE

As Brown, Ainslie, and Smith's maid all concur that Mr. Brodie was in Smith's house on the afternoon of the 5th March, it might appear a contradiction to this evidence; but Brown has fixed that it was very early in the afternoon, some time after two o'clock, but could not say that it was after three, so that it is evident the meeting in Smith's which they alluded to was between two and three o'clock, and before this witness came to dine with Mr. Brodie. *Vide* Brown's evidence.—*Creech.*

NOTE 16

From Mr. Brodie's house in Brodie's Close, Lawnmarket, to Bunker's Hill, is above half-a-mile, and Mr. Sheriff was home some minutes before eight o'clock.—*Creech.*

NOTE 17

Peggy Giles, Jean Watt's servant, said Mr. Brodie was in her mistress's house on Thursday afternoon; but this may have been between two and three o'clock, which she called afternoon, in the same way as Smith's maid said that the first meeting in her master's was on the Wednesday afternoon, which, by Brown's evidence, is fixed to have been before three o'clock.—*Creech.*

NOTE 18

A report having been circulated that Mr. Brodie was married to this witness in prison—which, if true, would have disqualified her from being a witness—it seems to have been the object of the Lord Advocate's questions to ascertain the fact.—*Creech*.

NOTE 19

The Tron Church is near a quarter of a mile from the Parliament Close.—*Creech*.

NOTE 20

This is inconsistent with Jean Watt's evidence, as she said that Mr. Brodie was not in her house at all on Thursday, and not till Saturday.—*Creech*.

NOTE 21

This doctrine, which had been suppressed in Scotland for above a century, was revived in the course of the memorable trial of Carnegie of Finhaven by the late Lord Arniston, the illustrious grandfather of the present Mr. Solicitor Dundas. Mr. Arnot, speaking of his address to the jury on that occasion, says, "He told them with a manly confidence, which conscious right inspired, that they must not be startled at the interlocutor of the Court." And they were not startled; for although the facts found relevant to infer a capital punishment were clearly proved, the jury returned a verdict finding the pannel not guilty, because they were of opinion that the interlocutor pronounced by the Court on the relevancy was erroneous.—*Morrison*.

NOTE 22

Old Norval's speech in "Douglas."—*Creech*.

NOTE 23

The particulars of this story are as follows:—Major had won a considerable sum of money the night before, and in such a manner as to lead to suspicion; two gentlemen, therefore, were determined to watch him, and for this purpose planted themselves the next night on each side of his chair, when, taking a proper opportunity, one of them seized his hand with the dice in it;

he grasped it close, and would not part with them; the other, seeing this, knocked him down, and in the fall the Major drew with him the first gentleman, who, however, would not let go his hold till he wrested the dice from him.

He then presented them to the company, who instantly saw and acknowledged the deceit. The Major was attempting some apology; the company would hear nothing, but turned him out of the room with every mark of disgrace and reprobation.

The dice were afterwards presented to the Jockey Club, in order to come to some resolution upon this transaction; but the President said, as their meeting referred more immediately to the turf, they could do nothing in it, but determined for themselves not to let such a man in future mix with them in any company. This resolution has been since followed in all the reputable gaming clubs.

Such is the story; the reflection that arises from it is very obvious, which is, that though this degraded man was so unfortunate for himself as to be detected, where is the public gaming table that is not surrounded with such? And where is the man, without a fortune of his own, that can spend from one thousand to two thousand pounds a year—as most of them do—without having some superiority, some dexterity, over the generality of those who play with them?

If the independent men who play at public tables and at public watering-places, therefore, were to look sharp, independently of the consideration of rank, title, or fortune, they would constantly find out more majors of this kind; but if they would do better, they would avoid all those places which are subject to the contamination of such men.—*Creech*.

NOTE 24

The using the word "pannel" in place of prisoner is peculiar to Scotland. It is believed it took its rise from the niche or place where the criminal was placed at the bar, which was called the pannel.—*Creech*.

NOTE 25

During the whole time of this trial the Court was uncommonly crowded, notwithstanding the fees of admission were raised so high as three, four, and five shillings. The heat was for a great part of the time intolerable; and the noise and tumult occasioned by orders given by the Court to clear certain parts of the house frequently interrupted the business of the trial. But the audience, who had paid for their places, were determined not to be turned out of them, and therefore maintained their ground, although the soldiers' bayonets were two or three times mentioned. The Court's being occasionally subjected to such inconvenience proceeds from the doorkeepers being allowed to extort money for admission—a practice directly contrary to the statute law of the land, and derogatory to the dignity of the High Court.

The doorkeepers not only demand money, but they claim the privilege of determining who shall and who shall not be admitted. They even presume to exclude, when they think proper, a great proportion of the members of the Court. Many of the agents during this trial were compelled to pay a crown for their places, and others were refused admittance upon any terms. When it is considered that the practice of the criminal law of Scotland cannot be acquired from books, nor by any one man in the course of his own experience, and that the agents are often charged with the conduct of trials, upon the issue of which the lives and fortunes of their fellow-citizens depend, it seems highly inexpedient, not to say unjust, to deny them the privilege of admission to the Court, where alone they can have an opportunity of acquiring that knowledge which it is highly necessary they should be possessed of. The Court, however, seem to think differently, for upon a late occasion, when an agent complained to them of being excluded by the doorkeepers, they gave him no redress.

I have only to add that if it is still thought proper to allow the doorkeeper to take money, a fare should be established for admission to each of the different parts of the house, in proportion to the accommodation they afford, that all His Majesty's lieges may be upon as equal a footing there as in other public places.—*Morrison.*

APPENDIX II.

A Brief Account of the Judges and Counsel Engaged in the Trial of Deacon Brodie.

Robert Macqueen, Lord Braxfield (1722-1799), eldest son of John Macqueen of Braxfield, Lanarkshire, sometime Sheriff-Substitute of the Upper Ward of that county, by his wife, Helen, daughter of John Hamilton of Gilkerscleugh, Lanarkshire, was born on 4th May, 1722. He was educated at the Grammar School of Lanark, and thereafter attended a law course at the University of Edinburgh, with the view of becoming a Writer to the Signet. He was apprenticed to Thomas Gouldie, W.S., Edinburgh, but finally decided to try his fortune at the bar, and, after the usual trials, was, on 14th February, 1744, admitted a member of the Faculty of Advocates. He was employed as one of the counsel for the Crown in the many intricate feudal questions respecting the forfeited estates which arose out of the Rising of 1745. He quickly gained the reputation of being the best feudal lawyer in Scotland, and is said to have received greater emoluments from his practice than any counsel before his time.

On the death of George Brown of Coalston, Macqueen was elevated to the bench on 13th December, 1776, and assumed the title of Lord Braxfield. He was also appointed a Lord Commissioner of Justiciary on 1st March, 1780, on the resignation of Alexander Boswell of Auchinleck. In the same year was published an anonymous "Letter to Robert Macqueen, Lord Braxfield, on his Promotion to be one of the Judges of the High Court of Justiciary" (Edinburgh, 12mo). This pamphlet, which points out the common failings of Scottish criminal judges is attributed by Lord Cockburn to James Boswell, the elder ("Circuit Journeys," 1889 p. 322).

On 15th January, 1788, Braxfield was appointed Lord Justice-Clerk, in succession to Thomas Miller of Barskimming, promoted to the Presidency of the Court of Session. He held that important office during a very interesting and critical period; and presided at the trials of Muir, Palmer, Margarot, and others, who were indicted for sedition in 1793-4, in the course of which he let fall from the bench the *obiter dictum*—"I never likit the French a' my days, but now I hate them." "In these," says Lord Cockburn, "he was the Jeffreys of Scotland. He, as the head of the Court, and the only very powerful man it contained, was the real director of its proceedings" ("Memorials of his Time," 1856, p. 116).

The conduct of Braxfield during these memorable trials has been freely censured in recent times as having been marked by great and unnecessary severity; but, the truth is, he was extremely well fitted for the crisis in which he was called on to perform so conspicuous a part, for by the bold and fearless front he assumed, he contributed not a little to curb the lawless spirit that was abroad, and which threatened a repetition of that reign of terror and anarchy which so fearfully devastated a neighbouring country. As an instance of his great nerve, it is recorded that Braxfield, after the trials were over, which was generally about midnight, always walked home to his house in George Square alone and unprotected, though he constantly commented openly on the conduct of the Radicals, and more than once observed in public, "They would a' be muckle the better o' being hangit!"

After a laborious and very useful life, Braxfield died at his residence, No. 28 George Square, Edinburgh, on 30th May, 1799, in the seventy-eighth year of his age, and was buried at Lanark on 5th June following. Before taking up his residence in George Square, Braxfield lived for many years in Covenant Close. He was twice married. By his first wife, Mary Agnew, niece of Sir Andrew Agnew, he had two sons and two daughters; by his second wife; Elizabeth, daughter of Lord Chief Baron Ord, he had no children.

Braxfield was the last of our judges who rigidly adhered to the old "braid Scots." "Hae ye ony counsel, man?" said he to Margarot, when placed at the bar, "Dae ye want tae hae ony appintit?" "No," replied Margarot; "I only want an interpreter to make me understand what your Lordship says!" "Strong built and dark, with rough eyebrows, powerful eyes, threatening lips, and a low, growling voice, he was like a formidable blacksmith. His accent and his dialect were exaggerated Scotch; his language, like his thoughts, short, strong, and conclusive" (Cockburn, "Memorials of his Time," 1856, p. 113). "Despising the growing improvement of manners, he shocked the feelings even of an age which, with more of the formality, had far less of the substance of decorum than our own. Thousands of his sayings have been preserved, and the staple of them is indecency, which he succeeded in making many people enjoy, or at least, endure, by hearty laughter, energy of manner, and rough humour" (*ib.* p. 114).

He domineered over the prisoners, the counsel, and his colleagues alike. Devoid of even a pretence to judicial decorum, he delighted while on the bench in the broadest jests and the most insulting taunts, "over which he would chuckle the more from observing that correct people were shocked. Yet this was not from cruelty, for which he was too strong and too jovial, but from cherished coarseness" (*ib.* pp. 115-116). Gerald, at his trial, ventured to say that Christianity was an innovation, and that all great men had been reformers, "even our Saviour Himself." "Muckle He made o' that," chuckled Braxfield; "He was hangit" (*ib.* p. 117). On another occasion he remarked to an eloquent culprit at the bar, "Ye're a vera clever chiel, man, but ye wad be nane the waur o' a hangin' " (Lockhart's "Life of Scott," 1845, p. 425).

Of Braxfield's grim humour in its unprofessional aspect but a few samples are now tolerable. Among these, however, is the following:—When a butler gave up his place because his mistress was always scolding him, "Lord!" exclaimed his master, "ye've little tae complain o'; be thankfu' ye're no marriet till her."

"Out of the bar or off the bench," says Stevenson, "he was a convivial man, a lover of wine, and one who shone peculiarly at tavern meetings." When Lord Newton, then Charles Hay, was one morning pleading before him, after a night of hard drinking—the opposing counsel being in the like case—Braxfield observed, "Gentlemen, ye maun just pack up yer papers and gang hame; the tane o' ye's riftin' punch and the ither's belchin' claret; there'll be nae guid got oot o ye the day!" ("Kay's Portraits," 1877, vol. i., p. 169).

A portrait of Braxfield by Sir Henry Raeburn was exhibited at the Raeburn Exhibition at Edinburgh in 1876, a delightful description of which is given by R. L. Stevenson in his essay, "Some Portraits by Raeburn" ("Virginibus Puerisque," 1881, pp. 219-236). Braxfield was, as every one knows, the prototype of Stevenson's "Weir of Hermiston," originally intended to be named "The Justice-Clerk," and of which the author wrote to Mr. Charles Baxter, on 1st December, 1892, "Mind you, I expect 'The Justice-Clerk' to be my masterpiece. My Braxfield is already a thing of beauty and a joy for ever, and, so far as he has gone, *far* my best character" ("Letters to his Family and Friends," 1899, vol. ii. p. 273)—a judgment which the literary world has unanimously sustained.

There is preserved in the Advocates' Library a copy of the "Latin Thesis on a Title of the Pandects" ("De Cadaveribus Damnatorum"), written by Sir Walter Scott on his admission to the Faculty of Advocates, 11th July, 1792, with the following dedication:—

VIRO NOBILI | ROBERTO MACQUEEN | DE BRAXFIELD, | INTER QUAESITORES DE REBUS CAPITALIBUS | PRIMARIO, | INTER JUDICES DE REBUS CIVILIBUS, | SENATORI DIGNISSIMO, | PERITO HAUD MINUS QUAM FIDELI JURIS INTERPRETI; | ADEOQUE, | IN UTROQUE MUNERE FUNGENDO, | SCELERA SIVE DEBITA SEVERITATE PUNIENDO, | SIVE SUUM CUIQUE TRIBUENDO ET TUENDO, | PRUDENTIA PARITER ATQUE JUSTITIA, | INSIGNI; | HASCE THESES JURIDICAS, | SUMMA CUM OBSERVANTIA, | SACRAS ESSE VOLUIT | GUALTERUS SCOTT.

SIR DAVID DALRYMPLE, Baronet, Lord Hailes (1726-1792), was the eldest son of Sir James Dalrymple, Bart., of Hailes, in the county of Haddington, Auditor of the Exchequer of Scotland, and Lady Christian Hamilton. He was born at Edinburgh on 28th October, 1726, and was descended on both sides from the nobility of the Scottish bar. His grandfather, Sir David Dalrymple, was the youngest son of the first Viscount Stair, Lord President of the Court of Session, and held the office of Lord Advocate for nineteen years. His mother was a daughter of Thomas, sixth Earl of Haddington, the lineal descendant of the first earl, who was Secretary for Scotland from 1612 to 1616, and President of the Court of Session from 1616 till his death in 1637. Dalrymple entered upon his studies at Eton, where he acquired a considerable knowledge of the classics and earned a high character for diligence and good conduct. He next re-visited his native city, and attended the University. From thence he went to Utrecht to study the civil law, returning to Edinburgh at the close of the Rising in 1746. He became a member of the Faculty of Advocates on 23rd February, 1748.

The death of his father two years later put Dalrymple in possession of a sufficient fortune to enable him to indulge his literary tastes; but he did not neglect his professional studies. As an oral pleader he was not successful. A defect in articulation prevented him from speaking fluently, and he was naturally an impartial critic rather than a zealous advocate. Notwithstanding this defect, he practised at the bar with much reputation for eighteen years. A great part of the business of litigation in Scotland at this time was conducted by written pleadings, and he became known as a learned and accurate lawyer.

On 6th March, 1766, Dalrymple was raised to the bench, on the death of George Carre of Nisbet, with the title of Lord Hailes, and on the resignation of George Brown of Coalston he was appointed a Lord of Justiciary on 3rd May, 1776. In the latter capacity he was distinguished for dignity, humanity, and impartiality—qualities at that times by no means characteristic of the criminal bench. The solemnity of his manner in administering oaths and pronouncing sentence specially struck his contemporaries. As a judge in the civil Court he was noted for his critical acumen and unswerving integrity. In knowledge of the history of law he was surpassed by none of his brethren, though among them were Elchies, Kaimes, and Monboddo.

At Edinburgh Lord Hailes lived some time in the Old Mint Close, foot of Todrick's Wynd; he next had a house in Society, Brown's Square; and latterly removed to New Street. His general residence was New Hailes, Musselburgh, where he died of apoplexy, the result of sedentary habits, on 29th November, 1792. Dr. "Jupiter" Carlyle, of Inveresk, who knew him well, summed up his character in a funeral sermon, in which he drew a glowing character of one of the most worthy of all the learned men of his time.

High as his memory stands as a judge, Hailes is better known to the world as a scholar and an author. His literary labours extend over a period of thirty-nine years—from the date of his first publication in 1751 till that of his last in 1790. "Lord Hailes was in some respects the very ideal of an historical inquirer. His mind was fair and dispassionate, and he reasoned with excellent logic. You will seldom find a mistake in fact or a conclusion not warranted by the premises in Lord Hailes' 'Annals.' He had some defects, too, and the greatest of them is an unnecessary and repulsive dryness of narrative" (Cosmo Innes' "Lectures on Scotch Legal Antiquities," 1872, p. 8). His publications, almost without exception, related to the early antiquities of Christianity, or to the antiquities and history of Scotland, which before his time had been critically examined by scarcely any writer. His most important work is the "Annals of Scotland," from Malcolm Canmore to Robert I., issued in 1776, and continued in 1779 to the accession of the House of Stuart. A complete catalogue of his numerous works will be found in "Kay's Portraits" (1877, vol. i., pp. 367-370).

SIR DAVID RAE, Baronet, Lord Eskgrove (1729-1804), son of the Reverend David Rae, of St. Andrews, an Episcopalian clergyman, by his wife, Agnes, daughter of Sir David Forbes of Newhall, was born in 1729. He was educated at the Grammar School of Haddington, and at the University of Edinburgh, where he attended the law lectures of Professor John Erskine (1695-1768). He was admitted a member of the Faculty of Advocates on 11th December, 1751, and quickly acquired a considerable practice. When the celebrated Douglas cause was before the Court he was appointed one of the Commissioners for collecting evidence, and in that capacity accompanied James Burnett (afterwards Lord Monboddo) and Francis Garden (afterwards Lord Gardenstone) to France in September, 1764, for the purpose of investigating the proceedings which had been carried on in Paris relative to the case.

After thirty years of honourable and successful practice at the bar Rae was, on the death of Alexander Boswell of Auchinleck, promoted to the bench on 14th November, 1782, and assumed the title of Lord Eskgrove, from the name of a small estate which he possessed near Inveresk. On 20th April, 1785, he was appointed a Lord of Justiciary, in succession to Robert Bruce of Kennet. He was one of the judges before whom Margarot, Skirving, and Gerald, the Reformers of 1793-4, were tried. He also assisted at the trials of the Rev. Thomas Fysche Palmer for sedition in 1793, and of Robert Watt and David Downie for high treason in 1794.

On the death of Lord Braxfield, Eskgrove was promoted to be Lord Justice-Clerk on 1st June, 1799, in which office he maintained the high character he had earned while at the bar. Henry Cockburn says of him, "Eskgrove was a very considerable lawyer; in mere knowledge probably Braxfield's superior. But he had nothing of Braxfield's grasp or reasoning, and in everything requiring force or soundness of head he was a mere child compared with that practical Hercules" ("Memorials of his Time," 1856, p. 118). He was created a baronet on 27th June, 1804; died at Eskgrove on 23rd October following, in the eightieth year of his age; and was buried in Inveresk churchyard. He married, on 14th October, 1761, Margaret, daughter of John Stuart of Blairhall, Perthshire, by whom he had two sons. Eskgrove resided for many years in No. 8 St. John Street, Edinburgh.

"A more ludicrous personage," says Cockburn, "could not exist. To be able to give an anecdote of Eskgrove, with a proper imitation of his voice and manner, was a sort of fortune in society. Scott in those days was famous for this particularly. Yet never once did he do or say anything which had the slightest claim to be remembered for any intrinsic merit. The value of all his words and actions consisted in their absurdity" ("Memorials," pp. 118-119). In the trial of Glengarry for murder in a duel, a lady of great beauty was called as a witness. She came into Court veiled, but before administering the oath Eskgrove gave her this exposition of her duty—"Young woman! you will now consider yourself as in the presence of Almighty God and of this High Court. Lift up your veil, throw off all modesty, and look me in the face" (*ib.* p. 122). Cockburn also narrates that, having to condemn certain prisoners who had broken into the house of Luss and assaulted and robbed the inmates, Eskgrove first, as was his almost constant practice, explained the nature of the various crimes, assault, robbery, and hamesucken—of which last he gave them the etymology; he next reminded them that they had attacked the house and the persons within it, and robbed them, and then came to his climax—"All this you did, and God preserve us! joost when they were sitten doon tae their denner!" (*ib.* pp. 124-125). Cockburn tells many other anecdotes of him, too numerous for quotation here; but it would be difficult to omit the following:—On condemning a tailor to death for stabbing a soldier, the learned judge aggravated the offence thus—"And not only did you murder him, whereby he was bereaved of his life, but you did thrust, or push, or pierce, or project, or propel, the lethal weapon through the bellyband of his regimental breeches, which were His Majesty's!" (*ib.* p. 122).

Lockhart states that, in Scott's young days at the bar, he was counsel for the appellant in a case before Eskgrove concerning a cow which his client had sold as sound. In opening his case Scott stoutly maintained the healthiness of the animal, which, he said, had merely a cough. "Stop there," quoth the judge; "I have had plenty healthy kye in my time, but I never heard o' ane o' them coughin'. A coughin' cow! that will never do—sustain the Sheriff's judgment, and decern!" ("Life of Scott," 1839, vol. i., p. 299).

A felicitous parody of Eskgrove's judicial manner is contained in the well-known "Advising" in the Diamond Beetle case ("Court of Session Garland," 1839, pp. 75-77). Notwithstanding, however, his many eccentricities, he was a man of the highest integrity of character, and "cunning in old Scots law."

JOHN CAMPBELL, Lord Stonefield (died 1801), son of Archibald Campbell of Stonefield, advocate, was admitted a member of the Faculty of Advocates on 9th January, 1748. He was subsequently appointed Sheriff of Argyll, an office which he long filled with the highest credit. On the death of Charles Erskine of Tinwald he was elevated to the bench, and took his seat, with the judicial title of Lord Stonefield, on 16th June, 1763. On the resignation of Francis Garden of Gardenstone, he was also nominated a Lord of Justiciary on 1st March, 1787. He resigned the latter appointment in the year 1792, but retained his seat on the bench till his death, which occurred at his residence in George Square, Edinburgh, on the 19th of June, 1801, after having been for thirty-nine years a judge of the Supreme Court.

It is somewhat remarkable that Stonefield and his two immediate predecessors occupied the same seat on the bench for a period of ninety years, Lord Royston having been appointed a judge in 1710, and Lord Tinwald in 1744.

Stonefield resided at one time in Elphinston's Court, and latterly at No. 33 George Square, Edinburgh. Of his professional history no record has been preserved. As a scholar his attainments were considerable, and as a judge his decisions were marked by conciseness of expression and soundness of judgment. He was a zealous and liberal supporter of every scheme tending to promote the welfare and improvement of his native country.

By his wife, Lady Grace Stuart, daughter of James, second Earl of Bute, and sister of the Prime Minister, John (the third earl). Stonefield had seven sons, all of whom predeceased him. The second of these was Lieutenant-Colonel John Campbell, whose memorable defence of Mangalore, from May, 1783, to January, 1784, arrested the victorious career of Tippoo Sultan, and shed a lustre over the close of that calamitous war.

JOHN SWINTON, Lord Swinton (died 1799), son of John Swinton of Swinton, Berwickshire, advocate, by his wife Mary, daughter of Samuel Semple, minister of Liberton. He was admitted advocate on 20th December, 1743, and appointed Sheriff-depute of Perthshire in June, 1754. In April, 1766, he became solicitor for renewal of leases of the Bishops' tithes, and solicitor and advocate to the Commissioners for Plantation of Kirks in Scotland, in place of James Montgomery, promoted to be Lord Advocate. He was elevated to the bench, with the title of Lord Swinton, on 21st December, 1782, on the death of Alexander Lockhart of Covington, and, on the promotion of Robert Macqueen of Braxfield in 1788, was also made a Lord of Justiciary. He retained both appointments till his death.

He died at his residence, Dean House, Edinburgh, on 5th January, 1799. Swinton married Margaret, daughter of John Mitchelson of Middleton, by whom he had six sons and seven daughters.

Swinton was the author of the following works:—(1) "Abridgment of the Public Statutes Relative to Scotland, &c., from the Union to the 27th of George II.," 2 vols., 1755; "to the 29th of George III.," 3 vols., 1788-90. (2) "Free Disquisition Concerning the Law of Entails in Scotland," 1765. (3) "Proposal for Uniformity of Weights and Measures in Scotland," 1779. (4) "Considerations Concerning a Proposal for Dividing the Court of Session into Classes or Chambers, and for Limiting Litigation in Small Causes, and for the Revival of Jury Trial in certain Civil Actions," 1789.

Lord Cockburn, in his "Memorials of his Time" (1856, pp. 112-113), remarks—"These improvements have since taken place but they were mere visions in his time, and his anticipation or them, in which, so far as I ever heard, he had no associate, is very honourable to his thoughtfulness and judgment." Cockburn also observes of Swinton—"He was a very excellent person; dull, mild, solid, and plodding; and in his person large and heavy. It is only a subsequent age that has discovered his having possessed a degree of sagacity for which he did not get credit while he lived. Notwithstanding the utter dissimilarity of the two men, there was a great friendship between him and Henry Erskine which it is to the honour of Swinton's ponderous placidity that Erskine's endless jokes upon him never disturbed."

SIR ILAY CAMPBELL, Baronet, Lord Succoth (1734-1823), was born on 23rd August, 1734. He was the eldest son of Archibald Campbell of Succoth, W.S., by his wife, Helen, only daughter of John Wallace of Ellerslie, Renfrewshire, and was admitted an advocate on 11th January, 1757. He soon obtained an extensive practice at the bar, and was one of the counsel for the appellant in the Douglas cause. During his last fifteen years at the bar his practice had become so great that there was scarcely any case of importance in which he was not engaged or consulted. In 1783 he was appointed Solicitor-General, in succession to Alexander Murray of Henderland, who was raised to the bench on 6th March of that year, but upon the accession of the Coalition Ministry he was dismissed, and Alexander Wight appointed in his place. Upon the fall of the Ministry he succeeded the Hon. Henry Erskine as Lord Advocate, and in the month of April, 1784, was elected to represent the Glasgow District of Burghs in Parliament, where he took an active share in all the important transactions of the time. The University of Glasgow conferred on him the degree of Doctor of Laws in 1784, and from 1790 to 1801 he held the office of Lord Rector.

After acting as Lord Advocate for nearly six years, on 14th November, 1789, Campbell was appointed President of the Court of Session on the death of Sir Thomas Miller, Bart., and assumed the judicial title of Lord Succoth. He was placed at the head of the Commission of Oyer and Terminer, issued in the year 1794, for the trial of those accused of high treason in Scotland at that disturbed period, and was highly commended by English lawyers for the manner in which he acquitted himself in that capacity.

Campbell held the office of Lord President for nineteen years, and upon his resignation was succeeded by Robert Blair of Avonton. He presided for the last time on 11th July, 1808, being the final occasion on which the old Court of Session, consisting of fifteen judges, sat together. After the vacation, the Court sat for the first time in two Divisions. On 17th September, in the same year, he was created a baronet. He died on 28th March, 1823, in the eighty-ninth year of his age.

Campbell was an able lawyer, but without any great forensic gifts. His written pleadings were models of perspicuity, force, and eloquence, but his speeches though admirable in matter, were unattractive in delivery. Cockburn says of him, "His voice was low and dull, his face sedate and hard. Even when heaving internally with strong passion, externally he was like a knot of wood" ("Memorials of his Time," 1856, p. 127). He was inferior to none of his brethren in depth of learning, and in private life was highly esteemed.

After his retirement from the bench, Campbell presided over two different Commissions appointed to inquire into the state of the Courts of law in Scotland, which he conducted with his accustomed industry and talent. He lived for many years in James's Court, Edinburgh; but during the later years or his life he chiefly resided at his paternal estate of Garscube, Dumbartonshire, where he kept his active mind continually engaged in various literary and agricultural pursuits.

Campbell was married to Susan Mary, daughter of Archibald Murray of Cringletie, one of the Commissaries of Edinburgh, by whom he had six daughters and two sons, one of whom only survived, viz., Sir Archibald Campbell of Succoth, Bart., who was appointed one of the Senators of the College of Justice on 17th May, 1809. He retired in 1825.

ROBERT DUNDAS of Arniston, Lord Chief Baron of the Court of Exchequer (1758-1819), the eldest son of Robert Dundas of Arniston the younger (1713-1787), Lord President of the Court of Session, was born on 6th June, 1758. He was a nephew of the celebrated Henry Dundas, Viscount Melville and Baron Dunira, whose daughter he afterwards married. He was educated for the legal profession, and became a member of the Faculty of Advocates on

3rd July, 1779, immediately after which he was appointed Procurator for the Church of Scotland. On the promotion of Sir Ilay Campbell to the office of Lord Advocate in April, 1784, Dundas, then a very young man, succeeded him as Solicitor-General; and on the elevation of the former to the bench as Lord President in November, 1789, the latter was appointed to supply his place as Lord Advocate, being then only in the thirty-first year of his age.

This office Dundas held for twelve years, during which time he sat in Parliament as a member for the county of Edinburgh (1790-6). He introduced into Parliament in 1793 a bill for defining and regulating the powers of the Commission of Teinds; but, from the little countenance extended towards it by the Ministry, and the strong opposition of the landed proprietors, he was under the necessity of withdrawing the measure.

Dundas conducted for the Crown, as Lord Advocate, the great prosecutions for sedition at Edinburgh in 1793-4; and on the occasion of the riots in connection with the Scottish Burghs Reform the windows of his house were broken by a hostile mob ("Kay's Portraits," 1877, vol. i., pp. 374-5). He acted as Dean of the Faculty of Advocates from 1796 to 1801; and, in 1799, was appointed Joint-Keeper of the General Register of Sasines for Scotland.

On 1st June, 1801, Dundas was appointed Chief Baron of the Exchequer in Scotland, on the resignation of Chief Baron Montgomery. He held this office till within a short time of his death, which happened at Arniston on 17th June, 1819, in the sixty-second year of his age. His town residence was in St. John Street, Canongate.

The excellences which marked the character of Dundas were many, and all of the most amiable and endearing kind. In manner he was mild and affable, in disposition humane and generous, and in principle singularly tolerant and liberal—qualities which gained him universal esteem. As presiding judge of the Court of Exchequer, he on every occasion evinced a desire to soften the rigour of the law when a legitimate opportunity presented itself for so doing. If it appeared to him that an offender had erred unknowingly or from inadvertence, he invariably interposed his good offices to mitigate the sentence. "It was in his private life, however," says his biographer, "and within the circle of his own family and friends, that the virtues of this excellent man were chiefly conspicuous, and that his loss was most severely felt. Of him it may be said he died leaving no good man his enemy, and attended with that sincere regret which only those can hope for who have occupied the like important stations and acquitted themselves as well."

Dundas was one of the few individuals who were spoken favourably of by the Rev. William Auriol Hay Drummond in his "Town Eclogue" (Edinburgh, 1804)—

"Let justice veil her venerable head,
When dulness sits aloft in robes of red!
Though with delight we upright Cockburn see,
With courteous Cullen, deep-read Woodhouselee;
In the Chief Baron's bland, ingenuous face,
Read all the worth and talent of his race."

Lord Cockburn, who knew him well, gives an interesting account of Dundas in his "Memorials of his Time" (1856, pp. 156-159).

WILLIAM TAIT, advocate (died 1800), was the second son of Alexander Tait, one of the principal Clerks of Session, who is referred to in "The Court of Session Garland" (1839, p. 50). He was admitted to Lincoln's Inn on 4th June, 1777, and became a member of the Faculty of Advocates on 19th February, 1780. He acted as Sheriff-depute of Stirling and Clackmannan from 1790 to 1797, and was member of Parliament for the Stirling District of Burghs from 3rd May, 1797, to 24th February, 1800. He died at Exeter on 7th January, 1800.

JAMES WOLFE MURRAY, Lord Cringletie (1759-1836), was the second son of Lieutenant-Colonel Alexander Murray of Cringletie, who had the honour to command the Grenadiers at the sieges of Louisburg and Quebec, and who died at Martinique in 1762. He was born on 5th January, 1719, and was named after General Wolfe, whose godson he was. He became a member of the Faculty of Advocates on 7th December, 1782, and was subsequently appointed Judge-Admiral. He was elevated to the bench on the death of Lord Meadowbank, and took his seat on 16th November, 1816, with the judicial title of Lord Cringletie, which he assumed from the family estate in Peeblesshire. He was also appointed one of the Commissioners of the Jury Court on 12th November, 1825. He resigned his judicial offices in 1834, and died on 29th May, 1836, in the seventy-eighth year of his age.

Murray married, on 7th April, 1807, Isabella Katherine, only daughter of James Charles Edward Stuart Strange, H.E.I.C.S., a godson of Prince Charles Edward Stuart, by whom he had four sons and nine daughters. He resided at one time in No. 17 Charlotte Square, Edinburgh.

References are made to Cringletie by Sir Walter Scott in his "Journal" (1891, pp. 322, 546); and an entertaining *jeu d'esprit* entitled "Notes by Lord Cringletie of the Trial, Douglas *against* Russell," will be found in "Appendix to the Court of Session Garland" (1839, pp. 7-14).

HENRY ERSKINE (1746-1817), second son of Henry David tenth Earl of Buchan, by his wife, Agnes, daughter of Sir James Steuart of Goodtrees, Bart., and brother of the celebrated Thomas Erskine, Lord Chancellor, was born in South Gray's Close, Edinburgh, on 1st November, 1746. After receiving some preliminary instruction at St. Andrews, he matriculated as a student of the United College of St. Salvator and St. Leonard on 20th February, 1760. In 1763 he proceeded to Glasgow University, and subsequently went to Edinburgh University, where, in 1766, he attended the classes of Professors Wallace, Hugh Blair, and Adam Ferguson. He was admitted a member of the Faculty of Advocates on 20th February, 1768. He had previously prepared himself for extempore speaking by attending the Forum Debating Society established in Edinburgh, in which he gave promise of that eminence as a pleader which he afterwards attained. His brilliant talents soon placed him at the head of his profession; and his legal services were as much at the command of the poor as of the wealthy. It was said of him that "no poor man wanted a friend while Harry Erskine lived."

In August, 1783, Erskine was appointed Lord Advocate in the Coalition Ministry, in succession to Henry Dundas (afterwards Lord Melville). He held office only for a very short period in consequence of a sudden change of Ministry in December, 1783. Anticipating this, Dundas offered, on the day of his appointment, to lend him his own silk gown, suggesting it was hardly worthwhile buying a new one; Erskine replied that no doubt Dundas's gown was made to fit any party, but that, however short his term of office might be, he declined to put on the abandoned habits of his predecessor. He was succeeded by Ilay Campbell (afterwards Lord President of the Court of Session).

On 24th December, 1785, Dundas having resigned the post of Dean of the Faculty of Advocates, Erskine was elected in his place by a decided majority, in spite of the influence of the Government, which was exerted against him. Lord Cockburn remarks, "His political opinions were those of the Whigs; but a conspicuous and inflexible adherence to their creed was combined with so much gentleness that it scarcely impaired his popularity. Even the old judges, in spite of their abhorrence of his party, smiled upon him; and the eyes of such juries as we then had, in the management of which he was agreeably despotic, brightened as he entered" ("Life of Lord Jeffrey," 1852, vol. i., p. 93).

Erskine had been annually re-elected Dean of Faculty since 1785; but in consequence of his having presided at a public meeting, held in Edinburgh on 28th November, 1795, to petition against the war, his political adversaries determined to oppose his re-election; and at the meeting of the Faculty on 12th January, 1796, Robert Dundas of Arniston, then Lord Advocate, was chosen Dean. Lord Cockburn, commenting on this incident, observes—

"This dismissal was perfectly natural at a time when all intemperance was natural. But it was the Faculty of Advocates alone that suffered. Erskine had long honoured his brethren by his character and reputation, and certainly he lost nothing by being removed from the official chair. It is to the honour of the society, however, that out of 161 who voted, there were 38 who stood true to justice, even in the midst of such a scene" ("Life of Jeffrey," vol. i., p. 94).

On the death of Lord Eskgrove in October, 1804, Erskine was offered the office of Lord Clerk Register, but declined it, refusing to separate his fortunes from those of his party. On the return of the Whigs to power in 1806 he once more became Lord Advocate, and was at the same time returned member for the Dumfries District of Burghs. The downfall of the Ministry in March, 1807, however, again deprived him of office, and the dissolution in the following month put an end to his Parliamentary career.

In 1811 Lord Justice-Clerk Hope was, on the death of Lord President Blair in May of that year, appointed his successor. Erskine, who was fifteen years Hope's senior at the bar, being disappointed of the preferment to which his professional standing and abilities entitled him, after a brilliant career extending over a period of forty-four years, retired from public life to his residence of Almond-dell in West Lothian, where he died on 8th October, 1817, in the seventy-first year of his age.

Erskine resided at one time in George Square, Edinburgh, next door to No. 25, where Scott's father lived. He removed in 1789 to No. 27 Princes Street.

Lord Cockburn calls Erskine "the brightest luminary at our bar," and adds, "His name can no sooner be mentioned than it suggests ideas of wit, with which, in many memories, the recollection of him is chiefly associated. A tall and slender figure, a face sparkling with vivacity, a clear, sweet voice, and a general suffusion of elegance, gave him a striking and pleasing appearance" ("Life of Jeffrey," vol. i., p. 91).

Erskine was twice married; his first wife, Christian, was the only daughter of George Fullerton of Broughton Hall, by whom he had several children, one of whom, Henry David, succeeded to the Earldom of Buchan on the death of his uncle, David Steuart Erskine, eleventh earl, in 1829. By his second wife he had no children.

ALEXANDER WIGHT, advocate (died 1793), was the son of David Wight, writer, Edinburgh. He was admitted a member of the Faculty of Advocates on 2nd March, 1754, and was subsequently appointed Solicitor-General to the Prince of Wales. He was vice-president of the Antiquarian Society, and was also a director of the Musical Society. He is said to have been long distinguished as an eminent counsel. He died at Edinburgh on 18th March, 1793.

Wight was well known as a legal writer, and was the author of "A Treatise on the Laws Concerning the Election of the Different Representatives sent from Scotland to the Parliament of Great Britain, with a Preliminary View of the Constitution of the Parliaments of England and Scotland before the Union of the two Kingdoms," dedicated to Lord Mansfield (Edinburgh, 1773, 8vo); and also of "An Inquiry into the Rise and Progress of Parliament chiefly in Scotland, and a Complete System of the Law Concerning the Election of the Representatives from Scotland to the Parliament of Great Britain" (Edinburgh, 1784, fol.).

Cosmo Innes says of him—"If we did not know his unhappy end we should call Alexander Wight, the author of the 'Law of Elections' and 'History of Parliament,' the most sensible, dispassionate, and clear-headed of historical lawyers. He had great difficulties to contend with in writing too early for correct versions of our Acts of Parliament; and the curious charters appended to his volume lose much of their value by the extreme inaccuracy of the only readings which he could procure" ("Lectures on Scotch Legal Antiquities," 1872, p. 11).

Wight is mentioned in "The Court of Session Garland" (1839, p. 47). It is recorded by Chambers in his "Traditions of Edinburgh" (1825, vol. ii., p. 159) that Wight was one of the earliest settlers in the New Town, where he built one of the houses on the south side of St. Andrew Square. He chose the situation of his new residence with a view to having the ancient part of the city still within sight, and especially St. Giles' steeple and clock, which had for many centuries directed the motions of his legal predecessors. In order to prevent the intermediate line of Princes Street from interrupting his beloved prospect, he purchased the feu of the ground which immediately intervened, and erected that house now occupied by the Sun Insurance Office (No. 40 Princes Street) upon it with a flat and low roof.

CHARLES HAY, Lord Newton (1747-1811), son of James Hay of Cocklaw, Writer to the Signet, was born in 1747. After the usual preparatory course of education, he passed as an advocate on 24th December, 1768, having just attained his majority; but, unlike most young practitioners, Hay had so thoroughly studied the principles of law that he was frequently heard to declare he was as good a lawyer at that time as he ever was at any later period. He soon became distinguished by his strong, natural abilities, as well as by his extensive knowledge of his profession, which embraced alike the minutest forms of the daily practice of the Court and the highest and most subtle points of jurisprudence. He was promoted by the Fox Administration to the bench on the death of David Smythe of Methven, and took his seat, with the judicial title of Lord Newton, on 7th March, 1806. This appointment was the only one which took place in the Court of Session during what was termed the reign of "The Talents"—a circumstance on which it is said he always professed to set a high value. Newton died unmarried at Powrie, in the county of Forfar, on the 19th of October, 1811.

Hay was, during the whole course of his life, a staunch Whig of the old school. Whilst at the bar his opinions were probably never surpassed for their acuteness, discrimination, and solidity; and as a judge he showed that all this was the result of such a rapid and easy application of the principles of law as appeared more like the effect of tuition than of study and laborious exertion.

Newton possessed an extraordinary fund of good humour, amounting almost to playfulness, and entirely devoid of vanity or affectation. There was a strong dash of eccentricity in his character, but his peculiarities appeared in the company of so many estimable qualities that they only tended to make him more interesting to his friends. He possessed great bodily strength and activity till the latter years of his life, when he became excessively corpulent.

Cockburn calls him "a man famous for law, paunch, whist, claret, and worth," and adds, "In private life he was known as 'The Mighty.' He was a bulky man with short legs, twinkling eyes, and a large purple visage; no speaker, but an excellent legal writer and adviser. Honest, warm-hearted, and considerate, he was always true to his principles and his friends. But these and other good qualities were all apt to be lost sight of in people's admiration of his drinking. His daily and flowing cup raised him far above the evil days of sobriety on which he had fallen, and made him worthy of having quaffed with the Scandinavian heroes" ("Memorials of his Time," 1856, p. 223).

Many quaint anecdotes are told of him. On the bench he frequently indulged in a certain degree of lethargy, and on one occasion a young counsel, who was pleading before the Division, confident of a favourable judgment, stopped his argument, remarking to the other judges on the bench, "My Lords, it is unnecessary that I should go on, as Lord Newton is fast asleep." "Ay, ay," cried Newton, "you will have proof of that by and by," when, to the astonishment of the young advocate, after a most luminous review of the case, he gave a very decided and elaborate judgment against him. The following story, says Chambers, was once told of Lord Newton by Dr. Gregory to King George the Third, who laughed at it very heartily. A country client coming to town to see him, when at the bar, upon some business, found on inquiry that the best time for the purpose was at four o'clock, just before Hay sat down to dinner. He accordingly called at the counsel's house at that hour, but was informed that Mr. Hay was then at dinner, and could not be disturbed. He returned the following day earlier in the afternoon, when to his surprise the servant repeated his former statement. "At dinner!" cried the enraged applicant; "did you not tell me that four was his dinner-hour, and now it wants a quarter of it!" "Yes, sir," said the servant, "but it is not his *this day's*, but his *yesterday's* dinner that Mr. Hay is engaged with. So you are rather too early than too late" ("Traditions of Edinburgh," 1825, vol. ii., pp. 276-277).

It is said that Newton often spent the night in all manner of convivial indulgences—drove home about seven o'clock in the morning—slept two hours—and mounting the bench at the usual time, showed himself perfectly well qualified to perform his duty. His Lordship was also so exceedingly fond of card-playing that it was humorously remarked, "Cards were his profession, and the law only his amusement."

Newton resided for many years at No. 22 York Place, Edinburgh. His portrait by Raeburn—"just awakened from clandestine slumber on the bench," as Stevenson describes it—is one of the most popular of that master's works.

JOHN CLERK, Lord Eldin (1757-1832), the eldest son of John Clerk of Eldin, the author of the well-known "Essay on Naval Tactics," and his wife, Susannah Adam, the sister of the celebrated architects of that name, was born in April, 1757. He was educated with the view of entering the Indian Civil Service, but, his attention having been turned to the legal profession, he was eventually apprenticed to a Writer to the Signet. After serving his indentures, he practised for a year or two as an accountant. Then, having qualified himself for the bar, he was admitted a member of the Faculty of Advocates on 3rd December, 1785.

Clerk speedily rose to distinction in his profession and acquired so extensive a practice that, it is said, at one period of his career he had nearly one-half of the business of the Court upon his hands. On 11th March, 1806, on the resignation of Robert Blair of Avonton, he was appointed Solicitor-General for Scotland, an appointment which he held during the twelve months that the Whig party was in office.

"Had his judgment been equal to his talent," writes Lord Cockburn, "few powerful men could have stood before him. For he had a strong, working, independent, ready head, which had been improved by various learning, extending beyond his profession into the fields of general literature, and into the arts of painting and sculpture. Honest, warm-hearted, generous, and simple, he was a steady friend, and of the most touching affection in all the domestic relations. The whole family was deeply marked by an hereditary caustic humour, and none of its members more than he" ("Life of Jeffrey," vol. i., p. 200).

His practice at the bar had been for some time falling off, and his health had already begun to fail, when, on 10th November, 1823, Clerk was appointed an Ordinary Lord of Session in the place of Lord Bannatyne. Assuming the title of Lord Eldin, he took his seat on the bench on 22nd November. As a judge he was not a success; his temperament was not a judicial one, and his faculties at the date of his elevation were seriously impaired. In consequence of the infirmities of age, after five years of judicial work, he resigned in 1828, and was succeeded by Lord Fullerton. He died unmarried at his house, No. 16 Picardy Place, Edinburgh, on 30th May, 1832, in the seventy-sixth year of his age.

As a pleader Clerk was distinguished by strong sense, acuteness, and the most profound reasoning. Throughout his entire career at the bar he delighted in defying, ridiculing, and insulting the bench; and it is recorded that his whole session was one keen and truceless conflict with judicial authority. He was in the habit of saying whatever he liked to certain of the Outer House judges without reproof. Lord Craigie especially, it is said, suffered a species of torture from him that required great natural sweetness and kindness of disposition to endure. Clerk, however, did not come off so well with the Inner House judges. On one celebrated occasion, having used somewhat threatening language towards Lord Glenlee in the Second Division, he was reluctantly compelled by the Court to make an apology to the offended judge. An account of this remarkable scene will be found in the "Journal of Henry Cockburn" (1874, vol. ii., pp. 207-210).

In politics Clerk was a zealous Whig. He had a considerable taste for fine arts, occasionally amused himself in drawing, painting, and modelling, and had such an attachment to cats that his house could always boast of half-a-dozen feline indwellers. It is recorded that at the sale of his collection of paintings and prints, which took place at his house in Picardy Place after his decease, the floor of the drawing-room gave way, and about eighty persons—one of whom was killed—"were precipitated into the room below, to the destruction also of much valuable china and numerous articles of vertu there displayed."

In appearance Clerk was singularly plain; he was also very lame, one of his legs being shorter than the other; and his inattention to dress was proverbial. It is related that when walking down the High Street one day from the Court he overheard a young lady saying to her companion rather loudly, "There goes Johnnie Clerk, the lame lawyer," upon which he turned round and said, "Na, madam, I may be a lame man, but no' a lame lawyer."

Clerk was of a convivial disposition, and the contrast between the crabbed lawyer and the good-natured *bon vivant* was strongly marked. He was a member of the Bannatyne Club, of which Sir Walter Scott was president. On one occasion, after the anniversary dinner, he is said to have fallen down-stairs and injured his nose, which necessitated his wearing a patch upon the organ for some time afterwards. On a learned friend inquiring how the accident happened, Clerk replied that it was the effect of his studies. "Studies!" ejaculated the inquirer. "Yes," growled Clerk; "ye've heard, nae doot, about *Coke upon Littleton*, but I suppose ye never heard tell o' *Clerk upon Stair!*"

An interesting account of Clerk's striking personality is given by Lord Cockburn in his "Life of Lord Jeffrey" (1852, vol. i., pp. 199-205).

ROBERT HAMILTON, advocate (1750-1831), son of Alexander Hamilton of Gilkerscleugh, Lanarkshire, distantly connected with the ducal house of Hamilton, was born about 1750. He entered the army, and was present at the Bunker's Hill and other battles of the American War of Independence, where he fought gallantly, and was severely wounded. He afterwards studied law, and became a member of the Faculty of Advocates in 1788. He was appointed Sheriff-depute of Lanarkshire in 1797, and on his resignation of that office, in 1822, he was appointed, on 5th February of the same year, Principal Clerk in the First Division of the Court of Session. He married a daughter of David Dalrymple of Westhall, one of the Senators of the College of Justice. He died on 13th December, 1831.

Hamilton was an intimate friend of his colleague, Sir Walter Scott, who mentions him frequently in his "Journal" as being incapacitated by gout from attending to his professional duties. They were both Commissioners of the Northern Lights, and went together the voyage of inspection in 1814, described by Lockhart ("Life of Scott," 1839, vol. iv., pp. 182 *et seq.*). Hamilton is noted therein as good humoured, even when troubled with the gout; "a very Uncle Toby in military enthusiasm, and a brother antiquary of the genuine Monkbarns breed." On his deathbed he gave Scott the sword he had carried at Bunker's Hill.

Hamilton was well known as a legal writer and genealogist. He had the credit of being a good lawyer, and, it is said, "obtained much professional reputation for getting up the case for Hamilton of Wishaw, which carried the peerage of Belhaven before a Committee of Privileges. He also drew up the elaborate claim of Miss Lennox of Woodhead to the ancient earldom of Lennox, an interesting production, but based on a fallacy."

APPENDIX III.

1. An | Account of the Trial | of | William Brodie, and George Smith, |
Before the High Court of Justiciary | on Wednesday, the 27th, and Thursday
| The 28th days of August, 1788; | For Breaking Into, and Robbing, | The
| General Excise Office of Scotland, | On the 5th Day of March last. |
Illustrated with Notes and Anecdotes. | To which is added, | An Appendix,
| Containing Several Curious Papers Relative | To the Trial. | By A Juryman.
| "Read this and tremble! ye who 'scape the laws." Pope. | Edinburgh: |
Printed for William Creech. M,DCC,LXXXVIII.

Quarto, pp. xii. + 125.

This, the first separate report of the trial, by William Creech, was published
on 5th September, 1788, "handsomely printed in quarto, price 3*s*., stitched,"
and contained three appendices. It was originally issued without the portrait
of Deacon Brodie, but on 15th September was advertised for sale as
"embellished with a full length portrait of Mr. Brodie by Kay, and reckoned
a very striking likeness. Price, 3*s*. 6*d*., or without the engraving, 3*s*. N.B.—
The former purchasers of the above account of this singular trial will be
accommodated with the print at 6*d*. each on sending their copies to Mr.
Creech's shop. A few copies of the print may be had separate from the trial
at 1*s*. each."

The advertisement adds—"A most shameful and mean piracy of the above
account of the trial has appeared. This may, no doubt, in some degree be
reckoned a compliment, as it is but fair to infer that when people are to pillage
they naturally wish to take what they think most valuable; but such a breach
of good manners and such a barefaced invasion of the right of another ought
to be exposed. Application has this day been made to the Lord Ordinary to
interdict the sale of this pirated edition." This intimation has reference to the
reports of the trial respectively published by Stewart and Robertson, as
aftermentioned.

2. The | Trial | of | William Brodie | Wright and Cabinet Maker in
Edinburgh, | and of | George Smith Grocer there, | Before the High Court
of Justiciary, | Held at Edinburgh on Wednesday the 27th, | and Thursday
the 28th August 1788; | For breaking into the General Excise-office at Edin-
| burgh on the 5th of March last. | Containing | The Evidence at Large for
and against the Prisoners; | Accurate Statements of the Pleadings of the
Counsel; | And the Opinions of the Judges on many | important Points of
Law: | With the Whole Proceedings. | By Æneas Morrison, Writer in

Edinburgh; | And Agent appointed by the Court to conduct the | Defence of George Smith. | Edinburgh: | Printed for Charles Elliot, Parliament Square; | and Sold by C. Elliot and T. Kay, No. 332 Strand, | London; and all Booksellers in Town and Country. | M,DCC,LXXXVIII.

Octavo, pp. viii. + 279.

Morrison's report of the trial, which is much the most accurate and complete, was published on 6th September, 1788. The editor writes in his preface, "It was thought better to state the proceedings by way of dialogue, in the same manner as all the English trials are published, than in the form of narrative—the usual manner or collecting both the depositions of witnesses and the pleadings of counsel in Scotland." This was an innovation which rendered the report more interesting and valuable than its competitors. An account of the trial by Charles Elliot, the publisher, had been announced, but it was arranged that Morrison should prepare it, Elliot furnishing him with his MS. and publishing the book.

It is interesting to know from a contemporary account that Deacon Brodie, while in prison after his sentence, "has read all the publications respecting his trial, and has given it as his opinion that Mr. Elliot's account was the best."

The advertisement states—"There will be published on Monday an appendix to this trial, which will be given gratis. Those who have already got copies may send for the appendix." With regard to this appendix, Morrison has a note that he had originally intended publishing certain interesting documents in his report, but had been informed by a friend of Brodie's "that Mr. Creech had engaged upon his honour not to publish anything in his account of the trial, either in the form of anecdote or otherwise, that did not occur in the course of the trial itself." Creech, however, published some additional matter, and Morrison considered "he was entitled to put the purchasers of his account on a footing with those who had purchased Mr. Creech's." The three appendices given in the first edition of Creech's report were therefore issued by Morrison, as above mentioned.

3. Extract from the Accounts of the | Trial | of | William Brodie and George Smith, | Before the High Court of Justiciary, | on Wednesday, the 27th and Thursday the 28th Days of August, 1788, | For Breaking Into, and Robbing | The | Excise Office of Scotland, | On the 5th Day of March last. | Illustrated with Notes and Anecdotes. | Containing also, | Several Curious Papers | Relative to the Trial; | as also, several | Transactions of the Criminals. | "*Read this and tremble! Ye who 'scape the laws.*" Pope. | Edinburgh: | Printed by A. Robertson, Foot of the Horse Wynd. | M,DCC,LXXXVIII.

Octavo, pp. vi.+72.

The advertisement of this account of the trial, which was published on 15th September, 1788 states—"The whole will be neatly printed on a fine paper and new type in three numbers at 9d.; the second number will be published on Saturday, the 20th; and the third on Friday, the 25th curt. And an additional number, price 3d., containing several occurrences, &c., from the day of their sentence till the 2nd of October next. *N.B.*—Commissions duly answered, for ready money only."

This was one of the pirated editions referred to by Creech, and is a literal reprint or his first edition of the trial.

The *Edinburgh Evening Courant* of Thursday, 18th September, 1788, gives the following account of the interdict whereby Creech endeavoured to stop the sale of this and Stewart's edition.:—"This day a new case in literary property was tried before Lord Dreghorn. Mr. Creech applied for an interdict against two piracies of his account of Brodie and Smith's trial. The interdict was granted, and parties were heard this day at eleven o'clock. Mr. Creech has sent up copies to Stationers' Hall by the mail-coach, with orders to enter the book in Stationers' Hall, according to the Act of Parliament 8th of Queen Anne; but the certificate of entry was not yet arrived. Lord Dreghorn declared both the copies complained on were gross piracies, but as the words of the Act of Parliament were express, he was sorry he could do nothing else than remove the interdict to the sale of the piratical copies until the certificate of entry was produced, and a new interdict might then be applied for, with action of damages. By this judgment it is necessary that the book be entered in Stationers' Hall before publication."

In advertising Part II. for sale the publisher made the following announcement:—"When Mr. Robertson published the first number of the above trial he copied it from Mr. Creech's account of it, not knowing or suspecting it to be property; but being since convinced that it is so, he applied to Mr. Creech for liberty to go on with his future numbers, which he obligingly consented to, although possessed of the certificate of the entry in Stationers Hall. The public will be regularly served, as advertised, with their numbers."

4. A Full Account of the Trial of William Brodie and George Smith, Before the High Court of Justiciary, on the 27th and 28th Days of August 1788, for Breaking into the Excise Office; With an Account of several other Depredations committed by them and their Associates. Edinburgh: J. Stewart, Lawnmarket, 1788. (Price, 1s. only.)

This was the other "piratical copy" of Creech's first edition, which was published on 15th September, 1788. No copy of the book is contained either in the British Museum or any other public library, so far as has been ascertained, and the above particulars are taken from a contemporary advertisement.

The publisher announced on 18th September—"J. Stewart informs his friends and the public that the interdict applied for by Mr. Creech was this day removed by the Lord Ordinary, and the sale goes on as formerly."

5. Anecdotes | and other | Curious Informations | concerning | William Brodie and George Smith; | also, of | James Falconer and Peter Bruce, | For Breaking into and Robbing the Dundee Banking | Company's Office, in Dundee, | With other Occurrences, since they received their Sentence till their | Execution. | Edinburgh: | Printed by A. Robertson, Foot of the Horse Wynd. | MDCCLXXXVIII. | Where may be had, the Trial in three Numbers, price 9d. | Also, | a striking likeness of William Brodie, price 3d.

Octavo, pp. 16.

Published on 2nd October, 1788, the day after the execution. It consists of two of Creech's appendices, together with some additional particulars concerning the prisoners not given by Creech.

6. An | Account of the Trial | of | William Brodie and George Smith, | Before the High Court of Justiciary, | On the 27th and 28th days of August, 1788; | For Breaking Into, and Robbing, | The General Excise Office of Scotland, on the 5th day of March last. | Illustrated with Notes and Anecdotes; | and the Portraits of Brodie and Smith. | To which is added, | An Appendix, | Containing several Curious Papers relative to the Trial; | and the Persons Tried. | By William Creech, | One of the Jury. | *Read this, and tremble! ye who 'scape the laws.* | Pope. | Second Edition. | Edinburgh: | Printed by and for the Author; | and sold in London by | T. Cadell in the Strand. | M,DCC,LXXXVIII.

Octavo, pp. xxii.+ 288.

This second edition of Creech's report, revised and corrected, was published on 3rd October 1788. The paragraphs in Smith's declarations, omitted in the former edition as having no immediate relation to the trial, were here given in full, and three further appendices were added to those contained in the first edition. The volume included the portrait of Deacon Brodie, already published, and an additional portrait, entitled "Smith at the Bar," also by Kay. The publication of this edition was delayed some days in order to give an account of the behaviour of the criminals at their execution.

7. The | Edinburgh Magazine, | or | Literary Miscellany. | Volume VIII. | [Quotation.] | Edinburgh: | Printed for J. Sibbald:—And sold by J. Murray, | London. | 1788. 8vo.

Report of the Trial—Monthly Register for August, pp. 114-120. Other references—pp. 101, 146-148.

8. The | Scots Magazine. | MDCCLXXXVIII. | Volume L. | [Quotation.] | Edinburgh: | Printed by Murray & Cochrane. 8vo.

Report of the Trial—August, pp. 365-372; September, pp. 429-437. Other references—pp. 358-359, 514-516.

9. The | Gentleman's Magazine: and | Historical Chronicle. | Volume LVIII. | For the Year MDCCLXXXVIII. | Part the Second. | [Quotation.] | By Sylvanus Urban, Gent. | London: | Printed by John Nichols, for David Henry, late of St. John's | Gate; and sold by Eliz. Newbery, the corner of St. Paul's | Church-yard, Ludgate-street. 1788. 8vo.

References—pp. 648, 829, 925.

10. The | Annual Register, | or a View of the | History, | Politics, | and Literature, | for the Year 1788. | [Device.] | London: | Printed for J. Dodsley, in Pall Mall. 1790. 8vo.

References—Vol. xxx., pp. 207, 214-215.

11. Traditions | of | Edinburgh. | By | Robert Chambers. | Vol. I. [II.] | Edinburgh: | Printed for W. & C. Tait, Princes Street. | MDCCCXXV. Post 8vo.

References—Vol. i., pp. 194-195.

12. The | Book of Scotland. | By | William Chambers. | [Quotation.] | Edinburgh: | Robert Buchanan, 26, George Street; | William Hunter, 23, Hanover Street; And | Longman, Rees, Orme, Brown, and Green, | London. | MDCCCXXX. 8vo.

References—pp. 327-328.

13. Minor Antiquities | of | Edinburgh. | By the Author of | "Traditions of Edinburgh," &c. | Edinburgh: | William and Robert Chambers, | Waterloo Place. | MDCCCXXXIII. Post 8vo.

References—pp. 165-168.

14. Reminiscences | of | Glasgow | and the West of Scotland. | By | Peter Mackenzie. | Vol. I. [II., III.] | Glasgow: | John Tweed, 11 St. Enoch Square. | MDCCCLXVI. 8vo.

References—Vol. ii., pp. 60-113.

15. A Series | of | Original Portraits | and | Caricature Etchings | By the late | John Kay, | Miniature Painter, Edinburgh | with | Biographical Sketches and Illustrative Anecdotes | In two volumes | Vol. I. [II.] | [Device.] | Edinburgh: Adam and Charles Black | MDCCCLXXVII. | (All Rights Reserved.) 4to.

References—Vol. i., pp. 96, 119, 141, 256-265, 399; vol. ii., pp. 8, 120-121, 286.

16. Edinburgh | Picturesque Notes | By | Robert Louis Stevenson | Author of "An Inland Voyage." | With Etchings by A. Brunet-Debaines | From Drawings by S. Bough, R.S.A., and W. E. Lockhart, R.S.A. | And Vignettes by Hector Chalmers and R. Kent Thomas. | Seeley, Jackson, and Halliday, 54 Fleet Street, | London. MDCCCLXXIX. Folio.

References—pp. 14, 35.

17. Cassell's | Old and New Edinburgh: | Its History, its People, and its Places. | By | James Grant, | author of "Memorials of the Castle of Edinburgh," "British Battles on Land and Sea," etc. | Illustrated by numerous Engravings. | Vol. I. [II., III.] | Cassell & Company, Limited: | London, Paris, and New York. | (All rights reserved.) N.D. [1884.] | 4to.

References—Vol. i., pp. 112-116, 217; vol. ii., 23; vol. iii., 367.

18. Etchings | Illustrative of | Scottish Character | and Scenery | By the late | Walter Geikie, R.S.A. | Sir Thomas Dick Lauder's Edition | with | Additional Plates and Letterpress | Edinburgh William Paterson | 1885 4to.

References—pp. 113-119.

19. Memorials of Edinburgh | In The Olden Time. | By | Sir Daniel Wilson, LL.D., F.R.S.E., | President of The University of Toronto, | Author of "Prehistoric Annals of Scotland," etc. | Second edition | [Device.] | Volume I. [II.] | Edinburgh and London: Adam & Charles Black, | 1891. | 4to.

References—Vol. i., p. 222; vol. ii., 23.

20. Deacon Brodie | or the Double Life | a Melodrama | In Five Acts and | Eight Tableaux. | By W. E. Henley | and R. L. Stevenson. | London: William Heinemann. | MDCCCXCVII.

Square 16mo, pp. viii.+182.

This play, of which Stevenson had prepared various drafts—the earliest in 1864—was first privately printed in 1880. A revised edition was printed "For Private Circulation Only" in 1888. The play was first published in "Three

Plays by W. E. Henley and R. L. Stevenson," 1892; afterwards in "Four Plays," 1896, and separately, as above, in 1897, as volume i. of "The Plays of W. E. Henley and R. L. Stevenson."

The play was first produced at Pullan's Theatre of Varieties, Bradford, on 28th December, 1882. The subsequent occasions on which it was performed were as follows:—At Her Majesty's Theatre, Aberdeen, in March, 1883; at the Prince's Theatre, London, on 2nd July, 1884; at Montreal, on 26th September, 1887; followed by a series of representations at Quebec, Toronto, Boston Philadelphia and other cities; and at the Star Theatre, New York, on 1st December, 1887. The cast of the play as performed in London and at Montreal is given in "Three Plays," 1892, and in subsequent editions.

21. Romantic | Edinburgh | By | John Geddie | London | Sands & Company | 12 Burleigh Street, Strand, W.C. | 1900. Crown 8vo.

References—pp. 22, 52, 69, 70, 106, 161.

22. Deacon Brodie | or | Behind The Mask | By Dick Donovan, | Author of "A Detective's Triumphs" [etc.] | [Device.] | London | Chatto & Windus | 1901 | (Rights of Translation reserved).

Crown octavo, pp. vi. + 258.

A novel founded upon the career of Deacon Brodie, and, so far as ascertained, his only appearance in fiction.

23. Edinburgh | and its Story | By | Oliphant Smeaton | [Device.] | Illustrated by | Herbert Railton | and J. Ayton | Symington | 1904 | London: J. M. Dent & Co. | New York: The Macmillan Co. 4to.

References—pp. 171, 224.

Reports of and comments upon the trial appeared in the three contemporary Edinburgh newspapers, viz., *The Caledonian Mercury*, *The Edinburgh Advertiser*, and *The Edinburgh Evening Courant.*

APPENDIX IV.

THE BRODIE FAMILY BIBLE.

THIS unique volume was recently acquired in the course of business by Mr. Richard Cameron, bookseller, Edinburgh. On finding it to be the family Bible of Convener Francis Brodie, father of the notorious Deacon Brodie, Mr. Cameron communicated his discovery to the Town Council, by whom it was purchased for the city on 28th June, 1904, and placed in the Edinburgh Municipal Museum, where it now finds a fitting resting-place among many other interesting memorials of the old burghal life.

This volume is valuable as throwing light upon the antecedents of Deacon Brodie, as to which little was previously known. It is a fine copy of the folio edition of the Holy Bible, printed by James Watson, the famous Edinburgh printer, in 1722, and comprises the Old Testament, the Apocrypha, the New Testament, and King James' version of the metrical Psalms. The book-plate of Francis Brodie appears within the front board of the book.

Francis Brodie has inserted between the Old and New Testaments a manuscript register of births, baptisms, and deaths occurring in his family, beginning with his own birth in 1708, and that of his wife, Cicel Grant, in 1718, their marriage in 1740 the births of their eleven children, most of whom died in infancy, and the deaths of other relatives.

It is noteworthy that the entry relating to the birth of his eldest child, William, has been cut out of the register, and the vacant space filled with blank paper. This was probably done in 1788, at the time of the Deacon's trial and execution, which took place six years after the death of his father. There still, however, remains in the register a record of William's birth. An entry appears with reference to the change of the calendar by Act of Parliament in 1752, whereby the Gregorian was adopted in place of the Julian calendar. In view of this, the events previously entered are repeated in accordance with the altered dates, each being eleven days later. In this new list the birth of the eldest son, William, is noted as occurring on 10th October, 1741.

The death of Francis Brodie on 1st June, 1782, is recorded by his daughter, Jean Brodie. Various later entries appear relating to members of the family, terminating in 1839 with the funeral letter of Jacobina Brodie (Mrs. Sheriff). Jean Brodie was the sister who kept house for the Deacon; and Jacobina Brodie was the wife of Matthew Sheriff, upholsterer in Edinburgh, who gave evidence at the trial in defence of his brother-in-law. Deacon Brodie refers to both sisters in his letters, which were produced in evidence against him.

The following is a copy of the entries above referred to, the original orthography being preserved throughout:—

Edinburgh, the 24 June 1708, was born I Francis Brodie, now Wright and Glass: Grinder in Edinburgh, Son to Ludovick Brodie, Writer to the Signet, and Hellen Grant his Spouse, was baptised by the Reverend Mr. Innes, in presence off

Edinburgh, the 17 August 1718, was born betwixt 11 and 12 att night, Cicel Grant (now my Spouse) Daughter to William Grant,

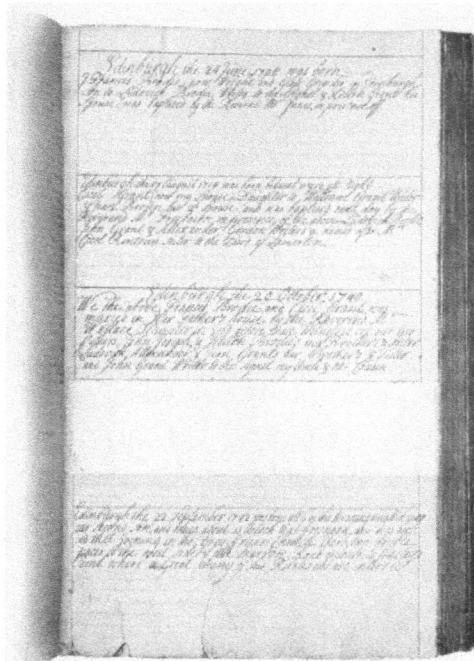

Facsimile of first page of MS. Register in the Brodie Family Bible.
(From the original in the Edinburgh Municipal Museum.)

Writer, and Jean Broun, his 2d spouse, and was baptised nixt day by the Reverend Mr. Freebairn, in presence of the above Ludovick Brodie, John Grant and Allexander Gordon, Writers &c., named after Mrs. Cicel Rentoun, Sister to the Laird of Lamerton.

Edinburgh, the 20th October 1740, We the above Francis Brodie and Cicel Grant was maried in Her Father's house by the Reverend Mr. Wallace, Minister in Edg. before these witnesses, viz., our two fathers, John, Joseph, and Hellen Brodie's my Brother's and Sister, Ludovick Allexander, and Jean

Grant's her Brother's and Sister, and John Grant, Writer to the Signet, my Uncle and her Cousin.

[Here followed the entry of the Deacon's birth, which has been cut out of the page, as above mentioned.]

Edinburgh, the 22 September, 1742, was born att 6 in the morning being Wednesday, our Second Son and deied about 11 oclock that Forenoon and was buried that evening in the Greyfriars Church Yard, two double paces to the West side of the narrow road opposite to Harley's Tomb, where a Great many of his Relations are interred.

Edinburgh, the 18 October 1745, was born betwixt 7 and 8 in the morning, being Friday, Hellen Brodie, our third child, and was baptised that same afternoon by the aforesaid the Reverend Mr. Mathieson, Minister in Edg., in presence of her two Grand Fathers, Hellen Brodie her Aunt, Ludovick Grant her Uncle, and John Grant, Writer, her granduncle, named after Hellen Brodie, her Grand Mother by her Father (who died the 15 December 1725).

The above Hellen Brodie contracted a sore throat, which in a few days occasioned her death on the 13th of August 1746 att 11 oclock forenoon, being Weddnesday, and was buried the nixt day in the evening att the above place beside her Brother. She was 9 months and 20 days old and a very agreeable Child.

Edinburgh, the 1st November 1747, was born 10 minutes after 5 in the morning, being Sunday, Ludovick Brodie, our Fourth Child and was Baptised that same afternoon by the Reverend Mr Glen, Minister in Edinr. in presence of his two Grand Fathers, Hellen Brodie his Aunt, and Ludovick Grant his Uncle, named after Ludovick Brodie his Grandfather.

The above Ludovick Brodie took a Chincouch, which in six weeks occasioned his death on the 14th of August 1748 att 12 oclock Forenoon, being Sunday, and was buried the nixt day in the evening att the above place beside his Brother and Sister. He was 9 month and 14 days old and a very agreeable, Strong Child.

Edinburgh, the 16th Jully 1749, was born half an hour after six in the morning, being Sunday, Francis Brodie, our Fifth and was Baptised that same afternoon by the Reverend Mr Glen, Glen, Minister in Eding., in presence of his Grandfather Ludovick Brodie, Hellen Brodie his Aunt, Ludovick Grant and John Brodie his Uncles, &c. Named after myself.

Edinburgh, the 16th October 1750 was born half an hour after Twelve in the morning, being Tuesday, Ludovick Brodie, our sixt Child and was baptised that same afternoon by the Reverend Mr Wallace, Minister in Eding, in presence of his two Grand Fathers, Hellen Brodie his Aunt, Mrs. Grant his Aunt, and Mrs. Grant his half Aunt, John Grant his grand Uncle, and John Brodie his Uncle, named after Ludovick Brodie his Grand Father.

By Act of the British Parliament, the Gregorian Kallender was introduced in Place of the Jullian, and in consequence of this, the day after the 2d of September (by leaving out eleven days) was the 14th of September, which makes the forementioned events to fall on the following days. viz.—

Francis Brodie (above designed) was born upon the 6 Jully 1708.

Cicel Grant, my Wife, was born the 28 August 1718.

We were married the 1st November, 1740.

Our First Child, William, was born, the 10 of October 1741.

Our Second Child was born and he died the 4 of October 1742.

Our third Child, Hellen, was born the 30 October, 1745 (her Grand Mother by the Father, whom she was named after died the 27 December, 1725) and she died the 25 August 1746.

Our Fourth Child, Ludovick, was born the 13 November 1747, and died the 26 of August 1748.

Our Fifth Child, Francis, was born the 28 Jully 1749.

Our Sixt Child, Ludovick, was born the 28 October, 1750.

Edinburgh, the 7th November 1752, betwixt 12 and 1 in the morning (being Tuesday) was born our Sevenths Child, and that same forenoon was baptised by the forementioned Mr. William Wallace, in presence of his two Grand Fathers, Mr. John Grant his Grand Uncle, Mr John and Mr James Brodie's his Uncles by the Father, Mr. William and Mr. Ludovick Grant's his Uncles by the Mother, and Mrs. Hellen Brodie his Aunt by his Father, named after John Brodie his Uncle.

The above John Brodie, upon the 15th January, 1753, (being Monday) took a Sudden illness and deied betwixt 6 and 7 in the morning and was buried in the before mentioned place. He was a very lively, well proportioned, well loock'd and thriving Child, to appearance, and was 9 weeks and 6 days old.

Edinburgh, the 28 February 1754, betwixt 2 and 3 in the morning (being Thursday) was born our Eight child, and that same day was baptised by the forementioned Mr. William Wallace in the presence of her two Grand Fathers, Mr John Grant her Grand Uncle, Mr James Brodie her Uncle by the Father, Mr William and Mr Ludovick Grant's her Uncles by the Mother, and Mrs. Hellen Brodie (now Mrs. Rintoul) her Aunt by the Father, named Cicel after her Mother.

Edinburgh, the 26 May 1756, ten minutes after two in the morning (being Wednesday) was born our ninth Child, and that same day was baptised by the Reverend Mr David Rintoul, one of the Ministers in Kirkcaldie, in presence of her two Grand Fathers, Mr John Grant her Grand Uncle, Mr James Brodie her Uncle by the Father, Mrs. Rintoul her Aunt by the Father, &c., named Margaret after her Aunt in Law Mrs Grant, spouse to Mr Ludovick Grant her Uncle by the Mother.

The above Ludovick Brodie, our Sixt Child, died the 3d of June 1756 (being Thursday) att four o clock in the morning of the Small Pox, aged 5 years 7 months and 6 days, and was buried in the above mentioned place; he was a beautyfull, genteel boy, had more prudence than most of his age, which, joined to a great deal of vivacity, benevolence, and kindness in his disposition, made him beloved by every one who knew him.

Mr Ludovick Brodie, Clerk to the Signet, my Worthy Father, died of a Fever, att his own house in Edinburgh, the 16 June 1758 att 1 o clock afternoon, aged 86, he was a very long time in business (and before he died was the oldest Clerk to the Signet) and bore a very fair character, being honest in his transactions and benevolent in his disposition, embracing every opportunity of doing good and charitable Actions to mankind in generall and to his Relations and Acquaintances in particular; Religious without ostentation, an affectionate Husband (to my Mother, Hellen Grant, his only wife, who died likewise of a Fever the 27 December 1725. She was a pious woman, a dutifull

Wife and an affectionate Mother,) and he was likewise a kind Parent and a constant and sincere Friend. As to his person, of a midle stature, strong, robust, and well proportioned, had an open and manly countenance, was burried the 19th Curt. in the above mentioned place.

Edinburgh, the 2d. February 1759, being Friday att ——— was born our tenth Child and that same day was baptised by the above reverend Doctr. William Wallace, in presence of her Grand Father Mr William Grant, Mr. James Brodie her Uncle by the Father, Mr. Ludovick Grant and Mrs Grant her Uncle and Aunt by the Mother, Mr. William and Hellen Grant's' her 2d Cousins by the Father, and named Jean after her Grand Mother and her Aunt by the Mother.

Edinburgh, the 31 of Jully 1760, being Saturday, att 1 in the morning, was born our eleventh Child and that same day was baptised by Doctr. Patrick Cumming, Minister in Edinburgh, in presence of her Grand Father Mr Willaim Grant, Mr James Brodie her Uncle by the Father, Mr Ludovick and Mrs. Grant's her Uncle and Aunt by the Mother, Mrs Gordon and Mrs Campbell her Aunts by the Mother, and Mrs Hellen Grant her 2d. Cousin by the Father, and named Jacobina after the above Mr James Brodie her Uncle.

Mr William Grant, Writer in Edinburgh, my wife's worthie Father, died of old age the 18 of January 1762, att 8 oclock in the morning, in the 100 of his age, he was a very long time in business, had a very fair character for honesty in all his transactions. Religious without ostentation, a good Husband, a dutiful Parent, and in his own lifetime did a great many good and Liberall actions, particularly to his Children, Grand Children and great Grand Children, who were very numerous. As to his person, he was of a midle stature, well Proportioned, of a Fair and comely Countenance, and was buried the 21 curt. in the above place.

On the 19th of February 1768, being Frieday, a little after one in the morning, died of a lingering illness, my eldest Daughter, Cicel, wanting 9 days to compleat her 14th year and during the long time she was indisposed, behaved with great Fortitude and Patience, her own distress never making her neglect nor abate that natural affability and good manners which she shewed to all, and particularly to her relations; when in health her person was tall and gentile and her countenance agreeable, her behaviour modest, polite and sensible, her capacity to learn was quick, and had a retentive memory, and as she was sincerely religious (without the least tincture of enthusiesem), there is no doubt that being both Good and Innocent, she is now extreamly, and will be eternally happy in the Celestiall Mansions.

On the 6th of March, 1776, being Weddensday, about seven in the evening, died of a linguring illness my (then) Eldest Daughter, Margaret, being 19 years 9 months and 11 days old, she had a Sollid Understanding, and without ostentation was firmly attached to the Cause of Truth, Virtue and Religion, Kind and Affectionate to her acquaintances but more especially to her Relations, and among her last words expressed her gratitude for the care they had taken of her, I believe her illness originated from a severe cold, which she contracted about 8 months presiding her death. She is now (I hope) enjoying eternall Bliss with her dear sister Cecil.

On the 22nd September 1777, being Munday night, one quarter after 11 oclock, died of a fever my dear wife, Cicel Grant, aged 59 years and 25 days and married to me 36 years and 325 days (which wants 40 days of 37 years.) She was a Chaste and dutifull Wife, and besides a great many good Qualities, she was equalled by few in the prudent and skillfull management of Her House and Family, was Religious without ostentation, Charitable and good to all, and is buried in the above place (two double paces west of the narrow road opposite to Harleys Tomb) where a great number of my and her Relations lyes interred: and there is no doubt she now enjoys Celestial happiness.

Mr. Francis Brodie, Wright in Edinburgh, my worthy Father, died of the Palsy att his own house in Edinr., the 1st of June 1782, att 5 oclock afternoon in the 74th year of his age. His character was that of an honest man, an affectionate husband, an indulgent parent, a faithful friend, and a generous master.

JEAN BRODIE.

My sister, Jean Brodie, died at her own house on the 22 of August 1821, at 10 oclock at night, aged 62 years and seven months, after a long and severe illness, which she bore with patience. She was a generous and affectionate sister and Aunt, a Sensible and Correct Woman in every respect, and is buried in the above mentioned place.

JACOBINA SHERIFF.

My Eldest daughter, Cecilia Sheriff, died at my house on the 30 of June 1831, at 6 oclock morning, aged 42. She was a humble Christian and dutiful daughter and most affectionate sister, and most faithfull friend. I trust she is now with the Lord, and is buried in the above mentioned place.

JACOBINA SHERIFF.

Her Dear and Affectionate Sister. 1831.

Jane Sheriff.

Jacobina Sherriff, my worthy mother, died at my house after three months illness in the 79 year of her age, she was the most affectionate parent, kind, indulgent in every respect, unopressive to all, humble in her opinion of herself, and I now trust she is beyond the reach of all sorrow.

Jane Sherriff
or Molleson

March 23
1839

Sir,

The favour of your Company to attend the Funeral of Mrs. Sherriff, my Mother-in-law from my House here to the Greyfriars Burial Ground, on Thursday the 28th currt. at 2 oclock afternoon, will much oblige.

Sir,
Your obedient Servant,
JAMES MOLLESON.

Edinburgh,
    3 Gloucester Place,
        March 25th, 1839.

APPENDIX V.

I.

Roll of the Knights Companions of The Cape.

Date of Admission.

1775 February 25th.

No. of Diplomas 232	Names of the Knights William Brodie	Titles of Knighthood Llhoyd

II.

Record of Cape Club Petitions, Vol. i.

No. 232.

To the Sovereign and Knights of The Cape
The Petition of William Brodie Wright in Edinburgh

Humbly Sheweth

That your Petitioner is very desirous to be admitted a Member of The Cape.

May it therefore Please the Sovereign and Knights to
admit your Petitioner and shall ever pray

WILLIAM BRODIE

The Candidate is recommended by

GILB. WAUGH
JAMES SYME

(Written upon the back of the Petition.)

PETITION OF WILLIAM BRODIE
1775
Grand Cape 25th Feb 1775.
Admitted D.S. Secry.
Sir Lhoyed.

III.

Minute of Meeting at which Deacon Brodie was admitted a Knight of The Cape.

Nineteenth Grand Festival of The Cape, held at
Capehall in Jas. Mann's, Craigs Close, 25th
Febry. 1775.

		Present	
		Sir Stick, Sovereign	
		Sir Westerhole, Depute Sovn.	
		Sir Fox, Treasurer	
		Sir Shirk, Secretary	
		Sir N. & A.,[29] Recorder	
		Sir Waterhole fifth	—Old Sovereigns
		Sir Scrape third	
		Sir Buildings	—Councillors
		Hall	
		Bejing	
		Bowl	
		Stone	
Sir	Wager, Chaplain		
Sir	Dive		Sir Padlock
	Brimstone		Kipper
	Silenus		Cellar
	Launce		Jawbone
	Fender		Corryarroch
	Surprise		Drawbridge
	Bolt		Toe

	Forgetful	Caltonhill	
	Marriage	Pole	
	Finger	Porter	
	Wig	Blott	
	Laverock	Sword	
	Dragon	Gutter	
	Pedro	Fine	
In	all 41	Bill £ : :	

Sederunt

The	following officers were this day duly elected vizt:—	
	Sir Stick, Sovereign	—Re-elected
	Sir Westerhole, Depute Sovereign	
	Sir Fox, Treasurer	
	Sir N. & A., Recorder	
	Sir Celler, Secretary	

Councillors:—

Sir	Tree	Sir Bank	—Re-elected
	Buildings	Bowl	
	Hayloft	Stone	
	Flatt	Fender	
	Vote	Finger	
	Be jing	Kipper	

The Recorded Protested that as Mr. Auld was irregularly ballotted at this Festival without his knowledge or consent the same shall not preclude him from an Appeal to any after Grand Cape if he chuses to enter the same and took instruments in the Secretary's hands and craved that this Protest be engrossed in the Minute of Sederunt of this Grand Cape.

The re-elected Sovereign after having taken the accustomed obligations to promote the Harmony of the Society was solemnly Crowned in the Chair of

State with all the usual formalities and with the other officers taking their proper places, the public business of this Festival was most harmoniously concluded.

APPENDIX VI.

I

Edinr. 15th October 1735.

Sederunt

James Simpson, Old D.G.	James Sime
Patrick Manderson	John Clerkson

Francis Brodie, Wright, compearing is made burges of this burgh as prentice to John Antonious, Wright, burges yrof. And gave his Oath &c. having payd for his duety to the Dean of Gild 13 Sh. 4 pennies & watches 24sh:——— Brodie B £1·6·7d.

II.

Edinr. 9th February 1763.

Sederunt

Patrick Lindsay, D.G.	William Good
John Robertson	William Mylne
Thomas Hepburne	Charles Howison

Francis Brodie, Wright, burges of this Burgh, Compearing is made Gildbrother thereof by right of Cecil Grant, daughter of William Grant, Writer, burges and Gildbrother thereof, his spouse and paid his dues and gave his oaths.——Brodie G £1·10·9d.

William Brodie, Wright, compearing, is made burges and Gild Brother of this Burgh by right of Francis Brodie, Wright, burges and Gild brother thereof, his father, and paid his dues and gave his oaths.——Brodie B & G £2·12·11½.

APPENDIX VII.

I.

Edinburgh the tenth day of September One
thousand seven hundred and eighty three
years.

Sederunt

Lord Provost	O.P.	T.C.
John Grieve	David Stuart	Thomas Simpson
		William Jameson
Bailies	O.B.	C. Deacons
James Dickson	William Galloway	William Fraser, Cr.
James Gordon	Francis Shaw	William Brodie
John Spottiswood		James Robertson
		John Douglas
D.G.	Old D.G.	George Chalmers
Thomas Cleghorn	Archibald M'Dowall	Robert Wemyss
Tr.	Old T.R.	
William Thomson	James Hunter Blair	
	M.C.:	
	Thomas Cleghorn, jr.	
	William Gillespie	
	David Willison.	

Extra^{ry} Deacons:—William Richie, William Young, William Inglis, Thomas
Hunter, Willm Forrester.

The Chamberlain produced in Council his Cash Book whereby it appears
there is a ballance due him of £306:13:10, Ballance due to Bankers

£5417:14:3, and paid in to the City's Cash Accompt with the Royal Bank £2385 Sterling.

Bailie Dickson from the first Bailie's Committee reported that they having examined the following accompts, vizt. an accompt due to William Brodie for Wright work done by him in the different public markets of the City, from Twentieth November seventeen hundred and eighty two to third July last, amounting to Sixty seven pounds, eighteen shillings and one penny; Item an accompt due to the said William Brodie for Wright work done by him in the Parliament House, Exchequer, &c., from twenty fifth September Seventeen hundred and eighty two to the eleventh of June last, amounting to Nine pounds, one shilling and four pence; Item an Accompt due to the said William Brodie for Wright work done by him in the Tolbooth and sundry other parts belonging to the City, from the fourteenth August seventeen hundred and eighty two to the seventeenth February last, amounting to Ten pounds, twelve shillings and two pence; Item an Accot. due to the said Willm. Brodie for Wright work done by him in making windows for St. Andws. Church, amounting to One hundred and twenty pounds, seven shillings and nine pence; Item an Accot. due to the said William Brodie for wright work done by him in making doors for the stalls in the New Flesh Markets and fitting up the new Veal Market, &c. from eighteenth November seventeen hundred and eighty two to seventeenth July last, amounting to One hundred and seventy six pounds, twelve shillings and five pence; Item an accot. due to the said William Brodie for Wright work done by him in the College, from ninth September seventeen hundred and eighty two to twenty first April last, amounting to Five pounds, eighteen shillings and nine pence; Item an accompt due to the said William Brodie for Wright work done by him in the different Churches of the City, from the twelfth of September seventeen hundred and eighty two to twenty fourth August last, amounting to Sixty six pounds, two shillings and one penny; Item an Accompt due to the said William Brodie for Wright work done by him in the Flesh Market, City Clerk's Chambers, and sundry other parts belonging to the City, from fourteenth September seventeen hundred and eighty two to twentieth July last, amounting to Fifty nine pounds, sixteen shillings and eight pence, all Sterling money, Did find the said Accompts right summed, calculated and sufficiently instructed, and therefore were of opinion the City Chamberlain should be authorised to pay the same, as the respective Reports under the hands of the said Committee bears—Which being considered by the Magistrates and Council, They approved of the said Reports, and authorize and appoint accordingly.

It was from the said Committee also reported that they having examined ... an Accompt due to William Brodie for Wright work done by him to the City's Engines, fire Cocks, &c. from twenty ninth November seventeen hundred and eighty two to twenty fourth May Last, amounting to Forty two pounds, three shillings and four pence Sterl; Did find the said Accots. right summed, calculated and sufficiently instructed and therefore were of opinion the City's Collector of the Cess and Watch money should be authorized to pay the same....

It was reported from the Committee on the New Gift that they having examined.... Item an Accot. due to William Brodie for Wright work done by him in repairing the Pier of Leith, from first September seventeen hundred and eighty two to Second July last, amounting to Forty nine pounds, nine shillings.... Did find the said Accompts right summed, calculated and sufficiently instructed; But in regard the City's Duty on Ale, &c. on which the said Accompts is chargeable is so much decreased that it cannot afford payment thereof, were therefore of opinion the City Chamberlain should be authorised to pay the same out of the City's proper Revenue, to be charged as a debt on the said duty and repaid and made good to the City how soon that fund can admit thereof....

JOHN GRIEVE, Provost.

II.

18th August, 1784.

... Upon a motion made in Council They remit to Convener Jameson, Deacon Hill, and Deacon Brodie to inspect the west wall of the Tolbooth and consider in what manner a Door or passage may be made thro' the same in order that criminals may be executed there, and to report:

III.

24th November 1784.

... Pursuant to a late remit to the Magistrates to consider as to the manner of fitting up a place adjoining to the Tolbooth of this City for the execution of Criminals, there was produced in Council a plan for that purpose with an estimate by Counr. Jameson of the Mason work amounting to Twenty-five pound two shillings and an estimate by Deacon Hill of the Wright work amounting to Twenty-five pound both Sterling, which being considered by the Council They ordain the work to be executed accordingly.

IV.

11th April 1785.

... An estimate signed by Counr. Jameson and Deacon Hill that the whole expense in rebuilding the shops and parapet at the west end of the Tolbooth shall not exceed in whole the sum of seventy pounds Sterling exclusive of the Wright work for the platform and the machinery for an Execution conform to a former Estimate being considered, the Council removed the shop mentioned in the minute of the eighth curt. and authorised the work to be executed with all possible dispatch.

V.

13th April 1785.

... Appointed the Dean of Guild and his Council to visit the west wall of the Tolbooth and to Report to the Magistrates their opinion if an opening can be made there with safety and without hurting the building for the purpose of executing Criminals on the west side of the Tolbooth, with power to the Magistrates to authorise the same to be done as formerly intended.

VI.

20th April 1785.

... The Magistrates produced the following Report:—"Edinburgh, 13th April 1785. The Dean of Guild and his Council agreeable to the Council's appointment visited the west wall of the Tolbooth and report their unanimous opinion that an opening can be made there with safety and without hurting the buildings (signed) Archd. McDowall D.G." and informed that in consequence thereof they had authorised the intended work to be completed.

The Magistrates represented that after the maturest consideration they had appointed the west end of the Tolbooth to be the common place for the public Execution of Criminals and moved that an Act of Council be passed for that purpose in order that Archibald Stewart now under sentence of death may be executed there in pursuance of his sentence, which being considered by the Council They approved of the conduct of the Magistrates and declared the west end of the Tolbooth to be the common place of Execution now and in all time coming.

VII.

4th May 1785.

... Read a letter signed by William Brodie and authorized charter of the lot in Princes Street feued by him last year to be granted to William Pirnie, Mason—William Brodie subscribing the same as consenter thereto.

VIII.

11th May 1785.

... Signed charter in favour of William Pirnie, Mason, with consent of William Brodie Wright, of fifty nine and one half feet in front of the Plot marked E north side of Princes Street agreed to have been feued to the said William

Brodie for payment of £3:14:4½ of feuduty commencing at Whitsunday 1785, and £10:13:4½ on the entry of each heir or singular successor. He paid to the Chamberlain Two hundred and eight pound five shillings Sterling of purchase money.

IX.

7th September 1785.

... Authorised Deacon Hill to make a moveable platform for the Execution of Criminals in terms of his estimate not exceeding sixteen pounds Sterling, to be executed at the sight of Baillies Eyre, Blair, and the Dean of Guild.

X.

12th April 1786.

... It was reported from the first Baillies' Committee that they having examined an accompt due to William Brodie for putting a roof on the new reservoir in Heriots Garden and compared it with the Estimate, found that the same exceeded the sum in the estimate in £2:4:6 but that the additional charge is on account of the building having been raised six inches higher than the original plan and therefore were of opinion the City Chamberlain should be authorised to pay the accompt amounting to £103:10:6 Stg.

XI.

13th September 1786.

... To Thomas Hill for work done by him in making a platform west end of the Tolbooth, Nineteen pounds seventeen 249 shillings and five pence half penny.... To Thomas Hill for erecting a second platform west end of the Tolbooth, Twenty-one pound seven shillings and eleven pence half penny.

XII.

20th September 1786.

... That part of the Sett entitled "Election in Special of Deacons" was read.

Then the said fourteen Incorporations being severally called, the following Persons were presented as their Deacons for the year ensuing:—

Surgeons—Forrest Dewar, Goldsmiths—Willm. Dempster, Skinners—James Brown, Furriers—Willm. Ritchie, Hammermen—John Milne, Wrights—Willm. Brodie, Masons—Robt. Dewar, Taylors—Jas. Richardson, Fleshers—Andrew Wilson, Cordners—Robert Moncur, Websters—Willm. Forrester, Waulkers—Thomas Tibbets, and Bonnetmakers—Adam Brooks.

It was reported that Edward Innes was elected Deacon of the Incorporation of Baxters.

The thirteen persons present were received, Sworn *de fideli* and authorized in their offices and qualified to Government by swearing the Oath of Allegiance and signing the same with the Assurance.

Then the chapter of the Sett entitled "New Council of Deacons" being read, the Council did proceed to make choice of six Council Deacons to be adjoined to the new Council for the year ensuing and elected the persons followings:—

Skinners—James Brown, Wrights—William Brodie, Masons—Robert Dewar, Baxters—Edward Innes, Fleshers—Andrew Wilson, Waulkers—Thomas Tibbets. All of whom compeared, except the said Edward Innes, who accepted of their offices, were sworn *de fideli* and qualified to Government by taking the Oath of Allegiance and signing the same with the Assurance.

JOHN GRIEVE, Provost.

XIII.

28th March 1787.

... On representation from William Forbes, Authorised Deacon Brodie to make a timber press for the use of the City Clerk in the office kept by the said William Forbes.

XIV.

31st October 1787.

... Read letter from Professor Andrew Dalzell addressed to the Lord Provost, that in the course of the night of the thirtieth current the College Library was broke into and the University Mace was stolen from thence. Ordered an advertisement to be published offering a reward of ten guineas to be paid by the City Chamberlain for discovering all or any of the Persons guilty thereof, or any person in whose possession the said Mace shall be found.

APPENDIX VIII.

ADVERTISEMENTS RELATING TO CERTAIN OF THE ROBBERIES
COMMITTED BY DEACON BRODIE.

(From the *Edinburgh Evening Courant.*)

1786.

On Friday evening last (the 12th August) the lock of the outer door of the compting-house of Johnston and Smith, bankers in the Exchange, was opened by some wicked persons, as supposed by a counterfeit key, and eight hundred pounds Sterling stolen out of their drawers, in the following bank notes, viz:—

Of the Royal, and Bank of Scotland	£194:	9:	0
British Linen Company	362:	2:	0
Dumfries	126:	0:	0
Glasgow Notes	64:	10:	0
General Bank of Perth	32:	0:	0
Dundee Notes (Jobson's) -	40:	0:	0
Several small Notes and Silver	11:	1:	0
	£830:	2:	0

It is entreated that every honest person will give the Magistrates of Edinburgh, or Johnston and Smith, notice of any circumstances that may fall under their observation for discovering the offenders; and farther, the said Johnston and Smith will give the informer a reward of Five Pounds Sterling for every hundred pounds sterling that shall be recovered in consequence of such information. As some smith may very innocently have made a key from an impression of clay or wax, such smith giving information, as above, so as the person who got the key may be discovered, shall be handsomely rewarded.

———

BY ORDER OF THE HONOURABLE THE MAGISTRATES OF EDINBURGH.

Whereas, on Sunday night last, the 14th inst. there was laid down or dropped at the door of the Council Chamber of this City, the sum of two hundred and twenty-five pounds sterling in bank notes, wrapped in a piece of grey paper, which was found by Robert Burton, a porter, and immediately after delivered by him to one of the Magistrates: This is to give notice, that the above sum is now sealed up, and in the hands of the City Clerks, and will be delivered to any person who shall prove the property thereof, with deduction of a reasonable allowance to the porter who found it.

1786.

SHOP BROKE INTO, AND ROBBED

In Parliament Square, Edinburgh.

WHEREAS betwixt the night of Monday the 9th, and Tuesday the 10th of October current, the shop of Mr. James Wemyss, Goldsmith in Edinburgh, situated betwixt the Goldsmiths' Hall and the Council Chambers of said City, was broke into and the following articles carried off, viz. 26 gold rings, some set with diamonds and the rest with stones; 24 plain gold rings; 5 seals set in gold; 1 gold broatch; 2 silver set broatches; 2 set crosses; 3 set ear-rings, one of them gold; 4 cut shank silver tea spoons, and one old plain silver do; 10 new silver table spoons; 1 silver tureen spoon, and the mouth of a dividing spoon; 2 silver punch spoons; 12 silver tea spoons, not quite finished but ready for burnishing; 1 silver seal with a ship on it, and one seal block; 12 silver stock buckles; 36 pairs silver shoe buckles; 3 single silver shoe ditto; 46 pairs of silver knee buckles, and four single knee ditto.

As the public, as well as the private party, are greatly interested that this daring robbery be discovered, it is requested that all Goldsmiths, Merchants, and other Traders through Scotland, may be attentive, in case any goods answering to those above mentioned shall be offered to sale, and to enquire how the persons who may offer them to sale came by them, and to get them examined before a Magistrate, and secured in prison, in case they cannot give a good account of themselves, and prove how they came by the said goods.

Letters containing information may be addressed to Mr. William Dempster, deacon of the Incorporation of Goldsmiths in Edinburgh, or to Mr David Downie, Goldsmith there, treasurer of said Incorporation, or to Mr William Scott, procurator-fiscal of the shire of Edinburgh; and in order that the person or persons guilty of the said robbery may be discovered, the Incorporation of Goldsmiths hereby offer a reward of TEN GUINEAS to any person who shall make such discovery, to be paid by Mr. Downie, their treasurer, upon conviction of the offender or offenders.

A SHOP BROKE.

Sheriff Clerk's Office, Edinburgh.

Dec. 28, 1786.

Between Sunday night and Monday morning last, a Hardware Shop here was broke into, and the following articles carried off:—A lady's gold watch, enamelled back, figure offering up a gift to Hymen—A large plain gold watch, caped and jewelled—A small secondhand gold watch; makers name of these three J. J. Jackson, London—One small single cased watch, maker's name Innes—Two silver watches, name Armstrong—Several gold rings, breast pins, and lockits, plain and set round with pearl for hair devices—A few pairs set knee and shoe buckles—Two lancet cases full of lancets, makers name Lavignie—All the rings, breastpins, lockits, and set buckles, are marked, in the under side with a sharp nail, the initials of the shop mark, and the selling price plain figures; so that if any attempt is made to erase any of these marks, it will easily be noticed.

Whoever will give such information, within three months from this date, to William Scott, procurator-fiscal of this County, as shall lead to a discovery of the person or persons who committed the above theft, shall, upon conviction of the offender or offenders, receive a reward of TWENTY GUINEAS, and the informer's name, if required, concealed.

WILLIAM SCOTT, Proc. Fiscal.

N.B. If any of the above articles are offered to sale, it is requested they may be stopped, and the person offering them detained till notice is given as above, for which a handsome reward will be given, besides all charges paid.

———

1787.

SHOP-BREAKING.

That in the Night betwixt Thursday the 16th and Friday the 17th of August instant, the Shop of John Carnegie, Grocer, at the foot of St. Andrew's Street, Leith, was broke into, and about 350 pounds of fine black tea stolen and carried off.

Whoever will give such information to William Scott, procurator-fiscal of the County of Edinburgh, within three months from this date, as shall lead to a discovering in the premises, will receive from him a reward of TEN GUINEAS, on conviction of the offender or offenders and the informer's name (if required) concealed.

N.B. It is presumed the above theft has been committed by some of those who stroll the country under the pretence of hawking tea, and who may have had access to know Mr. Carnegie's shop. The tea was turned out of the packages, and yesterday several parcels of tea were observed lying at different places on the Bonnington road, as if dropt from a parcel, which is a farther confirmation of the above suspicion, and that the tea stolen is carried to the country for sale by some hawker. If, therefore, any considerable quantity of tea is observed in the custody of any suspicious person or persons, it is intreated they may be secured, and notice given to said William Scott, who will pay all reasonable charges, besides a reasonable gratification for trouble.

Shop Breaking and Theft.

Sheriff Clerk's Office, Edinburgh, Oct. 29. 1787.

That in the night betwixt Saturday the 27th and Sunday the 28th of October Curt. a Shoemaker's shop in the Royal Exchange, Edinburgh, was broke into, and the following articles stole and carried off therefrom viz:—Ten pairs of Boots—Twenty pairs of Men's shoes—Three pairs of Men's slippers, red leather—One pair ditto, yellow—Eighteen pair white silk Queen's Uppers for shoes, embroidered with gold and silver—A silver watch, maker's name J. Dare, London, No. 2031—Another ditto, cracked on the outer Case, and having a leather string—A stone ring set in gold, having a man's head engraved thereon—A Lady's Pocket-book, of red Turkey leather, shut with a steel lock—Six pair of Men's silk Stockings, part white and part marled, marked J.C. and numbered—A hard leather Snuffbox, in the shape of a boot—Also, About four pound of bad halfpence, with papers of various kind, and in particular some parchments, and other rights of houses.

Whoever will give to William Scott, procurator-fiscal of this County, within three months from this date, such information as shall lead to a discovery of the person or persons who committed the aforesaid shop-breaking and theft; or will cause apprehend and imprison the said person or persons, shall, upon conviction of the offender or offenders, receive a reward of Ten Pounds, and the informer's name (if required) concealed.

N.B. If articles similar to the above are offered to sale, or discovered in the custody of any person of a suspicious appearance, it is entreated that the goods may be stopped and the person or persons in whose custody they are found secured, till notice is sent as above, for which a handsome reward will be given, besides all charges paid.

By the Right Hon: The

of the City of Edinburgh

WHEREAS, on the night between Monday and Tuesday the 29th and 30th current, some wicked persons did feloniously break open the doors of the Library of the University of this City, and steal the UNIVERSITY MACE, a reward of TEN GUINEAS, to be paid by the City Chamberlain, is hereby offered for the discovery of all or any of the persons above mentioned, or of any person in whose possession the said Mace shall be found.

Edinburgh, Oct. 31. 1787.

———

1788.

SHOP-BREAKING AND THEFT.

Sheriff Clerk's Office, Edinburgh, Jan. 9. 1788.

That this last night the shop of Mess. INGLIS, HORNER, & Co., Silk Mercers at the Cross of Edinburgh, was broke into, and the following articles stolen and carried off therefrom, viz.

A considerable quantity of black lutestrings, black armozeens, black florentines, and rasdimore silks, some of them whole, others cut pieces. Most of the armozeens and lutestrings have yellow lists or selveges, with some red threads on the outer edge; others of the lutestrings, and all the florentines have white selveges. All of the silks were rolled on pins or blocks, upon the end of most of which is the following mark I. L. S. with the number of the piece and quantity of the yards in figures. Several pieces of cambric, some whole, some cut—also a piece of plain white sattin. It is more than probable that the said goods may be cut in such a manner as to cause them, when exposed to sale, to have the appearance of remnants.

The value of the above goods is equal to from £400 to £500 Sterling, so far as yet discovered.

Whoever will give to William Scott, procurator-fiscal of this County, within three months of this date, such information as will be the means of leading to a discovery of the person or persons who committed the aforesaid shop-breaking and theft, or will cause apprehend or imprison the said person or persons, shall, upon conviction of the offender or offenders, receive a reward of One Hundred Pounds Sterling, and the informer's name, if required, concealed.

N.B. If articles, similar to those above described, are offered to sale or discovered in the custody of any person of suspicious appearance, it is intreated that the goods may be stopped, and the person or persons in whose custody they are found secured, till notice is sent as above; for which a handsome reward will be given, besides all charges paid.

SHOP-BREAKING AND THEFT.

Whitehall, Jan. 25. 1788.

Whereas, upon the night of the 8th or morning of the 9th of January instant, the shop of Mess. Inglis, Horner & Co., Silk Mercers in Edinburgh, was broke into, and articles taken therefrom amounting to upwards of £300 value; and as the persons guilty of this robbery have not as yet been discovered, notwithstanding every exertion that has been made; and the offer of £100 of reward for that purpose, his Majesty's most gracious pardon is hereby offered to an accomplice, if there was more than one concerned, who shall, within six months from this date, give such information to William Scott, procurator-fiscal for the shire of Edinburgh, as shall be the means of apprehending and securing all or any of the persons guilty of or accessory to the said crime.

Sydney.

Besides his Majesty's most gracious pardon, the sum of One Hundred and Fifty Pounds Sterling, in place of £100 formerly advertised, is now offered to any person or persons who will, within six months from this date, give to the above William Scott such information as shall be the means of leading to a discovery of the person or persons who committed the aforesaid Shop-breaking and Theft, or will cause apprehend and imprison the said person or persons in any sure prison, to be paid upon conviction of the offender or offenders; and the informer's name, if required, concealed.

And further, as a discovery in the premises, even although conviction should not follow, is of material consequence to the public, in case any person, within the above space, will give to the said William Scott satisfactory information by whom the said Shop-breaking and Theft was committed, a reward of Twenty Guineas will be given, whether the offenders are convicted or not.

The goods stolen from Mess. Inglis, Horner & Co.'s shop were a considerable quantity of black lutestrings, black armozeens, black florentines, and rasdimore silks, some of them whole, others cut pieces. Most of the armozeens and lutestrings have yellow lists or selveges, with some red threads on the outer edge; others of the lutestrings, and all the florentines have white selveges. All of the silks were rolled on pins or blocks, upon the end of most of which is the following mark I. L. S. with the number of the piece and quantity of the yards in figures.—Several pieces of cambric, some whole, some cut—Also a piece of plain white sattin. It is more than probable that the said goods may be cut in such a manner as to cause them, when exposed to sale, to have the appearance of remnants.

The value of the above goods is upwards of £300 Sterling, so far as yet discovered.

N.B. If articles, similar to those above described, are offered to sale or discovered in the custody of any person of suspicious appearance, it is intreated that the goods may be stopped, and the person or persons in whose custody they are found secured, till notice is sent as above; for which a handsome reward will be given, besides all charges paid.

———

Sheriff Clerk's Office, Edinburgh, March 12. 1788.

TWO HUNDRED POUNDS
OF REWARD.

WHEREAS WILLIAM BRODIE, a considerable House-Carpenter and Burgess of the City of Edinburgh, has been charged with being concerned in breaking into the General Excise Office for Scotland, and stealing from the Cashier's office there a sum of money—and as the said William Brodie has either made his escape from Edinburgh, or is still concealed about that place—a REWARD of ONE HUNDRED AND FIFTY POUNDS STERLING is hereby offered to any person who will produce him alive at the Sheriff Clerk's Office, Edinburgh, or will secure him, so as he may be brought there within a month from this date; and FIFTY POUNDS STERLING MORE, payable upon his conviction, by William Scott, procurator-fiscal for the shire of Edinburgh.

WILLIAM SCOTT.

DESCRIPTION.

WILLIAM BRODIE is about five feet four inches—is about forty-eight years of age, but looks rather younger than he is—broad at the shoulders, and very small over the loins—has dark brown full eyes, with large black eye-brows— under the right eye there is the scar of a cut, which is still a little sore at the point of the eye next the nose, and a cast with his eye that gives him somewhat the look of a Jew—a sallow complexion—a particular motion with his mouth and lips when he speaks, which he does full and slow, his mouth being commonly open at the time, and his tongue doubling up, as it were, shows itself towards the roof of his mouth—black hair, twisted, turned up, and tied behind, coming far down upon each cheek, and the whiskers very sandy at the end; high topped in the front, and frizzed at the side—high smooth forehead—has a particular air in his walk, takes long steps, strikes the ground first with his heel, bending both feet inwards before he moves them, again—usually wears a stick under hand, and moves in a proud swaggering sort of style—his legs small above the ancle, large ancle bones and a large foot, high brawns, small at the knees, which bend when he walks, as if through weakness—Was dressed in a black coat, vest, breeches, and stockings, a striped duffle great coat, and silver shoe-buckles.

APPENDIX IX.

Narrative of the Facts respecting the Breaking into the Shop at the Head of Bridge Street, belonging to John and Andrew Bruce, Merchants in Edinburgh, on the night betwixt the 24th and 25th December, 1786.

THE trial of William Brodie and George Smith being at present in the press for publication, Mess. Bruces furnished the publishers with the following facts, in order that they might publish the same along with the trial. These gentlemen, however, having declined to do so, as not being any part of the trial, Mess. Bruces now take this opportunity of laying before the Public the whole facts that have come out relative to the breaking of their shop; which, they have too much reason to believe, was meant to be concealed altogether. But, in justice to themselves, they wish to lay the whole candidly before the Public; and shall only add further that there is not one word in the following narrative but what is consistent with truth.

In the course of the precognitions taken by the Sheriff respecting the crimes committed by Brodie, Smith, Brown, and Ainslie, Mess. John and Andrew Bruce, Merchants in Edinburgh, applied to the Procurator Fiscal to know if any facts had come out respecting the breaking of their shop at the head of Bridge Street; and always received for answer, that whenever any thing occurred about breaking their shop, they would be informed of it. The Procurator Fiscal, however, never gave the Mess. Bruces any information on that head, although the very warrant on which Smith and Ainslie were incarcerated in March last, bore that it was on suspicion of breaking their shop.

When Smith and Brodie received their Indictment on the 19th of July last, it then appeared that no crime was specified in the Indictment but the breaking into the Excise Office. Mess. Bruces then applied to the Procurator Fiscal to know if any thing had come out, or was taken down in the precognition respecting the breaking of their shop; when he told them that nothing had been taken down thereanent; though Mess. Bruces were informed by Smith that he had, when examined before the Sheriff, declared every fact concerning it.

Mess. Bruces were at a loss to account for this extraordinary neglect of not taking down into the precognition all the facts that Smith had declared relative to their shop. They were in justice entitled to this, so as at least to have been satisfied in knowing who had done them the injury; and it might have led to a complete proof of the fact, so as to entitle them to restitution of the value stolen from them from the funds of those who had been guilty of the crime. They signified to the Procurator Fiscal that they wished still to have an examination of all concerned. But this he declined, by saying it was impossible to do it now—that they were indicted.

Mess. Bruce therefore drew up a memorial, and laid it before his Majesty's Advocate, in order to get, if possible, an examination respecting the breaking of their shop; when his Lordship was pleased to signify that it could still be done, and desired an application might be made to the Sheriff for that purpose; which was done accordingly by a Petition of the following tenor:—

Unto the Right Honourable the Sheriff-Depute of the County of Edinburgh, or his Substitute,

The PETITION of JOHN and ANDREW BRUCE, Merchants in Edinburgh.

HUMBLY SHEWETH,

That on the night betwixt the 24th and 25th days of December 1786, the petitioners shop, at the head of Bridge Street, was broke into, and several gold watches, seals, rings, and other articles, were carried off, to the value of about £350 Sterling. The petitioners applied to the Procurator Fiscal upon this occasion, who assured them that every step should be taken to endeavour to find out the persons who had robbed them of their property.

No intelligence, however, could be got respecting this business till the beginning of March last, when Brown gave information of him and his associates, Smith, Ainslie, and Brodie, being the persons who had committed so many offences of that kind; and, accordingly, the Procurator-Fiscal presented a petition to your Lordship, stating the fact of the petitioners' shop being broke, and referring to a list of articles stolen therefrom; and that there was reason to believe that Smith and Ainslie were the persons guilty of that crime, upon which they were apprehended, and incarcerated in the Tolbooth of Edinburgh, where they have remained ever since; and Smith and Brodie are now indicted to be tried for certain crimes, other than that of breaking the petitioners' shop.

When the petitioners learned that no notice of their shop was taken in the indictment, they applied to the Procurator-Fiscal to know what facts had come out in the precognition regarding the breaking of their shop, when he informed them that not a word respecting their shop had been taken down in the precognition, though he admitted, when Smith was examined before your Lordship, he had acknowledged the fact that he was the person who had broke the petitioners' shop, with the knowledge, and by the advice of Brodie: That Brodie had actually got part of the articles stolen therefrom, particularly some gold seals, and a gold watch-key, and some rings.

In these circumstances the petitioners were at a loss to know how to conduct themselves, in order still to get an examination of Smith, Brodie, and their associates, as there might be some difficulty in the matter, now that Smith and Brodie were indicted. However, as they are indicted for other crimes, the petitioners took the liberty of stating the matter in a memorial to His Majesty's advocate who is of opinion that Smith, Brodie, and all others concerned, or suspected, might still be examined with regard to the breaking into the petitioners' shop; and desired that the present application might be made to your Lordship for that purpose.

The petitioners are informed that Smith, though indicted, is still willing to declare every fact and circumstance respecting this matter. They are also informed that Brodie's watch, with some seals, are in the hands of Sir Sampson Wright, at London, and to be transmitted here. They, therefore, humbly trust that proper orders will be given to preserve these articles entire; and that inspection of them will be given to the petitioners, that it may be known whether they are any of the articles stolen from their shop.

May it therefore please your Lordship, to take the declarations of the said Smith, Brodie, Ainslie, and Brown, and anyother persons that may be thought necessary, and condescended on by the petitioners; and to give information to the petitioners when such examinations are to take place, that they, or their counsel, may attend, to put all pertinent questions to such as shall be examined respecting the breaking into the petitioners' shop; and to give inspection of Mr. Brodie's watch, seals, and other trinkets that may be along therewith, to the petitioners, so soon as they arrive.

According to Justice, &c.
JOHN and ANDREW BRUCE.

July 25th 1788.

The desire of the petition was granted by the Sheriff on the 26th of July; and, on the 28th of that month, the Sheriff-substitute, with the Procurator Fiscal, and Mr. Bruce, went to the prison to Smith; and the Sheriff-substitute informed him he was to come to take down his declaration respecting Mess. Bruce's shop-breaking, but not with regard to anything contained in his Indictment; and therefore hoped he would tell the truth. To which Smith answered, he had no objection to tell the whole truth; he thought it a piece of justice to do so; That he had formerly declared all he knew concerning that matter before the Sheriff, but he believed it was not taken down.

Smith was then examined, who declared, in substance, as follows:—

That, in the month of November, 1786, the declarant and Brodie had laid a plan to break into a hardware shop on Bridge Street, belonging to Davidson M'Kain: That they accordingly went there one night with a parcel of false keys and a small crow iron, and opened the door by unlocking the padlock and lock thereof with the false keys; after which they went and hid the false keys and crow iron, in case any of these articles should be found upon them, and then returned to the shop: That Smith was to go into the shop, and Brodie to watch at the outside of the door: That the declarant carried with him a dark lanthorn, which he lighted: That their intention was only to look at the goods, but not to carry them off that night: That the declarant remained in the shop for about half an hour; and, after being some time there Brodie called out "What made him stay so long—was he taking an inventory of the shop?"

That the declarant only brought away with him that night seventeen steel watch-chains, and a small red pocket-book. The steel chains the declarant afterwards sold along with some other goods of his own to an auctioneer, and the pocket-book he afterwards made a present of to Michael Henderson, Stabler in Grassmarket, his daughter.

That the declarant and Brodie afterwards, in about a fortnight, went back to rob M'Kain's shop completely, and opened the door as formerly, when Smith went in, and left Brodie to watch without; but he was not a few minutes in the shop, when he heard a person in the room immediately below rise out of his bed, and come towards the door; on which the declarant pulled up the shop-door, and ran straight into the street, without carrying any thing with him.

That he found Brodie had fled; and the declarant, on going up to the main street, found Brodie standing at the head of the entry into the Old Green Market: That, a little after this, the declarant and Brodie walked arm-in-arm down Bridge Street, in order to see what they could observe about the shop; and, in passing down the street, they saw a man looking out at the door immediately under M'Kain's shop, and a guard soldier standing opposite, at the head of the stair which goes down to the Flesh Market; so that the declarant and Brodie passed on along the Bridge, and afterwards went to their several homes, as nothing could be done further that night.

That Brodie told the declarant that the shop at the head of Bridge Street, belonging to Mess. Bruces, would be a very proper shop for breaking into as it contained valuable goods, and he knew the lock would be easily opened, as it was a plain lock, his men having lately altered that shop-door at the lowering of the streets: That the plan of breaking into this shop was accordingly concerted betwixt them, and they agreed to meet on the evening of the 24th of December 1786, being a Saturday, at the house of James Clark,

Vintner in the head of the Flesh Market Close, where they generally met with other company to gamble: That, having met there, they played at the game of hazard, till the declarant lost all his money; but at this time Brodie was in luck, and gaining money: That the declarant often asked Brodie to go with him on their own business; but Brodie, as he was gaining money, declined going, and desired the declarant to stay a little, and he would go with him.

The declarant, however, turned impatient, as it was near four in the morning, and the time for doing their business was going; he therefore left the room, and went by himself to Mess. Bruces shop, when he opened the door with false keys, and, after getting in, lighted a dark lanthorn, and took out of the show-boxes or glasses on the counter, and from the inside of the windows, ten watches, five of them gold, three silver, and two metal, with the whole rings, lockets, and other jewellery and gold trinkets in the show-boxes, all of which he put into two old black stockings, and carried them to the stable of Michael Henderson, in the Grass-Market, where he hid them under some rubbish below the manger, and afterwards went home to his own room in the Grass-Market.

That he staid there till near eight in the morning, and then went up to Mr Brodie's house, when the maid told him that Mr Brodie was in bed; and the declarant then left his name, and said he wanted to see him, and thereafter returned home to his own room: That, after staying there some time, Mr Brodie came and called for him, when the declarant told him what he had done, and desired Mr Brodie to stay there till he would go for the goods: That the declarant accordingly went to the stable, and brought the two black stockings, containing the goods, and poured them out upon a bed in a closet off his room, and then said to Mr Brodie, "You see what luck I have been in; you might have been there; but as you did not go, you cannot expect a full share; but there are the goods, pick out what you choose for yourself"; upon which Brodie took a gold seal, a gold watch-key set with garnet stones, and two gold rings: That the declarant and Brodie went twice over the goods, in order to ascertain their value; and the declarant, who was himself skilled in articles in that line, was of opinion they would have cost Mess. Bruces about £350 Sterling.

That, after this, the goods were again put into the black stockings, and carried back to Michael Henderson's stable: And, in the course of that day, being Sunday, the declarant and Brodie frequently passed Mess. Bruces shop-door, to see in what situation the door stood, and to learn if the robbery had been discovered; and nothing appearing, the declarant proposed to Brodie to go back that night, in order to sweep the shop clean; but Brodie objected to this, saying that a discovery might have been made, and a watch set to entrap them; on which account they desisted from the attempt.

That, after this, Brodie and the declarant had several meetings, consulting about the safest way to dispose of the goods: and, upon the Tuesday evening, it was concerted between them, that the declarant should go off next day for England with the goods; and at that time Brodie gave the declarant five guineas and a half to carry his expenses on the road; and, to evade suspicion, the declarant set out early next morning, and travelled on foot as far as Dunbar, where he took the mail-coach, and went to Chesterfield in England, and there sold the whole goods taken out of Mess. Bruces shop, except what Mr Brodie got, for £105 Sterling, to John Tasker alias Murray, who, he knew, had been banished from Scotland: That the declarant sent a twenty-pound note of this money in a letter to Mr Brodie, informing him of the sale, and desiring him to pay himself what the declarant had borrowed, and supply his wife with money till the declarant's return.

That the declarant staid for some weeks in England, during which time he had several letters from Brodie; and, on his return, gave to Brodie three ten-pound notes more of the money to keep for him, and to prevent suspicion by the declarant's having so much money about him, which money Brodie gave him as he wanted it, but gained a great part of it at play.

That among the goods sold to Tasker, there was a particular gold watch, which Tasker said he would wear himself, and, to prevent a detection, got the name and number altered by a man at Leeds, and which watch Tasker was wearing when the declarant left England.

Mr BRODIE was examined the same day, and being interrogated, declared, That he had been employed by the Magistrates of Edinburgh to alter the door of Mess. Bruces' shop, at the head of Bridge Street; that his men altered it accordingly, after the streets had been lowered.

And being interrogated, If he was at that time acquainted with George Smith, present prisoner in the Tolbooth?—declares, That he does not at present remember at what time he became acquainted with Smith—But, as the declarant has other business of his own at present to take up his time, declines to give any further answer to this or any other question at present.

Being further interrogated, If he recollects receiving from George Smith a gold seal, a gold watch-key, and two gold rings?—he declines to answer this or any other question, for the reason above stated.

And being desired to sign this declaration, he refused so to do.

ANNE HIBUTT, spouse of George Smith, was also examined, who declared, That one morning Brodie came to the room where her husband and she resided, and examined a parcel of jewellery goods; and she saw Mr Brodie get the seal, watch-key, and rings mentioned in her husband's declaration.

That she saw Brodie give her husband some money the night before he went to England; and, during her husband's absence, she received money from Mr Brodie.

ANDREW AINSLIE was examined, and declared as to the time of his becoming acquainted with Brodie and Smith: That he was at Glasgow at the time Mess. Bruces' shop was broke; but, on his return to Edinburgh, was informed of the particulars by Smith.

That he often saw, in Mr Brodie's possession, hanging at his watch, a gold seal and watch-key, which Brodie said, these, with some other trifles, were the only things he had got of what was taken out of Mess. Bruces' shop; and has often heard Smith and Brodie quarrelling, and Brodie grumbling and complaining that he had never got his proper share of the goods taken out of that shop.

JOHN BROWN, *alias* Humphry Moore, declared as to the time he became acquainted with Smith and Brodie: The first time he saw Brodie was supping in Smith's house: That he was not come to Edinburgh when Mess. Bruces' shop was broke.

That he has often heard Smith and Brodie talking with regard to that shop-breaking, and Brodie complaining that he had not got his proper share of the goods; and particularly, in a conversation betwixt Brodie and the declarant, after the shop of Inglis and Horner had been broke into, Brodie damned Smith for having broke into this last shop himself, and said he would treat him, Brodie, in the same manner he had done as to Bruces' shop, which was very ungenerous, after he had given him the information.

That he had often had Brodie's gold watch in his custody, and saw the gold seal and watch-key hanging at it, which Brodie often said were the only things he had got that were taken from Bruces' shop.

APPENDIX X.

STATE OF THE PROCESS AT THE INSTANCE OF JOHN HAMILTON, CHIMNEY-SWEEPER, IN PORTSBURGH, AGAINST WILLIAM BRODIE, WRIGHT AND CABINETMAKER, IN EDINBURGH, REFERRED TO AT THE TRIAL, RESPECTING THE LOADED DICE, WHERE THE CLUB, SO OFTEN MENTIONED IN SMITH'S DECLARATIONS, MAKES A CONSPICUOUS FIGURE.

THE process is in the form of a petition and complaint against Brodie, Smith, and Ainslie. It states that, on a certain night in January last, he, Hamilton, accidentally met with these persons in the house of Clark, vintner, at the head of the Fleshmarket Close; that when he joined them there playing at dice, that, suspecting no fraud or deceit, he had joined in the amusement, and, in a short space, lost six guineas, and some odd shillings; that, being surprised how this could happen, he seized on the dice, and had them examined, and discovered that they were loaded or false dice, filled at one end or corner with lead; and he concludes with praying for a warrant to apprehend and incarcerate the said persons, until they should repeat the sum of which he had been so defrauded, and pay a sum over and above, in name of damages and expenses.

Answers were given in for Mr. Brodie to this complaint, and separate answers for Smith and Ainslie.

They stated, in general, that, on the evening mentioned in the petition, they were innocently amusing themselves with a game at dice over a glass of punch, and that the petitioner intruded himself upon their company; that, if false dice were used on that occasion, it was unknown to the defenders, as the dice they played with belonged to the house; that, if the petitioner had lost the sum he alleged, it had not been gained by the defenders, as Smith and Ainslie had said, that, so far from gaining any thing that evening, they had lost, and Brodie said he had only gained 7s. 6d.; that the prisoner himself was a noted adept in the science of gambling; and it was not very credible that he would have allowed himself to be imposed upon in the manner he had alleged.

The replies for Hamilton to these answers are a curious production. After stating the nature of the complaint, and the defences that had been made to it for Brodie, Smith, and Ainslie, they say, "A wonderful story indeed! Smith and Ainslie, two noted sharpers at the business, in their answers, assert they were losers, and innocent Mr Brodie avers he was only a gainer in this paltry trifle of 7s. 6d.; and yet the petitioner finds himself out of pocket near as many guineas as that gentleman says he received of shillings. Certain, however, it is, that in their company, by undue means, he lost five guinea notes, two half guineas in gold, and six shillings in silver, before he suspected the fraud."

"Neither Dr Katterfelto, nor Breslaw, were present to transmute it. Unless, therefore, some of their learned pupils had not been very near him he would have been in possession of his money at this moment. Mr Brodie knows nothing about, and is entirely ignorant of such devices and always considered all dice to be alike. It is, says he in his answers, the petitioner who 'is such an adept in the science, as to be alone capable of using such instruments and of explaining the nature of them.'

"Miserable!—that the petitioner, a deemed sharper, should be taken in by a pigeon, to use the *lingua* of the Club. But so it has happened. Mr Brodie knows nothing of such vile tricks—not he! He never made them his study—not he! Never was at either pains or expense to acquire them, nor ever studied under Mr Breslaw, &c., &c., for that very special purpose—not he indeed! Mr Brodie never haunted night-houses, where nothing but the blackest and vilest arts were practised to catch a pigeon; nor ever was accessary either by himself or others in his combination, to behold the poor young creature plucked alive, and not one feather left upon its wings—not he indeed! He never was accessory to see or be concerned in fleecing the ignorant, the thoughtless, the young, and the unwary, nor ever made it his study, his anxious study, with unwearied concern, at midnight hours, to haunt rooms where he thought of meeting with the company from which there was a possibility of fetching from a scurvy sixpence to a hundred guineas—not he indeed! He is unacquainted altogether with packing or shuffling a set of cards—he is indeed! Mr Brodie, in all his innocent amusements, never met with any person, who, after having been fleeced of money to the amount or a hundred pounds, and detected of the vile and dishonest methods by which it had been abstracted from him, received, as a return for his moral rectitude, a very handsome incision on the eye—never he indeed! He never was in such company, nor ever met with such accident—not he! It is only the petitioner, or such like him, who are known and adepts in the devices—which Mr Brodie very modestly says he is innocent of—who could be guilty of such practices, and receive such returns.

"But, however certain Mr Brodie's innocence may be on these scores, previous to the 17th January current, it is as certain that on that night, both him and Ainslie, and Smith, had acquired more complete knowledge of the business of gambling than the petitioner; for, notwithstanding all his art, they went infinitely beyond him; he was totally at a loss when he observed the dice take such a run; not indeed but he was apprehensive something was going on unfair and ungenerous. At last, having been despoiled of his money, he seized them, and discovered the charm. For this unjustifiable procedure in the defender, the petitioner is confident every good magistrate will feel it their duty to give him reparation; and it is their business to check these infamous proceedings, be they followed by whatsoever person they may; for, the greater the man is, and the weightier his purse, the more is he the object of justice and example; and the lower the man is in rank or station, who suffers by such, the louder is the cry and more the demand for redress.

"If, so long ago as the 1711, the Legislature had perceived its pernicious consequences, how much is it the duty of those to whom its execution is entrusted to act up to its very letter; when it is a fact, that, in these modern times, gaming of every kind has pervaded all ranks; from the stable-boy to the Peer it is the subject of study and of practice; and some of every denomination have made it their chief business to attain the method or art how to cheat his neighbour the best; his neighbour, nay, his friend and companion, who never would have suspected such a latent serpent lay in his breast.

"There are living instances of men, who, though born to independence and enjoying most ample fortune, can intermix with the very lowest class of the multitude, and even court this company from motives prompted surely by the principles only of rapacity and avarice; and, without shame or remorse, use the most unjustifiable and dishonest practices to fleece them of their little pittance—pittances so much below their envy, that a relation of them would not bear the appearance of truth; and what must these men appear to be in the mind of every good person; yet still there are such who demean themselves to these practices, and, rather than associate with their equals, will descend to keep company with ostlers, pedlars, and stable-boys."

APPENDIX XI.

AN ACCOUNT OF MR. BRODIE'S BEING SEIZED AT AMSTERDAM.

JOHN DALY, an Irishman, residing at Ostend, had seen Brodie, who passed there under the name of John Dixon, at the house of one Bacon, a vintner, with whom he lodged.

Brodie was recommended to Bacon at Ostend by the following letter from Captain Dent, in whose vessel he went to the Continent:—

To Mr John Bacon, Vintner, Ostend.

Dear Friend,

The bearer, Mr John Dixon, was going passenger with me to New York, but, being taken sick, had a desire to be landed at Ostend. Therefore, I recommend him to your care, being a countryman and a stranger; on my account, I hope you'll render him every service in your power.

In so doing, you will oblige

Your most humble servant,
JOHN DENT.

Sir John Potter employed this Daly to go to Holland in pursuit of Brodie. He got notice of him at Amsterdam, by means of two Jews who attend the passengers that arrive in the treck schoots. He described Brodie to them, and a black trunk he had with him; and they, for a few stivers, showed him the alehouse where he had taken up his quarters.

Daly said Brodie was lodged in the first floor: that the landlord of the house informed him that the gentleman he enquired for was above. On this information, Daly went up stairs, knocked once or twice at the door, but no person answering, he opened the door, and went into the room. After searching about some time, he found Brodie in a sort of cupboard, and he addressed him, "How do you do, Captain John Dixon *alias* William Brodie?—come along with me." He then got him lodged in the Stadthouse. Daly came over to London, and got his reward.

APPENDIX XII.

ON Tuesday, the 1st July, I left London, and arrived at Harwich at three o'clock the next morning.

Wednesday, waited on Mr Coxe, the agent for the packet, with Mr Fraser's letter, and also on the Captain, who dined with me. At half-past four in the afternoon sailed out of the harbour, and lost sight of land at nine.

Thursday, got sight of Helvoetsluys at twelve next day,—dead calm four leagues from shore,—rowed into the harbour in the long boat, with Captain Hearne, and Carpmeal, (Sir S. Wright's officer), with the mail, and a woman going as Lady's maid to Sir James Harris's Lady,—drove back by tide, and almost out to sea again,—landed on sand, walked to several farmhouses, leaving the mail and baggage on the sand, guarded, in quest of a waggon,—refused;—a boor, at last, went at an extravagant price; we had walked seven miles on hot sands, and parched with thirst; at eight o'clock waggon came with the mail, &c.—set out for the Brill, but, within two miles, waggon broke down, and obliged to procure boors to carry mail, &c. arrived at the Brill at half past nine;—Brooks, the messenger, came from Helvoetsluys to meet us, where he had been waiting,—had heard nothing of any person (Englishman) being in custody at Amsterdam, which much alarmed me, nor had Hutchinson, the collector of the passports,—more alarmed;—delivered Mr Fraser's letter to Brooks;—at ten set off with Brooks for Maslinsluys, arrived there at half-past eleven, got to Delft at three-quarters past twelve;—arrived at the Hague at three in the morning in an open post waggon, with heavy rain, thunder and lightning.

Friday, waited on Sir James Harris at ten in the morning,—introduced to Brooks,—treated with great affability, and received a letter from Sir James, which he had already wrote, directed to Mr Rich, the consul, Sir James having first informed me that Brodie was safe in the Stadthouse,—consulted Sir James on the mode of obtaining him,—informed that, if the magistrates of Amsterdam required an official application to the States General, to come back immediately to him, and he would obviate all difficulties; but he did not think it would be necessary:—it was Sir James's opinion the magistrates would give him up without, if not, was certain they would detain him till an answer to Sir James's application to the States could be obtained;—set off for Amsterdam, and arrived there the same evening; waited on Mr Rich,—politely received; and we consulted on measures,—Mr Rich to wait on one of the magistrates that evening, and to send to me early next morning.—Waited on Mr Duncan, a Scots gentleman, and father-in-law to Mr Gerard, a minister at Amsterdam, with Mr Langlands's letter;—Mr Duncan seemed willing to identify Brodie; but on being called out into another room by Mr Gerard and his wife, on his return, Mr D. said as far as his word of honour as a gentleman would go, and his belief, he would say he was the man; but, if an oath was required he would not,—Saw then a manifest reluctance in Mr D. and had no doubt his daughter and the parson would endeavour to persuade him to decline troubling himself in the matter; but judged he could not go back from what he had said to Mr Rich.

N.B. No mischief but a woman or a priest in it,—here both.

Saturday morning, received a message from Mr Rich,—most of the magistrates gone to their country-houses,—nothing could be done till Monday;—Mr Rich entertained no doubt, but said a magistrate had informed him, that a formal requisition must be made by him, in writing, to the magistrates;—he produced the copy of one, requiring the person of William Brodie to be delivered up; I corrected it, by inserting "otherwise John Dixon," as the magistrates of Amsterdam knew of no William Brodie; Mr Rich agreed it was proper;—informed him of my suspicions respecting Mr Duncan, and the steps that would be taken by his family to make him, if possible, recant;—my fears further increased, as Mr Duncan lodged in the same tavern with me, I had frequent opportunities of conversation with him, and could plainly see a sorrow for what he had said, and a wish to retract.

Monday, waited on Mr Rich,—found, by a mistake in not inserting "otherwise John Dixon " in the requisition, that the business must be delayed till the next day ten o'clock, when a general meeting of the magistrates, with the grand schout, (high sheriff), to consider on the application;—mistake corrected, and requisition presented.

Tuesday, sent for by the magistrates to the Stadthouse;—from their manner, judged Brodie's delivery as predetermined;—Mr Duncan sent for.

MR. DUNCAN'S ACCOUNT TO THE MAGISTRATES.

That he was not a native of Edinburgh, but of Aberdeen; that he frequently came to Edinburgh on business; and that eight ten, or twelve years ago, he could not say which, the man who now called himself John Dixon was pointed out to him as Deacon Brodie, having asked a gentleman who he was.

That he had seen him several times after, and always understood him to be Deacon Brodie, but did not know his Christian name; had no doubt, and verily believed he was the same man; but would not swear he had no doubt and verily believed him to be the same.

———

BRODIE ORDERED TO BE BROUGHT IN.

SUBSTANCE OF EXAMINATION.

Q. What is your name?

A. John Dixon.

Q. That is the name you go by here—but is not your real name William Brodie?

A. My Lords, I stand here and claim the protection of the laws of this country, which require two witnesses, on oath, to prove me William Brodie.

You shall have the protection of the laws of this country, but they do not require two oaths to identify you; it requires that the magistrates shall be satisfied you are the same man.

Mr. Groves—I beg leave he may be asked, if he is not a native of Edinburgh?

Question put—the answer, I have been at Edinburgh.

Mr Groves—Is he a Deacon of Edinburgh?

A. I claim the protection of the laws.

Mr Groves—Does he know Mr William Walker, Attorney at law, of the Adelphi, London?

A. I know such a man.

Mr Groves—Then that William Walker procured the escape of this William Brodie from London, which I can prove by extracts of letters now in my pocket, the originals of which are here in the hands of your officers. I can swear to Mr Walker's writing.

Prisoner ordered to withdraw.

Here the Magistrates asked me if I was ready to swear that, from the pointed description of him and all said circumstances, he was, to the best of my belief, the man required to be given up?—I told them I was.

Mr Duncan was then asked if, from what he knew and what he had heard, he would swear he had no doubt, and believed him to be the man.

Mr Duncan's reply.—I am only a visitor here; and being called on such an occasion, it might, in my own country where I am a Magistrate, have the appearance of forwardness if I was to swear. I am a man of honour and a gentleman, and my word ought to be taken. I do believe, and I have no doubt, that he is the same man; but I decline to swear it; I'll take no oath.

The Magistrates expostulated, but unsuccessfully, on the absurd idea of saying, "I have no manner of doubt, and verily believe," and refusing to swear, "I have no manner of doubt!" &c.

As I had previously drawn up an information for Mr Duncan and myself to that effect, he was asked if he would sign it without swearing?—when Mr Duncan said he would.

The Magistrates then said that they should pay the same compliment to me they did to Mr Duncan, and take my signature to the certificate, without an oath, even to my belief.—Certificate signed.

The prisoner was then ordered in, and the certificate read to him, and asked, If he had not a father?—he replied,—None.

But you had a father, said the Judge—was not his name Brodie?

To this Mr Brodie replied,—"There are more Brodies than one."

Then by that, said the Judge, you confess your name is Brodie?

A.—A *lapsus linguae*, my Lord.

Brodie again insisted upon the oaths; but the Judge told him that all they wanted was to be satisfied, which they were from what Mr Duncan and Mr Groves had signed, and partly from a confession of his own.

He was told he should set off as that day; and it was settled at four in the afternoon.

The Judge told me I should have a guide, who would procure the means of conveyance, &c. I took my leave of them with thanks, &c.; waited on Mr Rich; at four was sent for to the Stadthouse, where there was a prodigious crowd; two carriages and four guides, with four horses in each carriage; and the prisoner, being properly secured, we put him into one, and got to Helvoet without much interruption next day at one o'clock; packet sailed at five.

N.B. I had wrote a letter to Sir James Harris on the Saturday, requesting the packet to be detained, who informed me by Mr. Rich, with whom I dined on the Monday, that it should be detained to the last moment.

Brodie was watched two hours alternately on board by the ship's crew; his hands and arms confined, and his meat cut for him, &c.

On Thursday night, eleven o'clock, we arrived at Harwich—supped—set off immediately, and arrived next day at noon at Sir Sampson Wright's, before whom, and Mr Langlands, Brodie confessed he was the person advertised.

APPENDIX XIII.

COPIES OF TWO AUTOGRAPH LETTERS OF DEACON BRODIE, HITHERTO
UNPUBLISHED.

[From Dr. David Laing's MSS. in the University Library,
Edinburgh.]

I.

[To the Right Hon. Henry Dundas (Viscount Melville).]

Right Honble. Sir

You are no doubt acquainted with my misfortunes. Extracts of the
proceedings against me are sent to London by my friends to endeavour to
procure a Remission or an Alteration

**Facsimile of Deacon Brodie's Letter to the Duchess of Buccleuch.
(From the original in Dr. David Laing's collection of MSS. in the**

of my Sentence. But I believe little respect is paid to such Aplications unless supported by respectable Personages. With which view I now most humbly Beseech your interposition and interest in support of this aplication making at London in my behalf and if possible prevent me from suffering an Ignominious Death to the disgrace of my numerous conections, even if it were to end my days at Bottony Bay.

I have wrote more fully upon this subject to His Grace the Duke of Buccleugh.

As the time appointed for my Disolution aproaches fast, I most earnestly intreat no time may be lost in writing to London in my behalf.

I now most humbly Beg that you will pardon this Presumption in one of the most unfortunate of the Human Race and whatever may be the result of this Aplication, I shall ever pray for your welfare and hapiness.

> I am with the greatest respect Right Honble Sir
> Your most obdt and huble Sert
> but most unfortunate
> WILL: BRODIE.

Edinr Tolbooth
10th Sepr 1788

II.

Madam,

Lett me beseech your Ladyship to pardon My Boldness in making the present address.

The wretched can only fly to the Humane and the powerfull for Relief.

As my triall is printed, it would Ill suit me to make any reflections on the unfortunate Issue; and this much I am convinced of, that the Current of Popular prejudice is so strong against me, that it will be well with me if I can Rescue my Life on any terms; and tho' my friends are making aplication above, I have little hopes of the success, unless some Respectable Characters who have had an oportunity of knowing something of those I have come of, and of my former life, Interest themselves in my behalf.

With all the fortitude of a man, I must confess to you, Madam, that I feel the Natural horror at Death, and particularly a violent Ignominious Death, and would willingly avoid it even on the condition of spending my Future years at Bottony Bay.

In that Infant Collony I might be usefull, from my knowledge in severall Mechanical branches besides my own particular Profession; and if your Ladyship and your most Respectable friend The Right Honble Henry Dundas, would Deign to Patronise my Suit, I would have little Reason to Doubt the Success. Capt John Hamilton too I think would be ready to assist in any measure Sanctified by your Ladyship.

Lett me again intreat you to Pardon my Boldness. My time flies apace, and the hand of Death presses upon me. Think for one moment, but no longer, what it is to be wretched, Doomed to Death, helpless, and in Chains, and you will excuse an effort for life from the most Infatuated and miserable of Men, who can confer no Compliment in subscribing Himself

> Madam,
> Your Ladyships Devoted
> huble Sert
> WILL:M BRODIE.

Edinr Tolbooth
in the Iron Room
and in Chains
10th Sepr. 1788.

P.S. I have requested Mr. Alexr Paterson my agent to Deliver this in Person to your Ladyship.

W. B.

—

APPENDIX XIV.

GEORGE SMITH was taken into custody on Saturday morning, the 8th of March, upon the information of John Brown *alias* Humphry Moore. On Monday, the 10th, remorse of conscience seized his mind, and he sent to the Sheriff, wishing to make a clean breast, and to tell the truth. From that time he has all along been humble, penitent, and resigned.

At his trial he intended to have pled guilty but was prevailed upon to take his chance of a trial. He meant to have asked for mercy on the ground of making an ample confession of the crimes committed and to be committed, and had prepared a speech in writing to that purpose, which he intended to have read.

On the Friday before the trial, Smith wrote a letter to the Board of Excise, saying that he was not to give them any trouble, for he would plead guilty.

By means of a humane and benevolent clergyman who attended this unhappy man with the most feeling solicitude and earnest discharge of duty during his imprisonment, we have been favoured with this speech, and the catalogue of crimes which were to have been perpetrated, which will strike every reader with horror and amazement.

It is in his own handwriting, and will be deemed curious by the public. It is remarkable that Smith spells much better in his writing than Brodie.

The speech is as follows:—

My Lords, and Gentlemen of the Jury,

I stand before this Tribunal, so dreadful to the guilty mind, a victim, in the first instance, to private revenge. The principal informer against me had suddenly become my mortal enemy, and thought of nothing, I fear, when he went to the Sheriff-clerk's Office, but my single ruin. I pray God to forgive him this cruel wrong, as I do from my heart.

Since I was committed to prison, it has been said against me that I was formerly a Smith by occupation, and made the keys that opened the Excise Office and other places; neither of which are true. I never was a Smith, nor ever made a key. Old keys were bought, and the wards of them altered; but I was not by any means the best in the execution.

It may be remembered against me that I tried to break out of prison. But, not to dwell upon the love of life, and the dread of an ignominious execution, both of which are so natural and strong, I not only sincerely repented of having made the attempt, but, as a proof of my sincerity, and, I humbly trust, as some kind of atonement, I prevented Peter Young and three others from doing so—who, with myself, could afterwards have escaped from prison—by freely discovering the plot to the turnkey.

I have, moreover, been falsely accused of advising my unfortunate wife not to speak at all when she should be brought to this Court; but I solemnly declare that the worst advice I ever gave her on that head, was to speak the truth. I have no fear of her evidence affecting my life. To make the wife the witness in law against the life of her husband, would be barbarous in any country. My great security here is that the justice and humanity of this country forbid it.

It was my full confession on my first imprisonment, that has made my offences capital. I have destroyed myself, otherwise no evidence could have condemned me.

I made that confession to prevent more dreadful mischief being done to this injured country from persons whom it least suspected; for God, who seeth in secret, only knows where the evil would have stopped. And, if possible, to make some small reparation for the violent wrongs I have myself been guilty of, I request the indulgence of the Court to suffer me to read over a list of such robberies as my accomplices and myself had determined to commit, had we not been timeously prevented.

- 1. On Dalgleish and Dickie, Watchmakers.

- 2. On White and Mitchell, Lottery Office keepers.

- 3. On a rich Baker near Brodie's close,—the name forgot.

- 4. The Council Chamber, for the Mace.

- 5. The Chamberlain's Office, for money.

- 6. Forrester and Co.'s, Jewellers.

- 7. Gilchrist and Co.'s, Linen-drapers.

[Besides these, and as depredations of greater magnitude,]

8. The Bank of Scotland (or Old Bank) was to have been broke into.

9. The Stirling Stage Coach, carrying a thousand pounds to pay the Carron workmen, was to have been stopped and robbed.

10. Mr. Latimer, Collector of Excise for the Dalkeith district, reported to have generally from one to two thousand pounds, was to have been robbed.

I do not here speak of those felonies which are set forth in my declarations, because some of them were made known by another.

With all humility, therefore, and a trembling heart, I urge the plea of having been the true cause—whatever may seem, or may be endeavoured to be proved to the contrary—of this wicked and dangerous confederacy being discovered and broken up, trusting my life to this one plea, and secure that it will have its full weight in the breasts of a discerning, unbiassed, and merciful Jury.

My most thankful acknowledgments are humbly returned to your Lordships for the appointment of such able and humane Counsel to plead for me. Forgive me for declining their kind help.

I have no warrant to be farther troublesome. My guilty conscience, in place of every other accuser and distress, has brought me to confess crimes for which avenging justice will sentence me to die, and I deserve my doom. I throw myself entirely on the mercy of the Court.

My Lords, to the charge brought against me in the Indictment, I Plead Guilty.

APPENDIX XV.

AN ACCOUNT OF THE EXECUTION OF THE PRISONERS, AND THEIR BEHAVIOUR AFTER THEIR CONVICTION.

(From Contemporary Sources.)

WILLIAM BRODIE appears to have been a man of a most singular and unaccountable character. During his confinement, and from the time of his receiving sentence till his execution, which was thirty-four days, he showed a mixture of character almost incredible. At times serious and sensible of his situation; and the next moment displaying jocularity and humour. He appeared to possess an undaunted resolution and at times even a daring boldness, frequently turning to ridicule his situation and the manner of his exit, by calling it "a leap in the dark." This disposition continued with him till almost the last moment of his existence.

He declared that, notwithstanding the censures and opinion of the world he was innocent of every crime excepting that for which he was condemned; and endeavoured to extenuate his guilt by saying that the crime for which he suffered was not a depredation committed on an individual, but on the public, who could not be impressed by the small trifle the Excise was robbed of. The hopes of obtaining a pardon or an alteration of his sentence to transportation seems strongly to have impressed his mind. In this view he immediately occupied himself in writing letters, and many of them were sensible, forcible, and well written; in particular, one to the Duke of Buccleugh, requesting his interest to be sent to Botany Bay. He complained much or the interruption he met with from the ministers attending him, and his fellow-convicts' singing of psalms, &c. Applications were also made to the jury, to the magistrates, and counsel, and many others, to second this view; and it was natural and commendable in his friends to use every exertion in his favour. The examples, however, of a Lord Ferrers, a Dr. Dod, the Perreaus, and Ryland, the King's engraver, are convincing proofs that the laws are not to be infringed with impunity, and that justice is impartial.

The situation of criminals in the prison of Edinburgh, after condemnation, is, from unavoidable circumstances, peculiarly irksome. They are chained by one leg to a bar of iron, along side of which they may walk; and their bed is made by the side of it. Mr. Brodie was allowed a longer chain than usual, a table and chair, with pen, ink, and paper; and the visits of any of his friends and acquaintances he wished to see, till the night before his execution, when none were permitted to visit him but clergymen.

To the same bar of iron on which he was chained, were, on this singular occasion George Smith, and two men condemned for robbing the Dundee Bank. Brodie was offered a separate room, but declined it.

Smith was uniformly devout and penitent—relished the conversation of clergymen, and joined fervently in religious exercises. Brodie said, upon some of these occasions, that he was so much employed with his temporal concerns he could not attend to them; but, when his business was finished, he would hear the clergymen. He remarked that the best of men had not thought it improper to employ even their last moments in the concerns of this world; that he was standing on his last legs, and it behoved him to employ his time sedulously; that he was determined to die like a man, and recommended the same to his fellow-sufferers. At times, however, he conversed with the clergy, and joined in their devotions. His conversation upon these occasions was directed to the principles of natural religion, not to the doctrines of revelation.

He lamented to a friend the impropriety of his first pursuits in life; that his inclinations at an early period led him to wish to go to sea; and though he did not possess much bodily strength, yet his courage and resolution were undaunted; that, instead of being in that disgraceful situation, his country might have looked up to him with admiration, and he might have been an honour to himself and family.

In the course of this trial he appears to have been naturally mild tempered and humane, but without principles of conduct, and easily led to crime. He writes in his letters affectionately of his children.

On the Friday before his execution he was visited by his daughter, Cecil, a fine girl of about ten years of age. The feelings of a father were superior to every other consideration, and the falling tears, which he endeavoured to suppress, gave strong proofs of his sensibility; he embraced her with emotion, and blessed her with the warmest affection.

On the Sunday preceding his execution a respite of six weeks arrived for Falconer and Bruce, the two people condemned for robbing the Dundee Bank. The news made Brodie more serious for a little time than he had before been, and he expressed his satisfaction at the event, declaring that it gave him as much pleasure as if mercy had been extended to himself. On Smith observing, "Six weeks is but a short period," Brodie, with some emotion, cried out, "George, what would you and I give for six weeks longer? Six weeks would be an age to us!"

He made frequent inquiries about the alterations that were making at the place of execution, which his friends declined answering out of tenderness. He observed that the noise made by the workmen was like that of shipbuilders; but for the short voyage he was going to make he thought so much preparation was unnecessary. On being visited by a friend on the Sunday evening he, with great calmness and composure, gave the needful directions respecting his funeral, and acknowledged with gratitude the attention that had been paid him during his confinement.

On the Monday preceding his death, at the request of George Smith, the two prisoners, Falconer and Bruce, for whom a respite had been obtained, were removed from the room in which they had all been confined. They parted from their companions in misery with great feeling and sensibility, and during the process of taking off their chains, Mr. Brodie, with great calmness, remained an unaffected spectator. Nothing appeared capable of shaking that fortitude which had attended him during the whole of his confinement.

On Tuesday morning, the day before his execution, a gentleman, who was visiting him, occasionally remarked the fatal consequences of being connected with bad women, and in how many instances it had proved ruinous. He began singing, with the greatest cheerfulness, from the "Beggar's Opera"—" 'Tis woman that seduces all mankind." The gentleman reproved this levity, but he sang out the song.

On the Tuesday evening, the 30th of September, the magistrates gave an order that none should be admitted to him but clergymen—a report having prevailed that there was an intention of putting self-destruction in his power. But of this order he complained, appearing to have full conviction of the dreadful consequences attending the crime of suicide; and declared that if poison was placed on one hand and a dagger at the other he would refuse them both, and not launch into eternity with the horrid crime of self-murder to account for—he would submit to the sentence of the laws of his country, and would wait his fate with calmness and composure.

The nearer the fatal moment approached the greater his resolution and fortitude appeared, without any adventitious aid, his manner of living being rather abstemious. He astonished every one that conversed with him, and his courage and magnanimity would have rendered his name immortal had he fallen in a good cause.

Late in the evening, while he was inveighing with some acrimony on the cruelty of not admitting his friends to him, he was suddenly agitated by hearing some noise, and, turning to Smith, he said, "George do you know what noise that is?" "No," said Smith. "Then I'll tell you; it is the drawing out of the fatal beam on which you and I must suffer to-morrow! I know it well." Soon after eleven he went to bed, and slept till four in the morning, and continued in bed till near eight o'clock without discovering any symptoms of alarm at his approaching fate.

At nine o'clock the next morning (Wednesday, 1st October) he had his hair fully dressed and powdered. Soon after a clergyman entered and offered to pray with him. Mr. Brodie desired he might use despatch, and make it as short as possible. During the remainder of his time he was employed in the most painful of all trials—parting with his friends, which he did with the utmost fortitude and composure.

At eleven o'clock he wrote the following letter to the Lord Provost, in a strong, firm hand:—

Edinburgh, Tolbooth,
Oct. 1. 1788, Eleven o'clock.

My Lord,

As none of my relations can stand being present at my dissolution, I humbly request that your Lordship will permit —— to attend, it will be some consolation in my last hour; and that your Lordship will please give orders that my body after be delivered to —— and by no means to remain in goal; that he and my friends may have it decently dressed and interred. This is the last favour and request of

Your most obedient,
but most unfortunate,
WILL. BRODIE.

About eleven o'clock the chains which had been on Mr. Brodie's legs since his condemnation were taken off. He was then visited by a few select friends, with whom he conversed with the greatest composure.

About one o'clock he ate a beef-steak and drank some port wine, and during this last repast he made some ludicrous remarks to Smith.

At two o'clock the guard marched up and surrounded the place of execution, at the west end of the Luckenbooths, and soon after the captain on duty informed the magistrates, in the Council Chamber, that all was ready. The magistrates then put on their robes of office; with white gloves and white staves, and followed by the clergymen in black gowns and bands, proceeded from the Council Chamber to the prison, attended by the proper officers.

At two o'clock a message came from the magistrates that they were in waiting, upon which Mr. Brodie said he was ready. He accordingly went downstairs, insisting that Smith should go first. Upon passing the room that Bruce and Falconer were in he took his farewell of them through the grate of the door, observing that, as His Majesty had given them a respite of six weeks, he did not doubt but he would at last grant them a pardon. When he entered the west stair a glass of cinnamon water was given him by some of his friends, with whom he still conversed most familiarly.

The magistrates reached the scaffold about ten minutes after two. The two senior magistrates only attended, as the other two gentlemen in the magistracy happened to have been on the jury of the unfortunate criminals; and in this singular case it was certainly a very becoming delicacy to excuse their attendance.

About a quarter past two the criminals appeared on the platform. When Mr. Brodie came on his scaffold he bowed politely to the magistrates and the people.

Brodie, at the first view of the immense multitude of spectators and the dreadful apparatus, said, "This is awful!" On passing a gentleman he asked how he did, and said he was glad to see him. The gentleman answered he was sorry to see Mr. Brodie in that situation. Brodie replied, "It is *fortune de la guerre*."

Brodie had on a full suit of black, his hair dressed and powdered; Smith was dressed in white linen with black trimming. They were assisted in their devotions by the Rev. Mr. Hardie, one of the ministers of the city, and the Rev. Mr. Cleeve, of the Episcopal, and Mr. Hall, of the Burgher persuasion. They spent some time in prayer, with seeming fervency. Brodie knelt, laying a handkerchief under his knees. He prayed by himself, nearly as follows:— "O Lord,-I acknowledge Thee as the Great Ruler of the world; although I lament much that I know so little of Thee, This much, however, I know, that Thou are a merciful God, and that, as I am a great sinner, Thou wilt have mercy upon me, through the merits of Thy Son Jesus Christ. O Lord, receive my soul! Into Thy hands I resign it. Amen."

When the devotions were over the great bell began to toll at half-minute pauses, which had an awful and solemn effect. When the executioner proceeded to bind his arms, Mr. Brodie requested that it might not be done too tight, as he wished to have the use of his hands, at the same time assuring his friends that he should not struggle. The criminals put on white night-caps; and Smith, whose behaviour was highly penitent and resigned, slowly ascended the platform, raised a few feet above the scaffold, and placed immediately under the beam where the halters were fixed. It is said Brodie tapped Smith on the shoulder, saying, "Go up, George; you are first in hand." He was followed by Brodie, who mounted with alertness, and examined the dreadful apparatus with attention, particularly the halter designed for himself, which he pulled with his hand. It was found that the halters had been too much shortened, and they were obliged to be taken down to alter. During this dreadful interval Smith remained on the platform trembling, but Brodie stepped briskly down to the scaffold, took off his night-cap, and again entered into conversation with his friends, till the ropes were adjusted. And though the dreadful moment of death was thus prolonged, he did not complain, but apologised himself by saying that it was on a new construction, and wanted nothing but practice to make it complete. He then sprang up again upon the platform, which was raised much higher than on former executions, but the rope was still improperly placed, and he once more descended, showing some little impatience, and observed that the executioner was a bungling fellow, and ought to be punished for his stupidity—but that it did not much signify.

Before he ascended the platform the last time he was addressed by his fellow-sufferer, George Smith; they then shook hands, and parted. Having again ascended, he deliberately untied his cravat, buttoned up his waistcoat and coat, and helped the executioner to fix the rope. He then took a friend, who stood close by him, by the hand, bade him farewell, and requested he would acquaint the world that he was still the same, and that he died like a man. Then pulling the night-cap over his face, he folded his arms, and placed himself in an attitude expressive of firmness and resolution. Smith (who during the interruption, had been in fervent devotion), soon after the adjustment of the halters, let fall a handkerchief as a signal, and a few minutes before three o'clock the platform dropped, and they, were launched into eternity, almost without a struggle.

The crowd of spectators within the street, in view of the place of execution, it has been calculated, could not have been less than 40,000, great numbers having come from all parts of the country. Luckily no accident of any consequence happened, which was much to be feared from the greatness of the crowd. One of the city officers fell from the platform to the top of the building where it was erected, and was considerably cut and bruised, but we hear not dangerously.

Brodie neither confessed nor denied the crime for which he suffered. To a gentleman who visited him the day before the execution, he said he thought it was hard to suffer for such a paltry sum, and appealing to Smith, he said, "George, it was not more than four pounds a piece." Smith answered he did not think it was so much, but he (Brodie) should know, for he counted the money.

Smith, with great fervency, confessed in prayer his being guilty and the justice of his sentence.

Much anxiety was shown that Brodie's body might not be detained in prison, and after the magistrates retired a vein was opened. It is said other means of recovery were used after it was taken away, but the neck was found to be dislocated.

Thus fell William Brodie, a just sacrifice to the laws of his country, and whilst we lament his fate we cannot but admire that impartiality, that integrity with which justice is administered; for however great, respected, or exalted the culprit, it affords no shield to protect from punishment or save from disgrace. This feeling would here suggest to bury with his bones his crimes, his follies, and his errors; and whilst we profit by his example, we cannot but lament how improperly those abilities were applied which might have done an honour to himself and family. His untimely fate claims the tribute of a tear, for if those who possess fortitude, courage, benevolence, and humanity claim our admiration, such was William Brodie.

APPENDIX XVI.

THE OLD EXCISE OFFICE.

(From the *Daily Review* of 24th January, 1873.)

ONE after another houses rich in historical associations and of a character that rendered the Old Town of Edinburgh remarkable, are being swept away by our Improvement Trustees. Their disappearance, while undoubtedly required for the sake of the sanitary welfare of their neighbourhoods, must excite in the minds of many a twinge of regret on several accounts; and as in the case of remarkable men, we cannot suffer their removal from the places that knew them so long to take place without directing attention to their distinctive features and history.

A tenement that would be a fit subject for antiquarian research is being levelled with the ground at present in the Nether Bow. It was one of the finest specimens of a class of houses which extended nearly the whole length of the High Street in former times—having wooden fronts projecting four or five feet in front of the masonry, thus giving the erection a more pasteboard appearance than the labourers who pull them down find to be in reality the case. While glass was still a luxury, and light to be enjoyed had to be sought for outside the dwelling, the old Edinburgh citizen, when building his house, took care to erect in front of its windows a wooden balcony, resting on sturdy pillars, that rose to the edge of the roof. Thus a piazza was formed on the ground floor under which the wares of the shop-keepers of the period were exposed, and a series of galleries above, where the burghers would step out from their houses of an evening to enjoy the air, and particularly the light, while watching the passers-by below, and where their children would play when the rain made the street not so agreeable for that purpose. In course of time, when glass came generally into use, the front of these balconies was boarded up and pierced with windows, and in many cases the shops below advanced a step, so as to keep flush with the frontage above. Hence the singular appearance of many of these tenements. Of this class was the old Excise Office. Its front was somewhat ornamental. Neat wooden pilasters divided the windows from each other. At its eastern corner, immediately below Baron Grant's Close, an outside stair that projected into the street before the alteration we describe led to a spiral stair, over the door leading to which was the pious inscription, "Devs Benedictat," and the date 1606. From this it would seem that the building was anything but new when taken possession of by the Hanoverian Excisemen. It is probable that it lodged more gentle persons and people who were held in better estimation than the officials that were regarded as the detested fruit of the Union. They took possession of the premises soon after that event in our history, stuck up the Royal arms on the face of the building, and set themselves to levy duty on the merchandise that entered the city by its principal gate, the Nether Port, the then direct avenue from the neighbouring seaport. Since George the Second's reign the Excise Office has had many a shift, and the building in Nether Bow many other strange occupants. While the character of the latter has been steadily declining, the prosperity of the Excise has been as uniformly increasing. The office was shifted to a more commodious house in the Cowgate, pulled down subsequently for the southern piers of George IV. Bridge; then to a house in Chessel's Court, in the Canongate, where the notorious Deacon Brodie committed his great robbery; next to Sir Lawrence Dundas' mansion in St. Andrew Square; afterwards to Bellevue House, in Drummond Place, since pulled down; and subsequently to where it is now. Two closes passed underneath the old Excise Office tenement; one was Baron Grant's Close, and the other Society Close. The Baron's fame has not descended to these days, and his name only lives on the wynd that once was his. But the other close has had rather a remarkable history. On its west side there was a curious old house with the following inscription over its main door:—"R. H. Hodie mihi eras tibi cur igitur curas." The date was obliterated by time. A curious turnpike stair led to the flats above. The tenement was the property of Aleson Bassendyne, the famous old Scottish topographer, who issued, in 1574, a beautiful folio Bible. The close at first bore his name; subsequently it was called after a Baron of Exchequer belonging to the house of Panmure, and last of all Society Close, from the circumstances that in a large stone mansion which the judge occupied, at the foot of the close, was afterwards housed the Society for the Propagation of Christian Knowledge founded in 1701, and erected into a body corporate by Queen Anne. There were many other buildings in the narrow wynd of great age and much interest, but they have been swept away. Now that these buildings have been removed, the obstruction presented to the traffic of the street by John Knox's house and church is more observable. But we would suffer much greater inconvenience ere we consented to the removal of the house of our venerable Reformer.

APPENDIX XVII.

An Account of the Proceedings against John Brown *alias* Humphry Moore at the Old Bailey in April, 1784.

Humphry Moore was indicted for feloniously stealing, on the 5th of February last, twenty guineas, value £21, and four pieces of foreign gold coin called doubloons, value £14 8s., the property of John Field, in the dwelling-house of John Brown.

The material circumstances of this case, as they appeared in evidence, were as follow:—The prosecutor, John Field, was walking along James Street, Convent Garden, when a person unknown joined company with him, and soon afterwards picked up a purse which was lying at a door. The prosecutor was persuaded to go to a public-house with him, being told that he was entitled to half the contents. From one end of the purse the stranger produced the following receipt:—"Feb. 2. 1784.—Bought of William Smith, one brilliant diamond-cluster ring, value £210, and received at the same time the contents, in full of all demands, by me, William Smith;" and from the other end he pulled out the ring itself. In the course of the conversation the prisoner entered the room, praised the beauty of the ring, and offered to settle the division of its value. Upon the stranger's lamenting that he had no money about him, the prosecutor said that he had forty or fifty pounds at his lodgings at Chelsea. "That sum will just do," said the prisoner. A coach was immediately called, and all three were drawn to the prosecutor's lodgings. The prosecutor and stranger went into the house, leaving the prisoner at the Five Fields, and they afterwards joined him at the Cheshire Cheese. The prisoner said, "I will give you your share of the ring if you will be content until to-morrow." The prosecutor put down twenty guineas and four doubloons, which the stranger took up and carried away, leaving the ring with the prosecutor, and appointed him to meet next day to have the money returned and £100 for his share of the ring. The prosecutor attended the next morning at the place of appointment, but neither of the parties came. The ring was of a very trifling value.

The jury were of opinion that the prisoner was confederating with the person unknown for the purpose of obtaining the money by means of the ring, and did therefore aid and assist the person unknown in obtaining the twenty guineas and four doubloons from the prosecutor. They accordingly found him guilty of stealing, but not in the dwelling-house subject to the opinion of the twelve judges whether it was felony.

Mr. JUSTICE WILLES (after stating the indictment and the circumstances that appeared in evidence, proceeded thus)—This matter was submitted to the opinion of all the judges, the first day of last Michaelmas term, except Lord Mansfield, who was absent, and they all agreed in the distinction between the parting with the possession and the parting with the property; that in the first case it was a felony, and in the last case it was not. Nine of the judges were of opinion that in this case possession only was parted with, it being merely a pledge, till the supposed value of the ring was delivered. Two of the judges thought that the doubloons were the same as money, and were of opinion it was a loan, and was a parting with the property; but nine of the judges were of opinion it was felony, and the judges could not distinguish this from the following case of the King and Patch. The prisoner was indicted for stealing a watch and some money. He picked up a ring and a purse in the street, and, pretending he had found it, offered to divide the money with the prosecutor, and opening the purse there was a ring and bill of parcels, stating the ring to be a diamond one, of £147 value, and a receipt for that sum. Different modes were proposed for the distribution; at last the prisoner asked the prosecutor if he would give him his money and watch and take the ring? Two other men that were in company took up the watch and money, and the prisoner got the prosecutor out of the room, under pretence he had something particular to say to him, and the two men ran away with the watch and money. The prosecutor was uneasy, and the prisoner said he knew the two men. The prisoner was apprehended, and the ring was found to be of the value of 10s. only. It was objected by the counsel for the prisoner that it was not a felony. But Mr. Justice Gould, Mr. Baron Perryn, and Mr. Justice Buller held it should be left to the jury to say what was the intention of the prisoner to get the money and watch, for if the whole was a scheme of the three men, it was felony, according to the case of the King and Peers, where a horse was hired for the day by two men who went directly and sold him; and Mr. Justice Gould left it to the Jury whether the prisoner and the other two men were not all in concert together. Upon the whole, therefore, of your case the majority of the judges are of opinion that you are guilty of the felony, and not merely of a fraud, and that judgment must be passed upon you accordingly.

Mr. RECORDER—Humphry Moore, when upon your trial I reserved this case; it was not from any doubt of your guilt, but doubting whether it was of that kind to support the indictment. That doubt has been submitted to the opinion of all the judges, and a great majority of them have concurred in opinion that the indictment was sufficiently supported, by the circumstances given in evidence against you. I never entertained any doubt that the offence of which you was clearly proved to be guilty, was deserving of as high a punishment as any felony committed under similar circumstances. If, therefore, no doubt in point of law had occurred I should have passed sentence upon you, to be transported for seven years. No reason occurs to me now for changing that opinion of your offence, but as the necessity of laying your case before the judges has occasioned some delay since your conviction, I shall take care the term of your transportation shall be computed accordingly. Therefore the sentence of the Court is, that you, Humphry Moore, be transported beyond the seas, for the term of seven years from the time of your conviction, to such place or places as His Majesty, by the advice of his Privy Council, shall think fit to direct or appoint.

FOOTNOTES:

[1] See Appendix I., Note 1.

[2] See Appendix I. note 2.

[3] See Appendix I. note 3.

[4] See Appendix I. note 4.

[5] See Appendix I. note 5.

[6] See Appendix I. note 5.

[7] See Appendix I. note 6.

[8] See Appendix I. note 7.

[9] See Appendix I. note 8.

[10] See Appendix I. note 9.

[11] See Appendix XVII.

[12] See Appendix I. note 10.

[13] See Appendix I. note 11.

[14] See Appendix I. note 12.

[15] See Appendix I. note 13.

[16] See Appendix I. note 14.

[17] See Appendix I. note 15.

[18] See Appendix I. note 16.

[19] See Appendix I. note 17.

[20] See Appendix I. note 18.

[21] See Appendix I. note 19.

[22] See Appendix I. note 20.

[23] See Appendix I. note 21.

[24] See Appendix I. note 22.

[25] See Appendix I. note 23.

[26] See Appendix I. note 24.

[27] Now the Head Office of the Royal Bank, St. Andrew Square.

[28] See Appendix I. note 25.

[29] The title of this member was Sir Nun and Abbess.

Milton Keynes UK
Ingram Content Group UK Ltd.
UKHW040832071024
449371UK00007B/744